Feeling Better, Getting Better, Staying Better

Feeling Better, Getting Better, Staying Better

Profound Self-Help Therapy for Your Emotions

Albert Ellis, Ph.D.

Impact ✻ Publishers ®
ATASCADERO, CALIFORNIA

ATTENTION ORGANIZATIONS AND CORPORATIONS:

This book is available at quantity discounts on bulk purchases for educational, business, or sales promotional use. For further information, please contact Impact Publishers, P.O. Box 6016, Atascadero, CA 93423-6016, Phone: 1-800-246-7228, email: sales@impactpublishers.com

Library of Congress Cataloging-in-Publication Data

Ellis, Albert.
    Feeling better, getting better, staying better : profound self-help therapy
for your emotions / Albert Ellis.
        p. cm.
    Includes bibliographical references and index.
    ISBN 1-886230-35-8 (alk. paper)
      1. Self-help techniques. I. Title.

BF632.E55 2001
152.4--dc21   2001024517

Publisher's Note

This publication is designed to provide accurate and authoritative information in regard to the subject matter covered. It is sold with the understanding that the publisher is not engaged in rendering psychological, legal, financial, or other professional services. If expert assistance or counseling is needed, the services of a competent professional should be sought.

Impact Publishers and colophon are registered trademarks of Impact Publishers, Inc.

Cover design by George Foster, Foster & Foster, Inc., Fairfield, Iowa.
Printed in the United States of America on acid-free paper.
Published by   ***Impact   Publishers*®**
POST OFFICE BOX 6016
ATASCADERO, CALIFORNIA 93423-6016
www.impactpublishers.com

Dedication

Once again, to Janet L. Wolfe, who has been of inestimable help to my theory, practice, and writing for the past thirty-six years.

Contents

Acknowledgements

I would most like to acknowledge my many clients over the years who have notably helped me to write this book and develop the theory and practice of Rational Emotive Behavior Therapy (REBT). Their collaboration with me was indispensable.

Emmet Velten and Kevin Everett FitzMaurice read parts of the manuscript of this book and made some valuable suggestions. Patrice Ward and Tim Runion labored mightily to word-process the manuscript. Bob Alberti edited the text with his usual remarkable skill and made the book much more readable than it would have otherwise been. Many thanks to all!

Introduction

This is going to be an experiment in writing as far as my use of language is concerned.

A few years ago I read the book, *Acceptance and Change,* and was struck by the chapter by Robert Zettle "On the Base of Acceptable Language." Zettle points out, following J.R. Kantor, N.W. Smith, and William James, that the study of attention, perception, memory, and cognition are more accurately stated as matters of attending, perceiving, remembering, and thinking. As Zettle notes, many nouns in psychology are misused instead of verbs and adjectives and *contructs* (which are actually fictions) are substituted for *events* (which are factual). Other psychologists, such as J.P. Guilford, also pointed this out for many years.

Consequently, I decided to favor verbs rather than nouns in several of my professional papers. As I was writing this book, I also read William Glasser's *Choice Theory* and found that he, too, deliberately uses verbs, such as "I depress" instead of nouns, as in "I suffer from depression." In doing so, Glasser promotes the view that negative feelings do not occur or exist in their own right, but that we have the *choice* of creating or not creating them for ourselves. We are the actors who actively act. We are not merely flotsam, the victims of external conditions.

Agreeing with Zettle, Glasser, and other writers, I decided in this book to talk about human thinking, feeling, and behaving as *verbs* rather than to construct misleading *nouns* for them. This is an experiment and I am partly trying it out for the first time in writing a book. We shall see how it works!

I previously wrote several books and articles in E-prime, a language invented by D. David Bourland. E-prime follows the General Semantic principles of Alfred Korzybski, and dispenses with all forms of the verb *to be*. Thus, instead of overgeneralizing and saying, "I am depressed," you say, "I depress myself right now." Why? Because "I am depressed" implies that you are *totally* depressed and will likely remain that way. So talking about depressing yourself — as in E-prime — discourages inaccurate and self-defeating use of language.

This book is not written in E-prime, because I found that it interferes somewhat with readability. But it uses few nouns to indicate action and favors verbs and adjectives in such cases. It thereby encourages the use of the kind of thinking that I employ and teach in Rational Emotive Behavior Therapy (REBT). This form of therapy has shown — ever since I created it in January, 1955 —that people do not merely get disturbing feelings — such as anxietizing and depressing — when undesirable events occur in their lives. Instead, they partly choose to upset themselves *about* these events — and they can therefore *refuse* to panic or depress themselves about them.

This book brings REBT up-to-date and shows you that in spite of many "bad" things that happen to you — or that you make happen — you have a *choice* of how to feel and behave about them. Glasser uses active language — favoring verbs and adjectives over nouns — in his book *Choice Theory*. I shall experimentally and partly try it here, hoping that it will encourage you to acknowledge that you largely *choose* — and can also refuse — to disturb yourself. Again, we shall see!

Editor's Note: Dr. Ellis would like to have carried his "experiment in writing" even further, but, alas, his editor is rather a traditionalist. The result is a compromise that we hope readers will find both accessible and challenging. — *REA*

1

The Difference Between Feeling Better and Getting Better

There are many ways you can get better and not just feel better — but I wouldn't count on most of them if I were you. When you've read this book, you'll be able to tell the difference between what *works*, and what merely *sounds good*.

The goals of effective psychotherapy and self-help approaches are twofold: (1) to help you disturb yourself less and (2) to enable you to lead a happier and more fulfilling life. When you seriously disturb yourself — with panic, depression, rage, self-pity — and when you function poorly — inhibit yourself, withdraw, act compulsively — you live less happily. Effective psychotherapy tries to help you reduce your self-disturbing beliefs and behavior, and also teaches you the skills of leading a more fulfilling, self-actualizing life. Without achieving the first of these goals, attaining the second is, though not impossible, damned difficult!

If you focus only on the first goal of therapy — minimizing your disturbing — you may find that achieving it is more complicated than it at first appears. Disturbing yourself less has two important aspects — feeling better and getting better (Ellis, 1972). Feeling better is important because you tend to function poorly when you feel bad, and you function better when you feel better. Feeling better is almost crucial to successful therapy, but usually short-lived. Fortunately, it's not the whole story.

Getting better is even more important — and more lasting. It consists of at least eight components: (1) feeling better; (2) continuing to feel better; (3) experiencing fewer disturbing symptoms (e.g., depression and needless inhibition); (4) seldom making your distress reoccur; (5) knowing how to reduce your distress when it reoccurs; (6) using this knowledge effectively; (7) being less likely to create disturbing reactions when new adversities occur in your life; (8) being less likely to *miserabilize* yourself, even when unusually bad events arise.

Getting better is different from feeling better and is usually much more difficult to achieve. There are many ways you can feel better — both in and outside of therapy. Thus, you can feel better on your own by arranging interesting and enjoyable distractions, by meditation, by Yoga and other kinds of physical relaxation, by socializing, by keeping yourself busy, by exercising, by using alcohol or drugs. With a therapist, you can be helped to feel better by his or her kindness, sympathy, cheeriness, optimism, acceptance, and support. There are thus almost innumerable ways, once you disturb yourself, of helping yourself to feel better. Billions of people have used them over the centuries. Try them and see for yourself.

Catch 22: For the most part, these techniques of making yourself feel better work temporarily — for a few minutes, a few days, or a few months. Why? Because they are often forms of distracting: of focusing on the good instead of the bad things in your life; or of focusing, instead of on the bad things, on some neutral events; or of concentrating on anything *but* adversity; or of thinking so intently of what you are doing — say, solving a problem or playing a sport — that you hardly have time to think of how poorly you are acting (or may soon act).

Your distracting thoughts and actions will often work very well — temporarily. For they shunt aside your panic and depressing thoughts that tell you that "bad" things (against your desires and interest) are happening, have happened, or most likely will happen. When you disturb yourself, you view these "bad" things as "awful" or "terrible" and think that they *absolutely must not* occur. When you upset yourself, you perceive something as bad, evaluate it as *very bad* or *awful*, and consciously or unconsciously demand that it *must* not be that bad — or even that it *must* not exist at all.

It doesn't really matter whether your evaluation of this "bad" event is accurate — whether most other people would see it as occurring and would appraise it the way you do. You *view* it as "terrible" or "horrible"; you think that it *must* not be as bad as it is — so you suffer. But, according to your conflicting belief, it *must not* be the way that you actually see that it *is*. Quite a paradox! What to do about it?

Does Meditation Work?

Let's suppose, for example, you are going to have an important interview for a job and you think that you *must* succeed at it or else it is *terrible* and you are an *incompetent person* who will *never* pass important interviews. Are your beliefs about failing the interview accurate? Most probably not: they are exaggerated, *catastrophizing* beliefs. No matter; you believe them, so you panic yourself about the upcoming interview. You have practically put your whole life at stake, depending on the outcome of the interview.

To relieve your worrying, you choose to meditate — a technique discovered in Asia thousands of years ago. So you choose one of several meditation methods:

♦ You say a mantra over and over again — such as "Om, om, om" or "Peace, peace, peace." You really focus on the word, and let nothing else enter your mind. You keep at it for ten or twenty minutes. Voila! — you close your mind to other thoughts, worrisome thoughts — and you are quickly unworrying. "Om" or "Peace" has replaced "It will be awful, horrible if I fail the interview! It will make me an incompetent person forever!"

♦ You meditate by training yourself to only *watch* your thoughts — whatever they are — and to *observe* them but not *evaluate* them. You focus on your thoughts. "I am thinking about the interview. I am seeing it in my mind. I am responding to the interviewer's questions. I am thinking about what he is telling me about the job. I am considering the merits of the job. I am seeing that it is different from my last job..." Watch, keenly watch, what you are thinking, but don't evaluate or measure your thoughts or the results you are predicting about the interview. Just observe. If you train yourself to do this — which is difficult! — you will distract yourself from *evaluating* to *observing*, and you will (at least for the moment) find it almost impossible to worry.

♦ You meditate by focusing *only* on your breathing, your breathing, your breathing. Don't evaluate *how* you are breathing or *how* you are focusing. Just keep concentrating on your breathing — or on anything *except* worrying about the interview and its outcome.

If you meditate — or focus — in any one of these ways, or use one of several other meditating (focusing) techniques, you will *not* think of the possible outcome of the job interview, will *not* evaluate it as bad, *will* think of quite different things, and therefore will not keep worrying about the interview (or anything else). Why? Because your mind normally focuses intently only on one thing at a time — particularly on catastrophizing. So when you concentrate on almost anything else, you will (temporarily!) stop your worrying. Yes, if you really, really focus on this other thing. Of course, you could focus not on the "horror" of having a poor interview, but on a number of other "horrors" — such as having a good interview, getting the job, and then failing on the job. Then you will still worry about something else — but *not* about the interview.

If meditating works — and there may be millions of instances over the centuries of its success in warding off catastrophizing — why should you not take it to its "logical" extreme and make yourself think of *nothing*. Why not have *no* thoughts?

That's not so easy. The human mind, even when you are asleep, thinks and thinks. When you are unconscious of what you are thinking, it still reflects. Therefore, it is possible for you, for a few seconds, to think of nothing — possible, but not easy! So you can try "mindless" meditation, though not for too long. Don't forget that to intently concentrate, or to meditate on *not* concentrating, still requires thinking. To will to be *will-less* requires some amount of thought. To desire to be desireless requires desiring. Maybe you can actually think yourself into a state of unconsciousness — if that *is* equal to non-thinking — but not for very long! Then you return to some kind of thinking. Why? Because you invariably do.

Reaching a state of "no mind," moreover, if you can really do it, is quite impermanent. It doesn't last and the relaxing that goes with it fades. That's the trouble with most meditation techniques. They work — briefly. Almost always, if you use them to interrupt an anxietizing idea — such as, "I must succeed in this project and it's awful if I don't" — they do interrupt it — temporarily. But they rarely help you to change it permanently. Sure as hell, it returns to plague you. So you *feel* better, all right, but hardly *get* better.

Relaxation? Exercise? Hobbies?

The same is true of other methods of cognitive distraction: physical relaxation, socializing, exercising, enjoyments. Acquiring a vital absorbing interest is one of the best methods Robert Harper and I recommend in *A Guide to Rational Living* (1997). All these methods have values and virtues in their own right. Physical relaxing shows you how you can calm and refresh your body. Socializing adds to your life. Exercising helps your health. Enjoyments, naturally, give you joy. A vital absorbing interest enables you to flow, grow, develop, and achieve longtime gains. All these methods may prove valuable to you. By all means experiment with them and often relish them.

Do they help you *get* better? Rarely. Or let's say only occasionally. For they may include changing your basic outlook or philosophy — as included in some forms of meditation. Or, even if your distractions are mainly physical — like Jacobson's Progressive Relaxation technique — they do include some thinking, such as *focusing* on relaxing your muscles — and may lead to related cognizing, such as rating your thinking highly and seeking to use it in other ways. As I shall keep noting in this book, because you are a unique human, you can think about your thinking and think about thinking about your thinking — and you often do.

So cognitive distraction *may* lead to permanent philosophic change and major psychological improvement. But usually it won't. For several reasons:

- It doesn't stress changing your basic attitudes — your demands that you must do well, that you're "no damned good" when you don't and that it's "terrible" when you don't get what you strongly want.

- It interrupts your disturbing — creating peace only for a while, and doesn't prevent your forcefully returning to it again.

- It often helps you so quickly feel good and relaxed that you have little incentive to see and challenge your disturbing thinking and feeling. Quite the contrary!

- It preoccupies you and takes energy and time away from your working against your neuroticizing attitudes.

It has short-term benefits that may lead to disillusioning when they fade and may therefore encourage you to give up on alternate, and perhaps better, forms of helping yourself.

Which means? That many good techniques, such as cognitive distracting, are palliating, work in the short-run, and may actually *interfere* with permanently getting better and staying better. That will be one of the main purposes of this book: to show you that *even good therapy can lead to weak results and can easily sidetrack you from better therapeutic methods.* Also, I'll show you which are the better — and especially more permanent — methods and how you can use them. I'll encourage you to use some methods that are moderately helpful, but I also hope to stimulate you to employ the more effective ones that this book presents.

How About Psychotherapy?

Is psychotherapy as it is practiced today generally helpful for self-disturbing people? Yes, hundreds of studies have shown it to be effective and hundreds more will probably show this in the future. A skeptical and efficient organization, Consumers Union, publisher of *Consumer Reports*, has shown that in about 80% of the cases, therapy produces good results.

Although some studies have also indicated that psychotherapy can be harmful, relatively little investigation of damage has been done. If further studies of harm were made, they would probably show some of the following potential and actual disadvantages:

+ Real harm may be done — therapy clients may become more disturbed — because the therapy is inadequate, or the therapy is adequate but the therapist uses it improperly.

+ Both the therapy and the therapist are efficient, but the clients are so disturbed that they may misuse it (almost any kind of treatment might be used to harm themselves).

+ The therapy may be beneficial in some respects, but it takes time, energy, and money, and discourages some clients from using methods that would be considerably more helpful. It therefore does relative — rather than absolute — harm.

In the first two instances, it can be easily ascertained if clients harm themselves by engaging in therapy. In the third case, it would be almost impossible to show that clients were self-harming only because they did not try alternative therapies that might have helped them more.

I'll try to show in this book the effective and ineffective results that people usually get from various kinds of therapy and self-treatment. I'll also show that they might have received *more* benefit from other kinds of therapy — such as Rational Emotive Behavior Therapy (REBT) and Cognitive Behavior Therapy (CBT). Thus, I shall "prove" — through hardly perfectly — that many of the therapies people have tried may have been *relatively harmful*.

Now, at first blush, this may not seem very important. If some people are helped by therapy, feel better, and lead happier lives, so what if they don't get still "better" therapy? So what if they don't *get better,* but merely *feel better*? Shouldn't they be thankful anyway?

Yes, in some ways. But shouldn't they also consider their potential losses, not just in the past, but right now, in the present and future? Shouldn't they feel sorry and regretful — though not necessarily depressed and angry — about that? Yes, I think they should. Why? For several reasons:

• It *is* regrettable if you make some *therapeutic gains,* but miss out on other *potential gains.* It would be nice, no doubt, if you were trained to be a paralegal, enjoyed this profession somewhat, and made a good living at it. But wouldn't it be regrettable that you were not, as you could have been, trained as an attorney, enjoyed it more than acting as a paralegal, and made more money at it? Let's be honest — isn't that lack of training fairly regrettable?

• After all, you only have one limited life; only so many possibilities and chances. If, then, you are helped by therapy to *temporarily* feel less depressed and make some gains because of that help, wouldn't it be better — much better — for you to use another form of therapy that would help you to be *permanently less depressable*? And wouldn't it be still better if this other form of therapy helped you to be *less depressable*, even when very strong adversities occurred in your life? Wouldn't that be considerably preferable for you, your loved ones, and for other people with whom you are close? Wouldn't the good results of this alternative therapy — if they actually could be attained — help more people more of the time?

• Although your therapy was perhaps good — though not good enough — its past effects cannot be changed. You may have had results and that were somewhat beneficial, but also relatively harmful. Too bad. But if you now see this and agree you can be helped decidedly more than you have been, that you can *get better* in addition to *feeling better*, you have plenty of opportunities ahead of you to try other aspects of therapy and to achieve this goal. Look what a boon that would be! Why should you not try to be helped significantly *more* than you have been?

No therapy is likely to be perfect — for you or any disturbed person. Any help you get from it, and from the particular therapist who works with you, can presumably be improved. I still contend it would be a damned shame if you got much less help than you could have gotten after spending time, energy and money! Not a holy horror, mind you — but quite disappointing! Why continue to put up with it? Why not try to correct it? This book will show you *how.* I believe it will probably help you to benefit more than the relatively inefficient therapy you may have had, and also give you new and better methods than you have used. A double benefit!

You are not likely to be a professional therapist, and this book is not designed to make you an authority on therapy. But, unlike other books, it is designed to teach you these important points about psychological treatment:

- *Techniques* that will very likely help you feel better if you are disturbing yourself, so that you may achieve a happier, more productive life.

- *Methods to avoid*, because they may help exacerbate your disturbing.

- *Procedures* that are likely to help you get better, stay better, and remain distinctly less disturbable.

Given this knowledge of what works, what doesn't work, and what works better, you will have more intelligent therapeutic choices. You are a unique individual, and therapy methods that work for you may well be different from those that benefit other people. This book questions what you *really* know about therapy, and tries to add appreciably to this knowledge. If, after reading it and using it, you want to stay with the therapy or self-help procedures you have used, fine. If you want to go beyond what you have now learned, very fine. Don't take anything the book says on faith. Think about it. Check it out. Experiment with it. Reject it if you will. Thoughtfully *consider* it. You don't *have* to use it. But you can *prefer* to do so, if you think it wise.

2

Don't Just *Feel* Better, *Get* Better!

Most ways of getting better require that you do several things that are interwoven with one another, such as changing your thinking and your feeling. But sometimes, almost by accident, one procedure will work; you may even do it on your own—without help from a therapist or anyone else.

Take Unconditional Self-Accepting (USA), for instance. Several ancient philosophers hinted at it about 2400 years ago — including Gautama Buddha and Lao-Tzu. In recent times, Paul Tillich, Carl Rogers, and I — among other thinkers — have ardently espoused it. Unconditional Self-Accepting means that you fully accept yourself, even when you perform badly and may be despised by significant others. You accept yourself just because you are alive, human, and unique. You exist, therefore you are an okay person. Or, in the more elegant Rational Emotive Behavior Therapy (REBT) version, you refuse to give your *self* — your personality, your being — *any* global rating.

I'll say more about this later, but let me say here that if you somehow achieve this benign and efficient state, no matter how you achieve it, you will go a long way toward *getting* better, instead of just *feeling* better. You will minimize your self-downing, even though you may do some execrable deed. You *will* also feel sorry, but not incredibly hurting, when others mistreat you, and will refuse to damn them. Finally, you may, because you have faith in your ability to cope with difficult situations, stop horrifying yourself about the frustrations of life and deal with them as well as you can. Therefore, you will find it difficult to seriously disturb yourself, even under unpleasant and unfair conditions.

It usually takes quite a bit of thinking and acting over a period of time to achieve USA. But you can also just decide to achieve it — and have it. You can decide to acquire it because someone else — such as a therapist — encourages you to do so. You can take it from religious teachings — for example, from the Christian maxim, "accept the sinner but not the sin." You can figure out that you'd darn well better adopt it because it works — and little else does. So in these and a number of other ways you can *choose* to acquire USA.

Great! If you make it happen that way. But since you were born — like all humans — with a tendency to globally rate your *self* as well as your *behavior*; since you were also taught to do this by your family and by society; and since you have trained yourself to practice various kinds of self-damning from childhood, you will probably have to work hard and long to achieve **Unconditional Self-Accepting (USA)**, and then work hard and long to retain it.

So I could merely describe what USA is and then tell you: "Now that you understand it, get it. Yes, push your ass (PYA) and get it!" Well, maybe you will, and maybe — more likely — you won't. For there is indeed a simple way for you to get USA. Just take it, for the asking, just as you choose to take *Conditional* Self-Accepting **(CSA)** — accepting yourself *on condition* that you perform well and earn the approval of others. You *chose* CSA, and you can similarly *choose* USA.

Simple, but not easy. Being a human, you think, feel, and act — and you do so interrelatedly and somewhat holistically.[1]

---

[1] See my discussion of this in my 1962 book, *Reason and Emotion in Psychotherapy* or in my revised version of this book, *Reason and Emotion in Psychotherapy, Revised and Updated* (1994).

Why? Because that's what humans do. This means that when you have a basic thought or philosophy — like USA — you think it fairly strongly, *and* you feel it (experience it in your body and gut), *and* you tend to act on it (behave as if it works). You do *all* these things together, largely unconsciously. But to change from one philosophy — such as Conditional Self-Accepting (CSA) —to USA, it will usually be necessary to *consciously* think, feel, and act. You can indeed achieve USA by deciding to just acquire it, but normally the process is much more complicated: you *decide* or *choose* to have it; you *work at* — yes, *work at* — several ways of feeling it; and you "force yourself" to keep *acting* on it.

In other words, you use several thinking, feeling, and acting ways to arrive at a basic philosophy like USA or CSA, and may be largely unaware of using them. But when you have *acquired* and *practiced* an attitude for a while, you have to consciously use several thinking, feeling, and acting processes to *change* it. Especially if you have a naturally bio-social tendency to have CSA — as I think we humans do — you may have to work hard and long to change it to USA. So resolving to change is an important part of the game — but only one part!

In the following pages, I'll describe several basic Rational Emotive Behavior Therapy (REBT) philosophies that give you an excellent chance of feeling better *and* getting better. First, let me show you how you often disturb yourself emotionally and behaviorally; and then let me describe some of the main methods you can use to make yourself less distressed and more *undisturbable*.

You Disturb Yourself!

The REBT theory of human disturbance differs radically from the "common sense" theory of most people (and many therapists, especially psychoanalysts). It essentially says that you don't just *get* disturbed from traumatic things that happen to you, you also *choose* to needlessly upset yourself about these traumas. Yes, you are a chooser, a constructor of how you react psychologically and, fortunately, you can *choose to refuse* to create your upset and to work toward more helpful ways of reacting.

This is a *constructivist* theory, originated thousands of years ago by Asian, Greek, and Roman philosophers. One of them, Epictetus, put it very clearly and succinctly, *"People are disturbed not by things, but by the view they take of them."*

Many modern therapists, especially psychoanalysts, have unfortunately distorted this into: "People are disturbed by things, and not by the view they take of them." Heed these therapists and you'll make yourself considerably less constructive — and more disturbable!

The REBT theory of how you disturb yourself is more comprehensive and precise than that of Epictetus. It says, "People disturb themselves by the things that happen to them *and* by their views, feelings, and actions." This is the philosophy of many modern thinkers, especially Alfred Korzybski, the founder of General Semantics. It is not *either/or*, but *both/and*. You disturb yourself by things *and* by thinking, feeling, and acting on them. You work hard — by thinking, feeling, and behaving — to upset yourself; fortunately, as a constructionist and a problem-solver, you can work at not doing so. You have *choices*.

REBT, as just noted, says that you actively think, feel, and behave to both create — and "uncreate" — your emotional problems. Take Joyce, for example. A talented teacher at 32, she was happy with her husband, Bob, and their two-year-old son, Todd. Then Bob suddenly announced that he was leaving her to live with his 19-year-old secretary, whom he had already made pregnant. Joyce felt severely depressed, threatened to kill herself, and was hospitalized for a month. Everyone said that Bob's infidelity and his leaving Joyce depressed her. They were partly — but not exactly — right.

The ABC's of Disturbing Yourself

Let me explain Joyce's depressing herself by using REBT's famous **ABC** theory of human disturbing. At Point **A** Joyce experienced *Adversity*: Bob had an affair, got his secretary pregnant, and announced that he was leaving her. At point **C**, Joyce felt the *Consequence*: depressing herself and desiring suicide. Many people, Joyce included, would say that the **A** (Adversity) caused

C (Consequences). Though partly correct — for Joyce probably would not feel self-destructive unless **A** had occurred — the formula **ABC** is lacking an important factor: **B**. **B** is Joyce's *Belief* about **A**, her core *view* of it.

Actually, Joyce's view (**B**) of the Adversity is complicated. It consists of strong perceiving and thinking — such as, "**A** is bad for me. It is not what I want. In fact, it is so undesirable that it *must* not occur! It is terrible and proves that I am a poor wife and an inadequate person!" Instead, Joyce could have had mild negative thoughts. For example, "It's too bad that Bob does not want me any more, but Todd and I can live happily without him." Or she could even have positive thoughts, for example, "If that's the unacceptable way Bob behaves, Todd and I are much better off without him! Good!" In which case, she would not depress herself, and might even encourage herself.

Second, at **B**, Joyce has understandably negative feelings that go with her negative thinking — feelings of loss, regret, surprise, shock, and horror — feelings that, again, help lead her to experience **C**, depressing herself. (Actually, **B** [Belief] also includes strong emotional and behavioral elements. Therefore, we can call it **Believing-Emoting-Behaving**.)

Third, at **B**, Joyce has action tendencies — such as to argue, fight, and escape — that accompany her thinking and feeling, and probably augment them. Again, they help lead her to depressing herself.

In other words, Joyce is not merely a *passive recipient* of Adversity experiences that lead her to react with depressing. She is a very *active reactor*, who responds with thoughts, feelings, and actions at **B** (Believing-Emoting-Behaving). Therefore, **C = A x B:** the Consequence is the *product* of the Adversity and her Beliefs (Emotions/Behavior) about it.

Although Joyce may have no control over what happens to her at **A** (Adversity), she has some degree of choice as to how she responds to **A** at **B**. In response to what happens to her at **A**, she largely *constructs* **B** in order to arrive at **C**.

When Epictetus "says," then, that Joyce's *view* of the Adversity — and not merely the **A** itself — creates her symptoms of depression, he seems to mean her *profound* view, which also includes her *feelings* (sensations and bodily reactions) and *action tendencies*. When people like Joyce bring on a strong reaction at point **C** —disturbing themselves — their **Believing (B)** just about always includes important emoting and acting elements. Why? Because thinking, feeling, and behaving go together and importantly affect each other (as I said in my first REBT paper in 1956!). So Joyce thinks-feels-acts about her **Adversity** to help create her symptom of depression.

♦ ♦ ♦ ♦ ♦ ♦ ♦ ♦ ♦ ♦ ♦ ♦ ♦ ♦ ♦ ♦ ♦ ♦ ♦

Important Note: REBT has long defined "**B**" as *beliefs* — rational beliefs (**RB**) or irrational beliefs (**IB**). The revised ABCs of REBT now define **B** as *Believing-Emoting-Behaving*. However, since this terminology is long-winded and somewhat awkward, I shall hereafter sometimes refer to B as *Beliefs*, in *italics*. I shall sometimes refer to Rational *Believing-Emoting-Behaving* as Rational *Believing* and refer to Irrational *Believing-Emoting-Behaving* as Irrational *Believing*. My use of italics in the words *Beliefs* and *Believing* will, I hope, keep reminding readers that when I use these capitalized words, I use them as shorthand for *Believing-Emoting-Behaving*.

♦ ♦ ♦ ♦ ♦ ♦ ♦ ♦ ♦ ♦ ♦ ♦ ♦ ♦ ♦ ♦ ♦ ♦ ♦

Who, Me Irrational?

The **ABC** theory of Joyce disturbing herself goes further, and distinguishes between her *rational* — self-helping — **Believing-Emoting-Behaving** and her *irrational* — self-defeating — **Believing-Emoting-Behaving**. She can choose to rationally consider the **Adversity (A)** that she sees occurring in her life (I like to call this "Adversitizing," or *perceiving* **Adversity**). Thus, she could strongly tell herself, "I see what Bob has done. I wish he had acted much differently. But if he decides to go with the bimbo instead of staying with Todd and me, that's unfortunate but not catastrophic. We can still live and be reasonably happy."

REBT theory says if Joyce really believed, felt, and acted on these *Rational Beliefs* (**RBs**), she would feel mainly the healthy, negative emotions (at point **C**) of sorrow, regret, and disappointment. These are relatively healthy negative feelings because they will help Joyce cope with her adversity, function effectively in her own and her child's life, and make a good adjustment to a bad, undesirable situation. Basically, they work.

On the other hand, Joyce can choose to pick several strong **Irrational Beliefs** (**IBs**), such as, "Bob is a bastard for what he has done! He absolutely *should not* have done it. It's *awful*. I *can't stand it*, and can't ever be happy *at all*. I might as well kill myself!" With this kind of self-defeating Believing-Emoting-Behaving (**IB**) she makes herself feel devastated, dysfunctional, and suicidal.

With either rational or irrational **B**'s, Joyce will create her own reactions and — sometimes strong feelings and behaviors (Consequences). But each will come out quite differently!

So REBT theory says that *Rational Beliefs* (**RBs**) — *preferences* that she do well and win approval from others — will lead to Joyce's *healthy* negative feelings when adversity occurs. *Irrational Beliefs* — *demands* that she *must* do well and be approved of, and that it's *awful* when she doesn't — will usually lead to *unhealthy*, or even destructive, feelings when she experiences serious Adversities. Therefore, she has a *choice* about disturbing herself!

"But I'm Really Upset About This!"

Don't for a moment think that REBT is trying to rob you of your feelings, or even get you to tone them down. Not at all. Feelings and emotions are fundamental to the human condition. As Peter Lang states, "Affects [emotions] are states in which the human organism is primed for survival actions and effectors are mobilized." Steven Reiss and his associates have, in a number of studies, shown that people have about fifteen basic motives and desires, and —verifying a core hypothesis of REBT — if they hold them very strongly they are more likely to *make themselves* anxious or panicked when they are not fulfilled. Variations in our desires, Reiss points out, make us unique individuals.

REBT, therefore, acknowledges and favors you having feelings, including strong feelings. But it gives you a choice, when your desires are thwarted, of *healthy* feelings — sorry, disappointed, frustrated, working to fulfill your desires — *or unhealthy* feelings — panic, depression, and anger. Unlike some other popular therapies, REBT recognizes that *you have a choice of how you feel.*

Is there evidence to back up this REBT theory? Yes! About two thousand experiments have been done by REBTers and other researchers to test what happens to people when they hold Rational or Irrational *Beliefs.* Almost all of them show that those who have more IBs and hold them strongly are more emotionally and behaviorally disturbed than those who have fewer IBs and hold them weakly. More than two thousand published studies also show that, when various kinds of disturbed and dysfunctional clients are helped to change their Irrational *Beliefs* to Rational *Beliefs*, they significantly improve. So REBT theory and practice has considerable empirical backing.

How Common Irrational Beliefs Lead to Emotional Disturbance

I presented my first paper on REBT at the 1956 American Psychological Association Annual Convention. At that time, I listed twelve common Irrational *Beliefs* (IBs) that my clients held when they were disturbing themselves. I went on to list over fifty common IBs. Upon giving this matter further thought over the years, I have realized there are *scores* of common IBs that lead to emotional disturbance. Fortunately they can be put under three major headings:

"I *absolutely must* perform well!"

"I *absolutely must* be treated fairly by others!"

"I *must not* find life's conditions very hard!"

Further research with REBT and IBs has shown that self-distressing people — such as Joyce — have one, two, or all three of these core IBs, with several subheadings under each of the three major ones.

Joyce, for example, had all three major Irrational *Beliefs* that she held strongly — that is, *emotionally*:

1. "I *must* not lose my husband, Bob, to another woman. Yet, although I must not, the fact is I *am* losing him, so I must be a rotten wife and a pretty worthless individual! Therefore, I'd better kill myself!"

2. "Other people *absolutely must* treat me fairly and considerately or they are no damned good! Bob has lied to me and treated me most unfairly, and therefore he is a rotten bastard!"

3. "The conditions under which I live *must not* be grim and frustrating, or else it's so *awful* that I *can't stand* it! Bob leaving me for his secretary creates very frustrating conditions that I can't bear! My life is *completely miserable* and *hopeless!*"

People create their severe upsetness with three powerful, major musts (and Joyce strongly held all three):

* "I *must* do well!"

* "Others *must* treat me honestly and fairly!"

* "Conditions *must* not be very frustrating or they are intolerable!"

If Joyce *preferred* these outcomes, but did not *demand* or *command* them, she would have had healthy negative, problem-solving experiences. She would have saddened, annoyed, and frustrated herself when Bob left her, but she probably would not have felt the depths of despair, depression, rage, and wishing for death.

What's more, by holding onto her Irrational *Beliefs* (IBs) strongly and forcefully, Joyce gave them an emotional and action-oriented quality. She *felt* — as well as *believed* — she was worthless for losing Bob. She viewed him as a bastard — and felt rage. She believed conditions were *awful* and felt that she couldn't bear them. Her powerful *Beliefs*, moreover, caused her to beat herself mercilessly, think and feel hopeless, and almost commit suicide. Her strong Irrational *Beliefs* included *emotional* and *activity* elements. They were not *merely opinions*; they were *powerful* opinions, feelings, and actions!

So What Can You Do About Your Self-Disturbing Beliefs?

Assuming it is correct that you and Joyce and other people disturb yourselves by powerful, emotive Believing-Behaving, how can you *see* what you are doing and *correct* it? For many years REBT has used a number of thinking, feeling, and behaving methods of actively disputing and counter-attacking IBs (Irrational *Beliefs*), using experiential and homework assignments to work against them. REBT persistently and forcefully questions and challenges them, and encourages you to change them back into RBs — healthy preferrings (Rational Believing-Emoting-Behavings).

In this book, I shall show you, as I showed Joyce, how to use some of the most effective REBT methods to vigorously rip up your Irrational *Beliefs* when you needlessly disturb yourself. I'll emphasize methods that you can use not only to *feel better*, but to *get better* and *stay better.* You can make yourself *less disturbable*, even when unusual and severe adversities occur in your life.

REBT, in other words, is a system of psychotherapy and self-help procedures which emphasizes that human values — or philosophic assumptions — are a prime source of disturbed or dysfunctional thoughts, feelings, and actions. As Robert Woolfolk pointed out, this was a minority view in 1955 when I originated REBT. Woolfolk notes that, at that time, "only Ellis, Jung, and the existentialists anticipated the conclusion [that] far from being a value-free endeavor, psychotherapy is a morally laden enterprise whose theories presuppose viewpoints both on an ideal functioning and on human baseness and peccability."

Woolfolk notes that *all* kinds of psychotherapy presuppose — consciously or unconsciously — a set of values which underlie change in the lives of clients. REBT consciously teaches that to get better, and not merely feel better, you must clearly recognize your present self-defeating values and change them to more self-enhancing values.

3

Feeling Better *and* Getting Better

When you acknowledge that your strong Irrational *Beliefs* (IBs) that lie behind much of your self-defeating emotions and actions almost invariably include absolutistic *shoulds, oughts,* and *musts,* and when you have learned to look for these grandiose demands and to actively Dispute them, you can then apply a new method of thinking to several important areas of your life.

Unconditional Self-Acceptance (USA)

Let us start with Unconditional Self-Acceptance — **USA** — one of the core attitudes that will help you prevent disturbing yourself, and minimize your disturbance when you do. This *Belief* may be contrasted with those of *non-accepting* and *Conditional Self-Acceptance* (CSA) — which can bring radically different results!

Non-acceptance means that you castigate and damn yourself, your being, for practically everything that you do "badly." Fortunately, complete non-accepting is rare. Some individuals almost ceaselessly damn themselves and think they are worthless, even when they do "good" deeds. For them, no good deeds are ever good enough. They thereby depress themselves. In this book, we will not consider these seriously disturbed people, and we'll assume that you are not one of them.

They can be treated with intensive psychotherapy and medication, but may not be able to adequately follow self-help procedures on their own.

Conditional self-acceptance (CSA) almost universally prevails, and means that you accept yourself when you think you have done well and have won the approval of others, and that you tend to blame yourself, your whole person, when you do badly. It has self-preservative usefulness — and that is probably why it is built into humans — because it motivates you to perform adequately and to get along with others. It sometimes encourages outstanding achieving and joy about this achieving. It is also called *self-esteem* — or esteeming yourself for your virtues and successes.

Since, however, conditional self-esteem includes a rating of your self, your being, as well as of your performance, it has enormous handicaps and leads to much self-downing, panicking, and depressing. For when you do badly, or think you do badly, or think that others see you as doing badly, you denigrate your whole self and feel worthless. Since you, like other people, are a highly fallible human and frequently make mistakes and do poorly, your conditional self-acceptance (CSA) often leads to self-damning. You hate yourself when you function badly; when you function well you see the danger of functioning badly tomorrow, and you worry and depress yourself. Conditional self-acceptance — or self-esteem — rarely is consistently effective.

USA works much better than conditional self-acceptance (CSA). It consists of your decision to accept yourself (and perhaps rate yourself as a reasonably good person) independent of your performances — *whether or not* you do well and *whether or not* you earn approval by others. You still very definitely rate or evaluate what you do and how you do it in order to live adequately in the world and to get along with others. And you may even hold high standards of how well you would *like* to do and how much you would *like* to be approved of by others. But you only *prefer* these standards — not escalate them into *absolute musts*. And you do not rate your self, your being, or your personhood on the basis of your standards. You merely accept yourself existentially because you *choose* to do so. With USA, you may like or dislike what you do, but you always accept *yourself* even when you don't like some of your thinking, feeling, and acting.

As I noted before, unconditional self-acceptance (USA), if you solidly choose to acquire it, wards off a great deal of your self-disturbing. It helps you to unconditionally accept others, and to cope when you are frustrated, because you will stubbornly refuse to put yourself down. It also rids you of much of your over-generalizing — which, again, is at the core of your disturbability. For when you believe, "I *am* what I *do*," and follow what Alfred Korzybski called "the *is* of identity," you over-generalize, and think illogically and unrealistically, thereby making yourself prone to many ills. I discuss this in detail in my books, *A Guide to Rational Living* and *The Albert Ellis Reader*.

Assuming that unconditional self-acceptance is highly desirable and will help you both *feel* better and *get* better emotionally, how do you go about achieving it? In several ways:

• Decide (choose) that you are a unique individual, that you are alive, and that you want to stay alive and be reasonably happy and free from pain. You make this choice because you make it — because it is your choice. You could, instead, decide to end your life or to continue it miserably. Well, choose!

• To stay alive and be reasonably happy, you try to perform many functions (such as finding and consuming food) and to live amicably with other humans who will aid you in remaining alive and being reasonably happy.

• To function properly, you rate or evaluate the things you do (and do not do) to see whether they aid you in continuing to live and be reasonably happy. If they do, you rate or evaluate them as "good"; if they don't, you rate them as "bad." This usually includes rating your relationships to other people: when you get along well with them, you judge that as "good," and when you get along badly with them, you judge that as "bad."

• Decide not to give your self, your being, your essence, your totality a global or general rating. For you do thousands of acts, some of which are "good," some of which are "bad," and many of which are fairly neutral. So giving your self, your being, a global or general rating is probably impossible and always inaccurate. Besides, if you did give yourself such a general rating, it would be short-lived, since the kind and degrees of "good" and "bad" acts that you do vary greatly over time, and continually change.

♦ Tell yourself, "What I did is good" or "What I did is bad" or, better yet, "That is good in some important ways." But do not give yourself any global or general ratings, such as "I *am* good" or "I *am* bad." You have a fairly clear-cut identity — for you are unique and somewhat different from all other individuals — but you had better not measure, rate, or evaluate this identity. You *perform* many things — poorly and satisfactorily — in accordance with your chosen goal of remaining alive and being reasonably happy. But you *are* not what you *do*. You are an ongoing, living process; it is probably impossible to rate accurately an ever-changing process — your "you-ness."

♦ You preferably stick to rating your thinking, feeling, and behaving, but refuse to evaluate your self, your being, globally. You will find it difficult to do this, because you are born with the tendency to rate what you *do* and, at the same time, to jump to global evaluations of what you *are* — to rate your entire being or personhood. You also learn to do so by social teaching — from your family, your friends, your teachers, and the mass media. When you measure yourself by using your innate tendencies and your social learning to do so, you keep practicing self-rating and make it habitual, easy, automatic. So for several reasons, you will find difficulty in only rating your behaving, and not simultaneously rating your self or totality. But it is possible for you to do so — at least, much of the time.

♦ If you find it difficult to refuse to rate yourself globally, and you want to use some degree of doing so, you can choose always to rate yourself as "a good person," because that usually is more valuable, more useful, than rating yourself as "a bad person" or "a neutral person." To judge yourself frequently as "a bad person" means that you think you are unworthy of living and enjoying yourself; that won't aid your original goals of continuing to live and be reasonably happy. Also, since you — like all humans — to some extent act the way you think, rating yourself as "a bad person" might cause you to act badly or inefficiently — and thus, once again, interfere with your staying alive and being reasonably happy.

    ♦ You can choose, if you wish, to rate yourself as "a good person" because it works; it aids your aliveness and your happy functioning. But you still had better realize that this kind of *global* rating is inaccurate and sloppy. The fact is, you often perform both well *and* badly; you are quite inconsistent over time! A global rating is a "simple" solution to the problem of self-worth. If you choose to use this approach, you may conclude, "I am a good person simply because I am alive, I am human, and I am unique." This is somewhat equivalent to your saying, "Now that I exist, I choose to continue to exist and be reasonably happy, so I will call myself — always — a good person, and thereby help myself continue to exist and be reasonably happy." You existentially choose to remain alive and try to be happy; and therefore you can existentially choose to define yourself as "a good person" to aid those goals.

    ♦ Defining yourself as "a good person" may well be practical and aid your remaining alive and being happy, but it cannot be empirically or logically "proven." It is true *by* definition. Still, it's better than the other choice: defining yourself as "a bad person." What's more, like most definitions, it is safe. If you say, "I am a good person *because* I perform well or because I am effective at winning people's approval," you are in jeopardy of performing badly later and losing people's approval. So you are only temporarily "a good person," and thus, you must keep "proving" to yourself that you still are one.

Defining yourself unconditionally as "a good person," whether or not you perform well and whether or not people approve of you, is much safer and more permanent. For you are then "good" because (a) you are alive, (b) you are human, and (c) are a unique individual. Well, that is pretty safe! As long as you are alive, you will surely be human and unique; therefore, your "goodness" as a person will remain until after you are dead. Then, what does it matter whether you are good or bad? If you choose to define yourself as "a good person" because you are alive, human, and unique, you will never be "bad," which will aid you in remaining alive and reasonably happy.

If you don't want to go to the trouble of refusing to rate yourself or your being, by all means use this definitional way of unconditionally accepting yourself. It works! It is only pragmatically, not absolutely, "true." But that's the one kind of "truth" —without a capital T — you are likely to get!

Let me add one caveat: If you define yourself as "too" good, as really "great," you may then easily slip into thinking of other people as "poor" or "bad." This type of thinking has led many who define themselves as "very worthy" to excuse themselves when they abuse others they consider "low."

◆ Unconditional self-acceptance (USA) also helps you change your behavior when you think that it sabotages your aliveness and your happiness. Because you then say to yourself, "My behavior is bad, but it is only a part of me, not the whole of me, and I have the power to change it. While if I, my entire self, was bad, how could I possibly change my poor behavior? I would be stuck with an essentially 'bad self.' Such a 'bad self' obviously cannot change its parts, its poor behaviors."

Furthermore, your behaviors only constitute *a part of* what you call your "self." They are not your self, per se. Similarly, the *behaviors* of the planets are not *the* planets. So, too, *you* are not your *behaviors*.

When you have USA, however, you watch yourself and your behaviors and often tell yourself, "The thinking, feeling, or acting that I experience is bad and self-sabotaging, but I, a total human, have the power to mold it and change it for the better. Therefore I can work at change!" So your unconditional self-acceptance aids you in growing and developing; while rating yourself as bad or inadequate tends to hinder you.

◆ You therefore may well conclude, "Since I am a person who is not generally 'good' or 'bad,' and since I have some control over my behaviors, I can choose to accept myself with my 'good' (helpful) acts and also accept myself with my 'bad' (unhelpful) acts, and thereby, once again, choose to prolong my life and to make it reasonably happy. I can also improve my 'bad' behaviors and increase my 'good' behaviors and lead an even better and happier existence."

Remember Joyce, the client I described in chapter 2? I helped her see her *musts* that drove her to suicidal thoughts. "Losing my husband to his secretary absolutely must never occur! My failure to keep him shows that I have serious flaws and makes me worthless!" With my assistance, she came to realize that her husband could have left her no matter how she behaved, but that if indeed he found her deficient in some respects, her failings didn't make *her* a failure. She had many virtues as a wife and mother in spite of his lack of appreciation. She was a live, unique *human*; for that reason alone she could rate herself as a *worthy person*. Better yet, Joyce saw that she didn't have to give herself *any* global or total rating, but could just accept herself, her being, with her "good" and "not-so-good" traits, and look for a partner who would do the same. With this attitude of unconditional self-acceptance (USA), she gave up depressing herself and looked forward to an enjoyable life.

Unconditional Other-Acceptance (UOA)

Along with Unconditional Self-Acceptance (USA) you had better learn Unconditional Other-Acceptance (UOA) in order to prevent yourself from becoming emotionally self-disturbing and to *get better* rather than merely *feel better*. UOA implies that you existentially choose to stay alive and to be reasonably happy, and you choose to do so not as a hermit, but as an ongoing member of the human race who inevitably interacts with other humans, usually from your birth to your demise.

You decide that you will live in a social group and you decide that it is in your best interests to get along reasonably well with the members of this group, and to relate intimately to a few of them. You also decide that, to a large extent, your well-being is allied to your group's well-being. You are dependent to a large extent on other group members, for example, for food, education, and social enjoyment, and would fare pretty badly without any such support. You want to be treated, at the very least, fairly and considerately by others, and therefore you had better treat them with reasonable fairness and decency. You do not want to be condemned, damned, or ostracized by people, therefore you unconditionally accept them — even though you may not approve of some of the things that they do to you and others.

As you do in unconditional self-acceptance (USA), you also can do with others—accept them (though not necessarily like them) with their good and with their "bad" behaviors, and refrain from rating them globally as persons. You accept them, as you do yourself, just because they are alive, are human, and are unique. You accept the sinners — but not their sins. You accept the social reality that they are all — every single one of them — incredibly fallible, and you accept them with their failings. Preferably you only rate or evaluate, in terms of your goals and purposes and those of the group in which you reside, the "goodness" or "badness" of people's thinking, feeling, and acting — and not of themselves or their being.

You largely give unconditional other-acceptance (UOA) to all humans because of your own self-interest. For, as just noted, they help you stay alive and enjoying life; you get along better with than without them; and you avoid disturbing yourself, especially enraging yourself, when they do not behave as you wish they would behave. But at the same time, in considering your own self-interest by unconditionally accepting others, you realize that you are a social animal, and that much of what you call your "you-ness," or your personality, is derived from the teachings of others and their reactions to you. Your individual personality is, in large part, really your social personality; the two are inextricably allied. Moreover, your very survival — and to a certain extent the survival of the human race — depends on the survival and well-being of your social group. If you conform to the group too much, too perfectionistically, you will be less of an individual. But if you conform too little, you will also be less of an individual — that is, get less of what *you* really want — and you may well not survive. You are part and parcel of your heredity and your environment — both/and, not either/or. By the same token, you are an individual person *and* are enormously influenced by, and react to, your social group.

To achieve unconditional other-acceptance (UOA), practice these methods:

• Just as you rate your own thinking, feeling, and behaving, but do not give a global rating to yourself, similarly rate the *behaviors* of other people, but not their total selves or being. Rate their deeds as "good" or "bad" in accordance with your own purposes and your group's purposes of staying alive and being reasonably happy. But do your best to only evaluate people's *acts and traits* and not their *total selves*. You will see, as in unconditional self-acceptance, that others do literally thousands of "good" and "bad" things, do them differently over time, and sometimes change the "good" to the "bad" and vice-versa. Therefore they cannot accurately be rated or evaluated as "good people" or "bad people." They are merely people who *do* "good" and "bad" things.

• When you see yourself designating a whole individual as "good" or "bad," realize that you more accurately mean something like "His character is 'good,'" or "Her ways of behaving with other people are 'bad.'" Even then, you are doubtlessly over-generalizing to some extent and had better remind yourself to be more accurate and add "much of the time" or "usually" to your observation.

• If you are exceptionally used to rating *people*, rather than merely their *thinking, feeling*, and *acting*, and you want to continue to somewhat sloppily see them as "good people" — because that will help you get along with them — you can tell yourself, "They are 'good people' because they are alive and kicking, because they are human, and because they are unique." Then you will always see them as "good people" as long as they are alive, human, and unique. This is a definitional concept of their "goodness," but it can work for practical reasons, not because it is absolutely "true." More details on the definitional nature of humans can be found in my pamphlets, "Psychotherapy and the Value of a Human" (1972), and "REBT Diminishes Much of the Human Ego" (1999).

♦ Continue to rate people's behaviors in respect to your own values and those of your social group. You can strongly like or dislike their deeds. If you like their behavior, you can continue to socialize with those people who have "likeable" traits and stay away from, if you feasibly can, those who have "dislikeable" ones. But don't deify the people with the "good" behaviors and don't devil-ify those with "bad" behaviors. Stick to your preferences and feel healthily sorry and disappointed, instead of unhealthily raging and punishing, when people act "badly." While unconditionally accepting them, even when they behave "badly," you keep from disturbing yourself — such as raging or self-depressing — and soon get over these feelings (if you have them), rarely recreating them.

When Joyce's husband left her for his secretary, she at first hated him, since she strongly told herself, "Bob has lied to me and treated me most unfairly, and therefore is a rotten bastard!" At the same time she used REBT to work on achieving unconditional self-acceptance (USA), she also used it to work on achieving unconditional other-acceptance (UOA). In doing so, she realized that Bob was, in some ways, distinctly irresponsible to her and their son, Todd, but he was not a completely *irresponsible person,* nor a *rotten father*. He was a person who did some good and bad *acts*. She strongly disliked his running off with his secretary, but she no longer hated *him*. She also showed Todd how to love his father while hating some of his actions. In achieving USA and UOA, Joyce was able to obtain an amicable divorce from Bob in spite of some of his "rotten" behaviors.

High Frustration Tolerance (HFT)

The three absolutistic kinds of thinking that, according to REBT, create nearly all human neuroses are, again:

♦ "I *absolutely must* do important things well and be approved by significant others, or else I am worthless."

♦ "You *must* treat me kindly and considerately or else you are a rotten person."

♦ "Conditions *absolutely must* be the way I want them to be and not unduly block me from my pleasures and goals, or my life is *horrible!* " It is the third of these "musts" that leads you down the garden path to low frustration tolerance (LFT), which is, again, involved in much self-disturbing.

High frustration tolerance (HFT) consists of disliking any person or thing that interferes with your important goals and values, and wishing — but not demanding — that that person or thing be abolished. It means that you view many things as bad — that is, not in your or your social group's best interest — and some of them as very bad, but you do not view them as *awful, horrible,* or *terrible.* For when you do view them as awful, you demand — consciously or unconsciously — that they *must* not be as bad as they actually are. You also often see them in an exaggerated light as even "worse" or more uncomfortable than they actually are. You frequently tell yourself, "Because these things are *awful*, I *can't stand* them. I *can't bear* them!" Ironically, since you see and feel them as more frustrating than they really are, you often make them — yes, *make them* — still more annoying.

Low Frustration Tolerance (LFT) very frequently gives you a double dose of woe. First, you awfulize about the hassles and problems that confront you, and feel depressed instead of disappointed, anguished instead of discomforted, panicked instead of concerned. Then, alas, you frequently have LFT about the disturbed feelings that you are creating by your original LFT. You insist that your self-depressing *absolutely should not* exist, that it is *awful* and *horrible*, and that you *can't stand it.* So you depress yourself about your self-depressing. Similarly, you insist that your panic is *awful*, must not exist, and that you *can't stand* it. So you anguish about your anguishing, make yourself panicky about your panicking. LFT easily begets more LFT!

In extreme — but not so unusual — instances, when you refuse to tolerate frustration, you really are claiming that you cannot, with your present problem or difficulty, be happy *at all*, and must be *completely* miserable. You either make yourself unable to enjoy almost anything, or you take part in some form of immediate gratification — like indulging in sweets or alcohol — that later brings poor results. LFT then becomes short-range hedonism: indulging in immediate self-gratifying in spite of its future consequences.

Don't think that you are unique by having LFT. Most probably not! In many ways, it is the human condition: innumerable people at times indulge in harmful pleasures, procrastinate at doing valuable tasks, whine and moan about the difficulties they face, seek help that they really don't need, lie and steal to get their way, act impatiently and defeat themselves, refuse to take care of their health, and do many other things that show they have abysmal LFT. Why is this so? Probably because early in the evolution of humanity, LFT had some distinct advantages, and perhaps helped preserve the human race. Loafing at doing useful chores, for example, may have enabled people to have more energy the next day to fight off human or animal enemies. Perhaps. Today most people have considerable LFT because of their innate tendencies and their social learning. So how can you minimize LFT and gain considerable high frustration tolerance (HFT)? In the following ways:

♦ Rate or evaluate the things that happen to you, or that you make happen, as "good" or "beneficial" when they help you stay alive and be reasonably happy, and as "bad" or "harmful" when they sabotage your goals and interests. Similarly rate things and conditions that are considered "good" or "bad" by your social community. Follow cultural conventions that are helpful but don't compulsively follow those that you think will harm you and other people. To some degree, think for yourself!

♦ When you rate events as "good" or "bad," try not to give them absolute or rigid evaluations, but also consider both their "good" and "bad" *aspects*.

♦ You are entitled to your personal tastes and distastes, to seeing things as "beneficial" or "harmful" for your own reasons. You learn many of these tastes and distastes from your own family, community, and society — for you are a social creature — but you still may view many things as "good" or "bad" differently than others do.

♦ Rate some of the things you dislike as "very bad" or "exceptionally bad" when they really block you from getting what you want or force you to do what you don't want to do. But don't insist that these things *should not* and *must not* exist and that it is "awful," "horrible," or "terrible" when they do. Realize that to some extent they must exist when they do. Though there are several reasons why you would *prefer* them to be better, there is no reason why they *absolutely must be*. Naturally, do your best to get rid of them or change them. But if they still are undesirable, they are! Acknowledge that, respect that, accept that.

♦ Labeling conditions that you find bad as "awful" or "terrible" implies that they are as bad as they can possibly be — 100% bad — which they practically never are. Again, it implies that they are so bad that they *absolutely must not* exist. You may also imply that they are even more than bad — 101% or more bad — which of course they cannot be. So they're bad! Awfulness is an invention, a horror in your head, that strongly implies that bad things are worse than they are — and definitely worse then they should be. It may start off by being factual, but then goes beyond that, to fiction. Force it back to being what, in fact, it is — that is, "bad" or "very bad" — according to your values and goals, but not a "horror."

♦ See that, along with your awfulizing and terribilizing, you often insist that you *cannot stand* very bad things. This is almost always false. If you really couldn't stand them, you would die of them. You can only do that once! If you really couldn't bear them, you would not be happy *at all*, and would always be *completely miserable* when they continue to exist. Thinking this, you may *make yourself* thoroughly miserable all the time, but the chances are exceptionally high that in spite of finding conditions bad, you can make yourself happy in several ways — if you try to do so.

♦ Realize that when you define things as "awful" — rather than merely as "very bad" — you thereby create disturbing feelings, which are sometimes worse than the "obnoxious" events that are occurring. Thus, you may panic and depress yourself— feelings that rarely do you any good. Again, you may withdraw from "awful" things and then stop yourself from changing them. Or you may discombobulate yourself so much that you unsuccessfully deal with your problems and thus make them "more awful"! As noted above, you may greatly depress yourself about your self-depressing, and thus encourage additional awfulizing.

◆ Tolerating frustrating events well increases your power to change what you can change. Accepting and bearing your diseases and ailments will help you deal better with them. Accepting difficult conditions will help you feel less horrifying about them and succeed better in spite of them.

◆ Watch the cost-benefit ratio of dealing with difficult people and situations. Hating them, running away from them, refusing to cope with them may be easier in the short run — but not in the long run. As Benjamin Franklin said in *Poor Richard's Almanac*, "There are no gains without pains." The pains are often worth it if you bear with them.

◆ Recognize that your self-disturbing is not easily corrected, and that only a good deal of working and practicing is likely to decrease it. See that this work and practice is beneficial in the short and the long run, because your self-sabotaging is painful, time- and energy-consuming, unproductive, and unenjoyable. It is well worth the time and trouble you take to reduce it — especially if you work at *getting* better and make yourself less *disturbable*.

◆ Look for the fun and enjoyment — not merely the pain and problems — of doing difficult things that are in your best interest. Try to focus on the joyous challenge of doing them, and not only on the trouble and effort. You may well see injustices and needless difficulties are bad, but they can be challenging and maybe even enjoyable to cope with and reduce.

◆ See that it is sometimes very hard to do an onerous task — such as to stop addicting yourself to overeating, but it is much harder, usually, not to do the task. You don't *have* to increase your tolerating of frustration, but it is highly *preferable* to do so. Thinking that you *absolutely have to* bear pain or else you are a worthless person will often make it still harder for you to bear it. But your strong preference, backed up by the work and effort to achieve HFT, will benefit you in both the short and the long run.

Joyce was afflicted herself with low frustration tolerance (LFT) when her husband, Bob, left their marriage to run off with his secretary. She told herself, "Bob absolutely *must not* leave me and our son in this very bad state. How *awful! I can't stand it!* My life is completely miserable and hopeless!"

Along with her self-downing and her considering Bob "a rotten bastard," Joyce's LFT made her exceptionally angry and depressed. In the course of her REBT sessions, I helped her, as noted above, achieve unconditional self-acceptance (USA) and unconditional other-acceptance (UOA). I also encouraged her to achieve higher frustration tolerance (HFT) by working at accepting (but not liking) these grim facts:

- Some aspects of her life were unfortunate, but that didn't mean that her whole life was "horrible."

- The misfortunes in her new marital status *should* exist, no matter how bad they were.

- Though her and her son's changed life was really unfair, she *could* stand it and didn't have to be completely miserable.

- If she accepted the "terrible" frustrations imposed upon her by Bob, she could focus on other relationships and quite likely enjoy them.

When Joyce stopped bemoaning her fate and tolerating (without liking) it better, she was able to build a much happier life for herself and her son, and to actually enjoy many things in life. Her accepting the Adversities that she could not change enabled her to arrange for considerable pleasure and much less pain.

Kevin Everett FitzMaurice suggests that REBT theory can include: (1) USA, Unconditional Self-Acceptance; (2) UOA, Unconditional Other-Acceptance; and (3) ULA, Unconditional Life-Acceptance, when you can't change conditions that you really don't like. If you acquire ULA, you indeed have HFT, high frustration tolerance! USA counteracts your self-downing, UOA counteracts your anger at others, and ULA counteracts your awfulizing and terribilizing.

Using Your Fine Constructivist Potential

Many types of psychotherapy, particularly psychoanalysis, stress that Adversities (A's) that occur, particularly in your early childhood, make you and keep you self-disturbing. They are partially correct about this, in that you may be biologically disposed to take seriously both childhood and later traumatizing, and to upset yourself about them. Each time you do this, your brain and neurological system are affected, making it easy for you to worsen or prolong your original reaction to traumas. It would be better, of course, if you were not plagued by severe traumas and if you were not so vulnerable to them. Often, however, they cannot be prevented.

Fortunately, you have the ability both to construct and to reconstruct your life, and thus you have considerable potential to change your reactions to traumatizing. As REBT theory says, you significantly contribute to the unfortunate things that happen to you by your *Beliefs* (Bs) about your Adversities (A's). While you frequently cannot change the A's, you definitely are able to change your reactions to A at point B.

After Adversities occur, you can change your traumatic reacting to them by *seeing them differently* and not *awfulizing* about them. Thus, you can react to a failure or a loss originally by depressing yourself; then by seeing it as unfortunate — but not catastrophic; and then by changing your reaction to a feeling of sorrow or disappointment.

Before Adversities occur, you can prepare in advance to see them as frustrating but not horrible, or as damaging but not devastating, and can train yourself to react more healthily to them and thereby make yourself less disturbable. If you develop a Believing-Emoting-Behaving outlook that is solidly anti-awfulizing, you can almost automatically stop horrifying yourself about life stressors. Thus, you can see a serious Adversity, such as the loss of a loved one, as an expectable and natural part of life and can remember experiencing many enjoyable moments with him or her that compensate for your loss. You will then feel, almost automatically, sorrowful, but not depressed, about your loss.

Your ability to create, control, and change your feelings by your *Beliefs* is not absolute and has some limitations. As Bertrand Russell once remarked, anyone who thinks that happiness comes completely from within had better be condemned to spend a night in a raging storm in rags in sub-zero weather! But if you acknowledge that you have considerable choice about how you feel under adverse conditions, and use your knowledge to help yourself cope with them, you can react with disappointment and regret, instead of holy horrorizing.

The main philosophizings that you can use to acknowledge and activate your remarkable constructive potentialities include the following:

♦ Recognize that Adversities frequently will happen, blocking you from getting what you really desire and delivering what you abhor. Rarely do you have control over these Adversities. What you almost always do have control over is your *thinking* and *feeling* and *behaving* about them. Even when you are so shocked that you momentarily lose control and respond in a devastating manner, you almost always have the ability to reflect and change your reacting, and thereby responding much differently. Clearly note that you have — and can use! — this constructive ability.

♦ The past Adversities of life may have strongly contributed to your present reactions and may have led you to disturb yourself. But you also significantly contributed to them with your *Beliefs about* past happenings; if you are still disturbing yourself about them, you are contributing to keeping them alive today. You made destructive conclusions about these past Adversities, and you are still, to some extent, making them. You can't change your past conclusions, but you can discontinue to hold them now.

♦ You can radically revise your disturbing *Beliefs* about the past and the present, first by gaining insight into them— recognizing what they were and what they still are; and second, by working and practicing to feel, think, and act against them. No matter how strongly you still irrationally *Believe* about the past, you can modify this tendency today.

• You can see that important elements of your *Beliefs* are the absolutistic *shoulds, oughts, musts*, and *demands* that you previously held about the Adversities of your life and that you still hang on to. You can work at changing them back to preferring and wishing, instead of demanding, by practicing strong preferential — instead of "musturbatory" — philosophizing, and by using the thinking, emotive, and behavioral techniques described in this book.

• Because you tend to innately hold your dysfunctional commanding, socially learn it, and habituate yourself to it for a period of time, you usually will require considerable work and practice to see it, challenge it, dispute it, act against it, and change the commanding into preferring. Moreover, once you give up *musturbating*, you have a nasty habit of easily returning to it. If you acknowledge this and see that you still stubbornly return to it, you'd better go back to the drawing board for more work and practice at minimizing it.

• If you desire to *get better*, and to steadfastly stop disturbing yourself even in the face of unusual Adversities, you can steadily review your panicking and depressing yourself and consistently work against doing so.

I've now described some of the most important ways of *getting better* that stress *thinking* and *philosophizing*. (More of that later!) The next few sections will describe some of the important ways of *feeling better* (and maybe — yes, maybe! — also getting better). Then I'll return to more important ways in which you can make yourself feel *and* get better.

4

Feeling Better I:
Thinking and Philosophizing Methods

ime now to consider some main ways of feeling better —
especially those that emphasize thinking and philosophizing.
As noted before, feeling better is good — *very good.* In some
respects it can be easier and quicker to achieve than getting better.
Moreover, since feeling *bad* tends to preoccupy you, and sidetrack
you from getting better, you may want to take some time, right
now, to feel better. If so, this chapter and the next two are for you.
If not, skip temporarily to Chapter 7. You can read Chapters 4, 5,
and 6 later, when you're ready.

Using Cognitive Distracting Techniques

As I noted in the first chapter of this book, many techniques of
cognitive distracting — such as meditating — work very well to
relieve your tendency to anxietize and depress yourself — usually
temporarily. But they may be used over and over again;
sometimes they become a habit with long-lasting effects.
Moreover, they all have emotional and behavioral — as well as
thinking — aspects; they may lead to profound philosophical
changes — and thereby to your *getting* better.

However, the techniques may present you with a dilemma. Take, for example, relaxing methods, such as Jacobson's Progressive Relaxation Technique, which I'll describe in a moment. Let us suppose you are anxietizing, indeed panicking, about speaking in public, and you freeze and cannot speak when called upon to do so. You focus on relaxing your muscles, from your toes to your head, and therefore find it almost impossible to think about the horror of speaking in public and falling on your face before your onlookers. Suddenly you cease panicking and are able to speak!

Great! But even if this relaxing technique works beautifully, it has several disadvantages:

…You'll have to keep using it every time you are called upon to speak in public.

…You may relax *too* much, and not have enough tension — good tension — to focus on speaking well.

…You may falsely conclude that you cannot speak in public unless you first use the Jacobson technique for twenty minutes or so, or resort to some other relaxing method.

Worst of all, your relaxing technique may work so well that it prevents you from tackling your main panic-creating *philosophizing*: "I absolutely *must* speak beautifully and greatly impress all the members of my audience, or else I am an inept, hopeless person." By relaxing, you marvelously *distract* yourself from seeing this Irrational *Belief* (IB) and from changing it. Despite your "helpful" distraction, your IB remains solidly in place. In fact, because you manage to live "beautifully" and speak in public successfully with this IB, you may unwittingly make it stronger than ever!

When you are panicking, should you abandon all distracting techniques, make sure that you get at the philosophical-behavioral sources of your panic, and forcefully uproot them? Not necessarily. You can, if you wish, use a combination of inelegant and elegant self-help methods. First, calm yourself down and enable yourself to speak well, despite your panicking, by temporarily allaying your panic with distracting techniques. Then persistently look for the Irrational *Beliefs* (IBs) behind your panicking, fully reveal them, and use REBT Disputing and other thinking techniques, as well as emotive and behavioral methods, to contradict and minimize your self-defeating convictions. If you use this combination, your public speaking (or other) panicking may disappear — perhaps permanently!

For example, you can use one or several cognitive distracting techniques, such as these:

♦ *Jacobson's Progressive Relaxation Technique.* Focus intently on relaxing your muscles, from your toes to your head, until your whole body is fully relaxed. The more you focus on relaxing each major muscle of your body, while telling yourself, "Relax, relax," the less you will be able to focus on worrisome, depressing, enraging, or awfulizing thoughts. Details of this relaxing technique are described in my book with Chip Tafrate, *How To Control Your Anger Before It Controls You*.

♦ *Meditation.* As I said in the first chapter, there are several forms of meditation. Some encourage you to focus intently on a key word, like "om" or "peace" or on your breathing, and some urge you to just observe your thoughts, but not evaluate them or take them seriously. Whichever technique you choose, by focusing so intently on a mantra, your breath, or passively observing your thinking (instead of *evaluating* yourself, others, or your thinking) you eliminate the opportunity to worry, depress, or enrage yourself. This distracting may work, but doesn't necessarily change your disturbing *musts*. However, it may at least convince you that you can — temporarily! — be free of (or side-tracked from) them.

Some forms of meditation directly or implicitly include a philosophy — such as the Buddhist, Taoist, or Christian philosophy. They may help you believe that all things are equally good, that "this, too, shall pass," that nothing is sacred, or that God will provide. This kind of philosophizing may promote profound change — either with or without meditating. Also, mere mechanical meditation — such as saying "om" repetitively — may show you that you have alternatives to worrying and may lead you to evaluating and questioning your musts and help you to ameliorate them. So, meditation may — or may not — lead to profound and lasting change.

• *Yoga* consists of gentle exercises that require you to concentrate carefully on your movements and distract yourself from your disturbing thoughts and feelings. It may give you a sense of peace, quiet, and gentleness that you may reflect upon, and thus acquire an "anti-awfulizing" attitude. But the exercises may not do so and may merely be distracting. Recently I saw a young woman who made a living teaching yoga. She herself practiced for two twenty-minute sessions every day and felt relaxed and happy each time. But at the age of 29 she was still frantically worried about not having a prospective spouse and being an "old maid." Her enjoyment of yoga, and the relaxation it brought, had not in the least changed her Irrational Believing-Emoting-Behaving: "I *must* have a guarantee that I will marry soon and not remain a 'worthless old maid.'"

Yoga may be accompanied by Hindu, Buddhist, and other philosophies that may help you to accept yourself, other people, and various grim realities (Adversities), and these may lead to profound philosophical changing. But in itself, it may only lead to your temporarily *feeling* — without *getting* — better.

• *Religious rituals and prayers* can be used as distraction methods — particularly as Catholics often use them. They, too, may lead to profound philosophic changes.

• *Pleasurable diversions.* There are almost innumerable diversions that you may engage in intensively. You can use reading, writing, painting, TV listening, music, internet surfing, shopping, computer games, sports, and other pleasures to distract you from worrying. As long as you are deeply involved in them, they can so thoroughly occupy your attention as to keep you from preoccupying yourself with disturbing thoughts and feelings. Go for it! But when you are no longer distracted, look for other, more philosophical ways of finding your self-disturbing convictions and changing them. Then your "relaxing" may lead to more permanent improvement.

Zack greatly anxietized that he would severely depress himself once again and be utterly miserable. The main way he allayed his anxiety was to turn on the sports channel on TV and watch game after game — baseball, football, basketball — anything to divert himself from his awfulizing. I had a heck of a time convincing this client to accept his potential self-depressing as distinctly *bad* but not *awful,* and by convincing himself that he could handle it if it reoccurred. When he finally acknowledged this, his panicking largely disappeared, and he also spent less time depressing himself.

Achieving a Vital Absorbing Interest

In the first edition of *A Guide to Rational Living* (1961), Dr. Robert Harper and I advocated that our readers vitally absorb themselves in some pursuit in order to create more self-actualizing, as well as to distract themselves to a long-range project — such as raising a family, building a business, writing a notable play or novel, working for a political cause, or otherwise being vitally absorbed, perhaps for thirty or forty years, with a big goal. Our views were that people who did this focused so well on long-range purposes that they had little time and energy for the usual kind of worrying, and thoroughly enjoyed their "magnificent obsession" even when their ultimate goal was not achieved.

A great deal of empirical and experiential evidence supports our view. In the 1970's, Mihali Csikszentmihalyi, a psychologist investigating human happiness, found that even short-term vital involvement can lead to "flow," or intense pleasure for the sake of immersion in what you are doing, instead of one-sided, worrisome concentration on the outcome. (He has described the process in his book, *Flow*.)

Gaining a vital absorbing interest in something, as long as you are not *overly* concerned about how well your project will turn out, is one of the best possible ways to distract yourself from anxietizing, depressing, and raging. If you prolong your vital absorption, so much the better! Your time and energy will tend to be healthily — instead of unhealthily — occupied.

I realize, now, however, that vitally absorbing yourself can be one of the best of the still palliative techniques of fulfilling yourself. Josephine, for example, had two vitally absorbing long-term interests: her three children, whose professional success she plotted and schemed for 30 years; and for 35 years her steady work on the Great American Novel. Both of these avocations brought her joyful involvement; and when I saw her, at the age of 55, she was still "progressing" with her novel. Fine! But Josephine, though unusually healthy, worried incessantly about herself, her husband, and their children dying of cancer, though there was little cancer in her family. Why? Probably because she was a natural "awfulizer." She horrified herself after a close friend died of cancer at the young age of 30, and never stopped worrying about it thereafter.

So you can awfulize about possible "horrors" *even though* you are vitally absorbed in a long-term cause or interest. Josephine probably awfulized less than she would have done without her two absorptions, but she still demanded — and never got — an absolute guarantee that her family would not be afflicted with fatal cancer. With my help, she began to see that there was no reason why she must have that guarantee, and that she could still enjoy life — including her children and her novel writing — even if a member of her family were fatally stricken with cancer. She lost most of her hypochondriacal panicking and became absorbed in some healthy practices that might help her and her three daughters reduce the risks of developing breast cancer.

Using Self-Efficacy

In the first edition of *Reason and Emotion in Psychotherapy* (1962), I distinguished between achievement-confidence and self-confidence — which at that time were often confused in the psychological literature. They still are.

You gain *achievement-confidence* when you actually believe or prove to yourself that you are able to do a task well. Because of your observation or your (sometimes deluded) thought, you predict that you will continue to be competent at this task, and because you have faith in your competence, you often increase your probability of doing it well.

Achievement-confidence, however, is not *self-confidence*, which I defined in 1962 as your steady confidence in yourself as a person — *whether or not* you think you are able to perform well at certain tasks. I now call self-confidence *unconditional self-accepting*. You decide to accept yourself regardless of your performances — and regardless of whether other people approve of you — just because you are alive and kicking. When you have unconditional self-accepting (USA), you usually assume that you can perform well, and consequently do so. But you could have USA, perform poorly, and still decide that you are okay.

In the 1970's, Albert Bandura came up with the notion of *self-efficacy*, and he and his associates performed many experiments showing that when people are self-efficacious — which is about the same thing as having achievement-confidence — they believe (rightly or wrongly) that they can do well in certain tasks, and therefore they actually tend to do better at them. If, on the other hand, they have a sense of self-*in*efficacy, they believe that they will do poorly in some tasks, and they actually tend to do poorly. Thus, if you are confident that you can do well at tennis or public speaking, you will tend to perform better at these tasks than if you believe, for whatever reasons, that you will perform poorly.

Studies by Bandura and others have shown that self-efficacy aids in your performances. It is also correlated with self-confidence, but with *conditional* self-confidence or *conditional* self-accepting (CSA). Thus, if you see yourself as being efficacious at important things — such as school, work, and socializing — you will tend to be self-accepting *because* you perform well. But you will not have *unconditional* self-accepting (USA), which is independent of perceiving how well you perform.

Acquiring a sense of self-efficacy is good, because it helps you to do more of the things you want, and often to do them well. But even the people who have it — millions of people, probably including you — often anxietize about important achieving. "After all," goes their thinking, "I could always fail and then I'd feel inadequate and not self-accepting."

Let us therefore not put down self-efficacy. It is good for many purposes, especially for achieving. It makes you feel good

— very good — about what you do, and often (temporarily) about yourself. For you know, when you have it, that you can perform important tasks well, and that is quite satisfying. But unless you have self-efficacy *together* with unconditional self-accepting (USA), you'll still create much anxiety for yourself.

Take Helen, for example. She especially wanted to be good at socializing and to win the favor of many people she considered important. Because she worked hard at doing so — seeing the good qualities of others and complimenting them on what she saw — she had many friends. But she was always afraid that she would fail to befriend new people and would lose some of her present friends. So she panicked herself about this, which interfered with presenting herself well, especially to new people. She therefore failed to do what she knew would work! Even when she initially succeeded, she kept worrying about bollixing up the relationships in the future.

Helen's self-accepting was conditional and shaky. Sometimes — when she succeeded in pleasing others — she felt very good about herself; other times — when she thought she might be disapproved of — she felt very inadequate. In her case, as in most others, conditional self-accepting didn't work too well.

With my help, Helen kept her interest in befriending others but gave up her *dire need* to do so. She learned to make her social relationships *important* but not *sacred*. When she thought she was failing to win the approval of someone, she convinced herself that that was too bad, but it wasn't the end of the world. She could be happy — though maybe not *as* happy — without that person's approval. She began to deliberately take the chance of being herself with her best friend, Mary, whom she had been panicked about displeasing. Helen told Mary what she really thought about some things that Mary was interested in, thereby risking the friendship. Mary not only took this well, but actually said she found it more fun to be with the "interesting Helen," rather than the "always agreeing Helen." That convinced Helen to be much more herself with other people and not to go out of her way to agree with them. Changing her "dire need" for the approval of others into "strong desire" worked much better. She lost a few friends, but kept the great majority — and felt much less panic.

Don't stop trying to keep friends, get good marks at school, achieve at your job, and work for other goals. But don't connect your *achievements* with your *personal worth*. Enjoy what you accomplish, but be determined to accept yourself unconditionally, *whether or not* you succeed. Then you can try for the best of both worlds: to achieve well and earn the advantages of doing so, but to always accept yourself fully as a person even when *you don't*.

Self-efficacy is worthwhile, but it's not enough. You can have it *with* unconditional self-acceptance (USA). You can feel good about yourself whether you're achieving or not.

Staying in the Present

Because much of your worrying is about what you may do and what may happen to you in the future, some therapists and philosophers recommend cultivating the habit of focusing on and staying in the present. This has certain advantages. Most sports, arts, and scientific pursuits that you are likely to experience occur in the present. If, therefore, you worry obsessively about what is going to happen to you in the future, you'll miss these present experiences — and much of the pleasure of the one life you will ever have. You never can be sure what will happen to you tomorrow, however wisely you plan and scheme to provide for it. And you can easily make this kind of planning frantically preoccupying.

Sam did reasonably well in life, making a good living as an attorney, and enjoyed spending time with his family. But in all these respects, he kept worrying about terrible things that might happen in the future, and therefore never fully enjoyed his work or his family relationships. Most of the things he worried about — clients suing him for malpractice; his children failing at school — never actually happened. When they did, he was able to cope with these disruptive events and figure out solutions to them. But he spent an inordinate amount of time trying to make the "dismal" future not happen. He let the present go by, mechanically coping, but not really enjoying it.

Sam had read in several self-help books about the virtues of staying in the present and focusing on the immediate pleasures at hand. At times he succeeded in doing so, and worried less about the future. But he soon returned to thinking about miserable business or family events that *could* happen; and he worried about and planned detailed solutions to problems that seldom actually materialized. Though he realized that his worrying was useless, he kept at it obsessively.

I showed Sam, in our first several REBT sessions, that his Irrational Believing-Emoting-Behavings included: "Terrible things *must not* happen to me at work or in my family life. If they do, I might not be able to handle them and that would prove that I am not really a competent person. Either I *must* head them off and see that they do not occur, or else I *must* be totally prepared for them and have a detailed plan of dealing with them and improving them. Because my work and family life are so important to me, I must always be on top of them and prove that I am a competent attorney and father. Otherwise they may overwhelm me and show how essentially inadequate I am!"

Under my direction, Sam actively disputed these dysfunctional *Beliefs* and came up fairly consistently with some healthy philosophizing:

 ◆ "Bad things may well happen at work and at home, but they will merely be unfortunate and not terrible."

 ◆ "Seeing that they are merely unfortunate makes me also see that truly "terrible" things are unlikely."

 ◆ "If bad or very bad things do happen, I can deal with them even if they are suddenly sprung on me."

 ◆ "If for some reason I don't ward off or deal with problems efficiently, that doesn't at all affect my worth as a person. I am okay even if my solutions to problems are not very good."

 ◆ "My wife and children, as well as my law partners, are quite capable of handling most of their problems with their own resources, and don't require that I be available every minute to help them."

◆ "I can enjoy many pleasures of the moment if I permit myself to focus on enjoying them, and can have a much more fulfilling life doing so than I would have by obsessively worrying about the future."

◆ "Even if Adversities somehow happen and I am not able to cope too well with them, focusing on the pleasures of the moment gives me an enjoyable life and makes me able to bear better the misfortunes that may, but often don't, arise."

This kind of a philosophizing helped Sam considerably. He also used several other REBT techniques to help him stop obsessively worrying:

◆ He realized he was naturally obsessive, and deliberately restricted his obsessive worry to no more than fifteen minutes a day, forcing himself to think of other things and projects instead.

◆ He made himself constructively engage in sculpting in his spare time. (This activity not only distracted him from a good many of his worries, but he also found it pleasurable in its own right; when he absorbed himself in it, he achieved the process of flow by intently focusing on its problem-solving aspects.)

◆ He practiced Rational Emotive Imagery, and made himself imagine that some of the worst things that he dreamed of actually happened. (He felt very anxious and depressed when he did so, but he changed his disturbed feelings to feeling only keenly disappointed about these "terrible" events. By doing this several times, he became accustomed to automatically feeling disappointed about such bad events when they occasionally occurred.)

Through forcing himself to stay in and focus on the present, Sam distracted himself from his obsessive worries, and also added to the enjoyment of his life. By focusing on today's enjoyments, along with several other "elegant" REBT cognitive-emotive-behavioral methods, Sam effected a profound change in his attitude that helped him both feel better *and* get better.

Similarly, you can make good use of focusing on and staying in your present, even if you are not too seriously disturbed about anything. Rather than let your present pass by in order to "ensure" your future pleasures, take some time out to think about the virtues of living *today*. Then take more time to focus on how you can enhance your *now* interests and involvements. Absorbing yourself in the present can give you real presence — and presents! Otherwise, you may let today go by, but take little advantage of it. Just as becoming vitally absorbed in music, art, or science takes deliberate time and effort, the same concentrating is required for you to figure out and implement ways of *being* present in the present. Don't let your today go to waste by letting it passively pass. That pathway is easy to take — but not sufficient for experiencing a fuller life.

Carpe diem! (Seize the day!)

Making Responsible Choices

I have somewhat wrongly put psychologist Nathaniel Branden, author of *The Psychology of Self-Esteem*, in the "self-esteem camp" for many years, and pointed out that he demands that people like themselves *because* they accomplish. That's not exactly true. My recent correspondence with him reveals that he really encourages people to *responsibly* accomplish: that is, work for goals and values that have "good character" and social responsibility.

Well, that's a little better — but it still seems conditional to me. You will find it *highly desirable* to *responsibly* help yourself and other people; but, please, don't make even that type of accomplishing *necessary* to your self-accepting. If you do, you'll still make yourself prone to anxiety and depression.

Try, instead, the goal of *preferential responsible choosing*. Select and work for aiding goals that help you, other people, and the environment in which humans reside. In doing so, be *responsible* to yourself, others, and the world. Social interest and global interest go along with *self*-interest. According to REBT, you still have a choice — meaning some (not a total!) degree of "free will." Choose it!

5

Feeling Better II: Emotive, Evocative, and Experiential Methods

There are many emotive-experiential methods you can use to help yourself feel better when you are beset with woes and tribulations and are reacting — or overreacting — badly to them. Psychotherapy and self-help materials are full of them. These methods almost always work, probably because emotional exercises serve several functions. First, they are absorbing in their own right, and thereby can distract you from becoming emotionally disturbed about problems. Second, they are largely pleasurable, either immediately or in the long run. Third, they help you see the good side and possibilities of life, and hence make you aware of the cost-benefit ratio of indulging in anxiety and depression. Fourth, they provide alternative ways of thinking and acting, and help you abandon the idea that you *absolutely must* do this or *must not* do that. Fifth, they involve and include cognitive — and, especially, behavioral — processes that encourage change. In fact, in significant ways, the methods themselves *are* thinking, feeling and behaving *differently*.

The trouble with many — perhaps most — of the emotive-evocative methods of making yourself feel better is that they do not necessarily aid your making a *profound philosophical change*; sometimes they might even sabotage your efforts. Let's take a look at one of them to see how this works.

Other-Approval and Self-Approval

Perhaps the most common way people try to help themselves feel better when they've disturbed themselves is to seek the approval of other people, including their therapists. Trudy was a classic case in point. Although reasonably competent in most of the important things she did, she had perfectionistic standards of how well she *should* do — consequently, she felt she never did well enough. She was especially efficient at her computer programming job, made a good living at it, and received regular increases in salary. But she always found someone — often the head of her group — who was more adept than she, and compared herself woefully to him or her, berating herself mercilessly for her "ineptness." She did the same thing in other aspects of her life — such as dieting and sports — and consequently chronically depressed herself.

Noting this when she was still in her teens, but refusing to give up her need to perform perfectly, Trudy focused instead on winning the approval of others. She figured out that flattery would get her somewhere, so she told other people how bright and attractive they were, and she was exceptionally nice and helpful to them. Naturally, she had many friends; several who were devoted to her. Putting herself down for her "ineptness" added to other people liking her. They realized her competence, but found it unthreatening because she always downplayed it.

Trudy's good relationship with others kept her partly distracted from her own self-downing. It provided her with enjoyable relationships that added to her life. Because of external approval, she found life worth living in spite of her "failures," knowing that she would always have friends. When she did not succeed with some people, she saw that there were others who really liked her, so she didn't need the love of all the people all the time. This approval from others helped her to accept herself when she did not achieve her standards of perfection.

Consequently, Trudy lived a "good" life in spite of depressing herself about her lack of outstanding accomplishments. However, she was so distracted by her preoccupation with social relations, that she gave little thought to the source of her self-disturbing: her obsession with achieving perfection. In fact, she used her social "successes" as a tradeoff against her achievement "failures," and got by in spite of them. She was wildly happy when she socialized, and felt depressed when alone, but she knew that she could always enjoy old and new intimacies, so at least she led a half-way decent life. Though an ardent problem-solver in her computer programming activities, Trudy gave little thought to how she was depressing herself with her perfectionism and didn't try to solve this problem. She was too busy making and keeping friends.

When she came to see me, Trudy was startled to discover that she was largely depressing herself with her *insistent demands* that she do remarkably well at work, school, and sports. I had to force her to discuss her perfectionistic demands, because she kept side-tracking us by talking about her relationships. Either she talked about new friends she had made, or discussed techniques of keeping old friends. So, we had lots to talk about — except her perfectionism about accomplishments! I kept bringing her back to this, especially when she felt depressed, but she continued to escape into approval-seeking topics.

I finally made a rule that we would only discuss her social affairs for half the session — and spend at least the other half on her depressing herself about her perceived lack of accomplishments. This eventually worked. Trudy became more aware of her own demands to perform outstandingly, and her view that she was worthless when she didn't. Eventually she did some Disputing of her Irrational *Beliefs* and partially surrendered them. She depressed herself less, and devoted more of her time to accomplishing — *reasonably* well — some of the projects she had been avoiding. She still enjoyed being with her friends and intimates — but acted less compulsively about spending time with them and winning their approval.

Let's not quibble about this. Winning the love and approval of significant other people is one of the great joys of life; millions of people devote much time and energy doing this. If you enjoy it, by all means cultivate this garden. But watch out for *compulsive* socializing because you consider yourself unlovable and worthless if you don't win the favor of others. Also, don't merely seek approval to compensate for your other lacks and deficiencies. Try to remedy some of these deficiencies and, if you can't improve them, *unconditionally accept* yourself as a person in spite of them.

You can experience the joys of relating with people as a satisfaction in its own right, and not to make up for or distract you from your other failings. When Trudy stopped needing others' approval to compensate for her accomplishment failures, she chose to have fewer friends — and as a result had better relationships with them. She selected them for their intrinsic virtue, and not for their ability to make up for her deficiencies. A number of her friends were not that interesting, and she quietly dropped them. She found the time spent with the remaining, well-selected friends was more valuable.

If you enjoy winning social approval, try doing so to *get* better and not merely to *feel* better. Realize that you *like* your friends — and even *love* some of them — but you don't absolutely *need* them. Figure out ways of making new friendships and maintaining old ones — but don't do so compulsively. See how quality counts more than quantity — especially since you have a limited amount of time and energy to cultivate a friendship.

Apply a cost-benefit analysis to whom you befriend and whom you ignore. Weigh those choices against your own interests, values, and goals. Observe how effective people usually divide their time between social affairs and other aspects of their lives. Pick friends you can learn from — including learning how to disturb yourself less and enjoy yourself more. Leave yourself some time for being alone and for doing some of the things you can usefully do when you're by yourself.

Devote some of your time alone to creative pursuits that are not possible when you are immersed with others. But also see if you can be collaboratively creative when you're with your friends, as well as when you're by yourself. Use some of your time with your friends to accept them unconditionally, even when they act badly. Work on your over-sensitivity when you are with some of your sometimes-irritating friends. Don't get rid of them too easily. Recognize that you are disturbing yourself about their behavior. Try not to sacredize or to devil-ify your intimates. Once again, use gaining their approval to both feel better *and* (preferably) to get better.

When the "Other" is a Therapist

If you pick a therapist to help you with your problems, beware of becoming obsessed with loving or being loved by him or her. Good therapists can support and help you. They will care for you as an individual, and they have an incentive to help you become happier and less disturbed. Some of them may come to care for you personally, and would if they had met you outside the therapy office. But this also has its dangers. A therapist who cares too much for you personally may not see clearly what is needed to help you work on some of your basic problems. She may be too kind to you — too lenient and lax — and may not want to "hurt" you with needed honest confrontation of your self-defeating behaving. This type of "caring" may encourage you to have more therapy sessions than you actually require.

If a therapist personally *dislikes* you, of course, that may have its own hazards — such as seeing you as "sicker" than you are, giving you a deliberate hard time with homework assignments, wanting to get rid of you too quickly, or unconsciously wanting you to suffer. Real problems!

There are also several dangers if you feel too close or maybe even in love with your therapist. You may not want to reveal your failings. You may want to keep disturbing yourself and stay in therapy for a long period of time. You may want to change mainly for the therapist and not for yourself. You may unthinkingly do what the therapist wants you to do and not what you really want to do in life.

If you are over-attached to your therapist, you may put your worth on the line for his or her love. This is the Achilles heel of some so-called "humanistic," person-centered therapies. Carl Rogers, for example, rightly emphasized, as does REBT, the therapist giving you *unconditional* accepting, in order to show you how to model it for yourself. But that approach may help you to accept yourself for the wrong reason: *because* your therapist accepts you. That is *conditional* self-acceptance!

If your therapist correctly teaches you how to achieve *un*conditional self-acceptance (USA), you achieve it *whether or not* anyone else, including your therapist, accepts you. Quite a thing! So by all means pick a therapist who accepts you unconditionally — whether or not you do well at therapy or anything else. But don't let his or her acceptance help you to conditionally accept yourself. As usual, watch it, and think for yourself!

Getting the approval of others is great in its own right, and may, in several ways, distract from your self-disturbing. But *getting better*, rather than *feeling better*, means that you must take a penetrating look at how you sabotage the way you function — and minimize it! This can be done, along with getting approval, by first thoroughly accepting yourself and stopping your self-sabotage. As a result, you'll have greater ability, more time and energy, and more incentive to win social approval as a healthy companion to your self-approval.

Using Support Groups

Support groups have long been available for self-disturbing and self-handicapping people. When you make yourself panicked or depressed, finding a group of people who have something in common with you, and meeting regularly with them, can help you see that there are others with problems similar to yours. Perhaps they have experiences or ideas to share about ways of coping. You may also find a religious, political, social, or athletic group that interests you. Getting involved in discussing and working for common goals may distract you from your disturbing feelings and behaviors.

Support groups, which usually concentrate on one particular kind of self-disturbing behavior, have become very numerous and popular in recent years. Thus, you can find groups of people who are suffering from depression, manic-depression, panic, grief, obsessive-compulsive disorder, etc. Some groups include victims of domestic violence, substance abusers, holocaust survivors, and AIDS patients.

Thus, in a support group you can find people who similarly "disturb themselves" and are very willing to listen and talk with you. Some of them have more information about your distress than you have. Most of them tend to be sympathetic and supportive. You can use some of them as good coping models. You can personally befriend some of the members, who may help you in various ways. The group itself may be an advocate for your kind of distress and may help fight prejudices against it. The group may provide reading and recorded materials that are useful. For these and other reasons, you may be helped by joining and regularly attending such a group.

However, support groups may also have their disadvantages when they are not led by a well-informed and fairly rational leader. Alex, one of my clients who had AIDS, joined a group in which all the other five members also were afflicted with AIDS. Alex had previously been in one of my regular therapy groups, where we helped him considerably to overcome his anxiety, so he knew something about REBT. In his AIDS support group, however, Alex found that most of the other members got together every week mainly to bitch and complain about how horrible their disease was and how their lives were completely ruined by it. After a few weeks of hearing this, he was panicking more than ever about having AIDS, so he returned to one of my groups, where the seven other members had the usual problems of depression, anxiety, and rage about various misfortunes in their lives.

Alex almost immediately perked up with the use of REBT, helped the other group members dispute their Irrational *Beliefs* (IBs) about their life hassles, was encouraged and given homework assignments to dispute his own IBs. He soon was less depressed and anxious. After a few months, he became too ill to continue with the group; he died a year later. Several group members who kept visiting Alex reported that he remained in good spirits till the end. He was hardly deliriously happy, but was minimally panicked and depressed.

The usual kind of support groups, then, have their disadvantages. Some of them are cultist and promulgate unrealistic and unhelpful ways of coping with self-disturbing behavior. Others spend much time in endless wasteful discussions of trivia. Some of them include disruptive people who bother the other members and are hardly helpful.

Many support groups — at best — are palliative rather than curative, only helping people to *feel better* rather than to *get better*. A friend of mine, Julie, was a member of a grief group after she lost her father and mother during the same year. She got a good deal of sympathy and support from most of the members of the group, but some of them blamed her for not grieving enough, and some tried to persuade her to be very angry at God and the universe for taking away her parents. The group did nothing at all to distinguish between grieving and depression, and did not show her how to stop "depressing herself" by giving up her demanding that her parents *should not* have died when so young. Some group members also encouraged her to castigate herself for not being with her parents more while they were still living.

Julie did not want to buy these notions, so she quit the group and helped herself by reading a few REBT books that showed her how she could strongly grieve without depressing herself. She concluded that it was extremely sad that she had lost both her father and mother in the same year, but that they would not have wanted their deaths to devastate her. They were both in their sixties and it was expected that they would live much longer. But Julie was able to see some good that they died in the same year, since they each would have had a hard time living without the other. Julie loved them both, but that was hardly a reason why they shouldn't die, nor that they shouldn't die in the same year. She decided that she would spend more time with her father's brother and her mother's sister with whom she had compatible interests. With attitudes like these, Julie bore up quite well; she was sad and grieving for the next year or so — but not depressed. She did much more to help herself with some REBT philosophizing than the support group had done for her.

In your own case, if you are sincerely grieving over the loss of a loved one, you can try a support group and perhaps receive a great deal of benefit from it. You can do so if you have a physical disease or are emotionally distressed. At the same time, especially if you receive limited help from the support group you pick, you can use REBT to look at your *demands* — such as demands that you not be physically or emotionally afflicted — and turn them back into strong *preferences*. You can thereby get what help you can from the support group you select and still use some of the main cognitive, emotive, and behavioral techniques in this book to work on your basic attitudes, feelings, and behavings.

Religious Faith

Many people have helped themselves over the centuries by using religious and spiritual methods when they are emotionally disturbed. In doing so, some of them have acquired a profound philosophy of self-help that has supported them in their deepest crises. The Buddhist philosophy teaches that life includes a considerable amount of pain, but that you can cope with this if you don't strongly need or demand pleasure. It shows how you can even surrender your strong desires for pleasure and achievement and get along unmiserably. The Christian ideal, as several REBT practitioners have shown (e.g., Stevan Nielsen, Brad Johnson, Steve Johnson, Hank Robb, Mitchell Robin, Ray DiGiuseppe, and others), teaches that you can accept the sinner but not the sin; you can accept yourself and others despite your sinning; you can unconditionally accept yourself and other people.

Various religious philosophies overlap with the teachings and tenets of REBT and other proactive attitudes. If you follow them, you may make a profound philosophical change, accept yourself and others, and develop a strong ability to tolerate frustration. You can achieve these goals if you are agnostic or atheistic, but certain religious outlooks may appreciably aid or enhance them. In a recent book, *Counseling and Psychotherapy with Religious Persons,* Stevan Nielsen, Brad Johnson, and I have shown how REBT is highly compatible with some kinds of religions — especially with religions that posit a kindly, forgiving God.

At the same time, religious views and actions often lead their devotees to *feel* better even when they do not, in an REBT sense, encourage them to *get* better. Thus, the essence of several religions is that God will provide a major source of support, help you in your hour of need, and take care of you in important ways. Some of these religious concepts, however, are, again, palliative, and will help you definitely to *feel* better rather than to *get* better.

There are several reasons why this is so:

◆ You have to depend on and have faith in a supernatural force or deity, even though you have no way of proving empirically or scientifically that such an entity exists. When you are not specifically helped by this force in the manner that you want to be, you may easily make yourself disillusioned with it and may suffer setbacks.

◆ Ideally, mental health seems to consist of faith and confidence *in yourself*, with no intervening variable, such as a God or spirit on whom to rely. Dependency on some hypothesized "god" may weaken your faith in yourself and make it more provisional.

◆ When you believe devoutly in some kind of God or supernatural force that you cannot factually support, you are likely to resort to some element of dogma or absolutism. But mental health, as stressed in REBT, is allergic to dogmatic, absolute conceptualizing and is open-minded, flexible, and scientifically-oriented.

◆ Some religions tend to hold absolutistic, inflexible rules of conduct, which needlessly restrict your freedom, and which again are somewhat opposed to flexible, democratic rules and practices favored by mentally healthy individuals.

There are, of course, many different kinds and degrees of religious believers. Some are much more self-directed, unconditionally self-accepting, socially interested, and accepting of uncertainty and ambiguity than are others. Nonetheless, devout religious faith and belief are, in many respects, safe, secure, and reliable. They do have, for many people, some advantages. Therefore, it is not totally unwise to adhere to them, at least in part. Too-rigid adherence to religious rules and attitudes may indeed be harmful to many people — and even some Catholic priests oppose what they call "scrupulosity" or rigid adherence to Catholic rules. But more liberal and compromising forms of religion may use the advantages of profound faith unfounded on fact, and blend it with the factual "realities" of the world. Even if religious views are merely palliative — helping people to feel better rather than to really get better — they still may aid people with disturbing feelings to suffer less.

Spiritual Beliefs

The use of spirituality in helping to disturb yourself less is a somewhat different matter than the use of religiosity. The word "spiritual" stems from the term spirit, or ghost, or supernatural entity; as such it is almost the same as the terms *religious, supernatural,* or *God-oriented*. In regard to this view of spirituality, we may say much the same things as we just noted about religion. Spirituality of this sort has its drawbacks and limitations, but you also may use it to distract yourself from and to have faith in overcoming your self-disturbing. But since it is again somewhat opposed to factual "reality," it may help you — temporarily — to feel better rather than get better.

There is another, and rather different, kind of spirituality, that many therapists employ to try to help people live better with and to sometimes minimize their distressing. Consider the dictionary definition of *spirituality*: "spiritual (of the mind) etc. Refined, sensitive. Connected with the spirit, etc. Not with external reality (his spiritual home)." This can be significantly different from god-oriented or supernatural spirituality. "Spiritual" includes two different definitions of *sensitive*. On the one hand *sensitive* means receptive to esthetic experiences. Thus, you may be sensitive to art, literature, and music. But on the other hand, *sensitive* means emotionally vulnerable — which is often a form of over-sensitiveness to adversities and over-vulnerability to criticism by others. Artistic and esthetic sensitivity are usually beneficial, while emotional sensitivity or vulnerability can be harmful.

Somewhat similarly, "spiritual" can mean being out of touch with reality, since you can be too romantic or convinced of magical and supernatural entities. Or spiritual can mean having an optimistic, purposive, vital absorbing interest in things, which in some ways puts you in better touch with reality and better able to cope. This second kind of spirituality is often encouraged by therapists and experts on happiness.

Jerome Frank, among others, noted a good many years ago that when self-distressing people have this second kind of spirituality, they nicely get into the spirit of things, have great hope for the future, take an optimistic view of how they can cope with difficulties, and especially are constructively purposive. They have distinct goals and values in life and they focus on achieving these purposes, frequently on a long-range basis. They are determined and forceful in pursuit of their major aspirations; they often have a concerted philosophy of life that helps structure their thinking and doing — such as devotion to a system of ethics or to a humanitarian cause. This kind of spiritual seeking can be valuable and happiness-producing to practically anyone; it is particularly useful if you are prone to anxiety and depression and want to overcome these tendencies.

Let's look at a case in point. Peggy seemed to have been born and raised to have depressive tendencies — as both her father and mother often depressed themselves and taught her to have a pessimistic view of the world. She realized that she had mood swings during her adolescence, particularly when she compared herself to her younger brother, Paul, who took an optimistic view of life and was sure that even the worst events would turn out well and that he could handle them. Peggy felt, instead, that things would normally turn out badly and that she would not be able to deal adequately with them. Then, when she depressed herself about this, she berated herself and made herself seriously melancholic.

Noting that she *absolutely needed* others to approve of her, and was seriously affected when they didn't seem to do so, Peggy first made a habit of helping her peers in order to win their steady approval. She then acquired a philosophy of helpfulness, making it a central theme of her life, and devoted herself to the cause of serving others by deciding to become both a nurse and a nun. She found the monastic life too academic and lonely so she eventually gave it up, but still devoted herself to nursing.

Peggy built her life around helping others in several important ways. She made a fetish out of truthfulness and always made sure she was exceptionally honest with people, even at her own expense. She was an active member of several charitable agencies that assisted underprivileged children and adolescents. She served as a volunteer mediator in marriage and family disputes, and taught a course on ethics at a social service center, encouraging her teenage students to follow ethical rules.

After awhile, Peggy's preoccupation with helping others, and particularly with helping them to be ethical, was no longer something of a ploy to get people to like her — for by this time she was widely respected and had plenty of friends — but became an avocation in its own right. She constantly taught, preached, and acted in humanitarian ways; although she was no longer religious, she consistently lived in accordance with the doctrines of St. Francis.

Peggy was so absorbed in her work and in promulgating ethical and helpful philosophizings that she had little time for self-depressing behavior. When something sorrowful happened in her life — the death of her mother; the affliction of her dear friend with Hodgkins Disease — she threw herself more than ever into her humanistic pursuits and concentrated on helping others with their sorrowful situations. She was so absorbed in this that she didn't have time to depress herself.

Untypically, however, Peggy fell in love with one of the doctors she worked with, a real lady's man who had affairs with every attractive woman he could take to bed. He showed no interest in Peggy, who was reasonably attractive but no real beauty. To make matters worse, he could see that Peggy was deeply enamored of him, craving his reciprocation, and making something of a nuisance of herself when they were working together. In order to put her off, he became deliberately critical and cruel toward her, almost arranging to get her fired for incompetence. His cruelty broke her heart and she seriously depressed herself about it. She went into a shell, only performing some desultory nursing for awhile, and stopping all her "do-good" activities. Nothing seemed to matter any more; she returned to her adolescent state of self-depressing.

When I saw Peggy for therapy, we soon determined that she had at least two Irrational *Beliefs* that led to her self-depressing. First, she flagellated herself for being unattractive to the doctor she was in love with and for bothering him so much with her attentions. Second, she berated herself for stopping her devotion to helping activities. Peggy also realized that her compulsion to help people was something of a diversion from her basic urge, at the age of 33, to have a husband and children. She had originally picked the nursing profession because it was such a good thing to do, and brought her genuine acclaim. But her worth as a person was really highly conditional and depended on her chosen goal of being kind to others and winning their approval.

In the course of therapy, Peggy realized that her do-goodism was a fine pursuit, and that it largely had distracted her from her negative self-rating tendencies, but by no means had eliminated them. Her life was constructive and purposive; she truly enjoyed, to a large degree, helping others. But she accepted herself largely *because* she did good deeds, not unconditionally. She had to work hard to give up the idea that she must *earn* self-accepting by aiding others. So for several months Peggy fought to surrender this conviction. She finally accepted herself as a somewhat "selfish" person, who basically wanted to devote herself to a husband and children, and only secondarily to humanity in general. When she accepted this "failing," although she still enjoyed her nursing and helping others, she primarily worked at finding a suitable husband. In fact, she made that her main — though not frantic — goal in life.

The moral of this story is that being purposive, optimistically centering your life around a big goal, and being spiritual in this sense, can bring excellent results. It can distract you from your anxietizing and self-depressing and give you enjoyment in its own right. But it can also be used to cover up your lack of *unconditional self-accepting*, and thereby prevent you from dealing with important issues. It therefore can help you feel better without getting better — and may in fact interfere with this latter goal.

Feeling better is good, but getting better is better. If you elect to follow spiritual methods to get better, keep in mind these four key guidelines for a healthy spiritual approach:

  • First of all, try to be *spiritually purposive*. Have goals and values — including long-range ones— that structure your life to some extent and give you something to work for. If you can acquire purposes that help others as well as yourself, and that are viewed as "worthy" by society, that is all to the good. Pick your goal, give it some real thought, and then work at accomplishing it.

  • Second, pick a purpose that *you truly enjoy*, and not an aspiration that you think that you *should* select. Choose it because you like it and because you think there is a good chance that you will enjoy working for it.

  • Third, beware of egotistical reasons for choosing your purpose! If you have practical ego reasons — you want to achieve something because doing so will win you friends or material things you enjoy having — that's not so bad. You are entitled to go after what you want because it brings you rewards. But watch out for egotistical, self-centered reasons for striving for your goal (e.g., public recognition, awards, financial gain, political power). Success of this type will not make you a better person, nor make you deserving of happiness, "perfume your wormhood," or get you into heaven. Thinking this way will give you highly *conditional self-accepting* — and make you always liable to a pratfall when, for any reason, you do not achieve this kind of "worthiness."

  • Fourth, pick a basic goal or purpose that includes or is allied to a philosophy of *getting better* as well as *feeling better*.

Thus, make it your goal to not only achieve unconditional self-accepting (USA), but also to teach it to others, through talking to them, holding classes, writing about it, and otherwise "spreading the gospel according to REBT." Perhaps sponsor a contest. Apply it to business, education, and sports. Try to model it for others. Make it as much a part of your life as you can — just as you would do if you favored a political or religious philosophy and tried to promulgate it for others to follow.

Take these same steps for other basic self-helping philosophies that enable you to get and stay better emotionally. Try, as well, to aid others in developing helpful core philosophies. Spread the word on unconditional self- and other-accepting, and promote other rational attitudes. Work at achieving them yourself; but also take them up as causes and see if you can help influence other people to think about them and act on them. Promulgating unconditional self-accepting (USA), unconditional other-accepting (UOA), and high frustration tolerating (HFT) may well become your social interest. It may also serve as a model, an encouragement, and a rehearsal for your own self-fulfilling changes. Double consummation!

6

Feeling Better III:
Behavioral and Activity Methods

REBT has always favored real-life practice or risking beneficial exposure as a method you can use to feel better and get better. In fact, I used it successfully on myself at the age of 19 — before I ever thought of becoming a psychotherapist! If you force yourself to change your behaviors, you can sometimes change your feelings quickly and effectively. In addition, you may profoundly change part of your underlying philosophy.

Over the centuries many religious, spiritual, and other groups have found this to work. Thus, the famous Zen Buddhist teaching says, "When you meet the Buddha on the road, kill him!" This paradoxical directive lets you see that no one but yourself can basically help you, and that unthinking devotion to a guru or cult has great limitations. To improve, you have to take suitable, self-changing risks yourself.

The trouble with some of the most popular behavioral methods of self-changing is that they are distracting and often enjoyable in their own right, but they may not help you change your fundamentally self-disturbing outlook. The Yoga teacher in chapter 4 enjoyed doing Yoga for two twenty-minute sessions every day, and hardly worried about her important goal of marrying *while* she was doing it. But after the exercises were finished, she often went right back to catastrophizing about the fact that she was twenty-nine years of age, still far from having a permanent mate, and might indeed never have one. Horrors!

I shall now describe some of the most popular heavily behavioral self-help methods that you can use to help yourself feel better, and I'll show you how they can, sometimes, also help you to get better.

Using Breathing Exercises

As Robert Fried has shown, one of the best forms of relaxing and helping your mind and body get ready for successful living is breathing exercises. Frequently, especially when you are self-disturbing, you breathe incorrectly — for example, you may hyperventilate. This both leads to, and results from, emotional dysfunctioning. Read Dr. Fried's book, *Breathe Well, Be Well*, and see for yourself.

Some of the main points emphasized in Dr. Fried's breathing exercises are:

♦ Chest breathing tends to be rapid and shallow. Sitting comfortably, place your left hand on your chest, your right hand on your navel, and breathe normally for one minute. If your left hand is almost motionless while your right hand moves when you inhale, that is good; you are a belly breather.

♦ If, however, your left hand rises noticeably, or if both hands move more or less simultaneously, that is bad; you are a chest breather.

♦ To become a belly breather:
   ✓ stop sucking in your gut
   ✓ avoid tight clothing
   ✓ breathe through your nose instead of your mouth
   ✓ practice belly breathing at least twice a day for about four minutes each time.

♦ At the same time, practice muscle relaxation. Imagine that the tension in the muscles in your forehead is flowing out of your body each time you exhale. Do the same thing, breath by breath, with your jaw, neck, shoulder, arm, hand, leg, and feet muscles.

This form of breathing, like most relaxation techniques, will temporarily distract you from anxietizing and self-depressing and help you feel much better. If you also want to get better, use breathing exercises along with the other thinking-feeling-behaving profound methods of self-therapy described in this book.

Exercising Methods

Exercise is good for the body — and frequently for the soul. It may stir up your endorphins and help you depress yourself less when you are in a dismal mood. It may interrupt your anxious or other obsessive thinking and encourage you to have more healthy ways of thinking. It may lead to pleasurable experiences that sidetrack you from your disturbances and add to your life so that you see living as much more satisfying than you previously did. It may provide experiences — such as unique uses of your body — that let you see that you can choose alternative purposes and goals, and not merely stick rigidly to old ways.

On the other hand, devotion to exercise can sometimes interfere with your rational thinking-feeling-acting and sidetrack you from arriving at elegant solutions to your self-disturbing. Nonnie, for example, got so many benefits from her devotion to running and calisthenics that she tried to induce all her close friends, male and female, to also participate. She kept so busy that she had little opportunity to depress herself. When she felt bad about her work or her relationships with men, she vigorously interrupted her mood with some form of exercise. She enjoyed this so much, and got her body working so well, that she almost immediately felt okay.

This kind of distraction and pleasure stopped working as Nonnie became older. She failed to get a steady boyfriend — partly because some potential partners resented her obsession with exercise, and objected to her insisting that they also relish it. She felt stuck in her boring teaching job, but could make a good living at nothing else, so "had to" keep at it another ten years before she could retire with a pension. Although she had beautifully tolerated the hassles of exercising and keeping in good physical shape with dieting, she *couldn't stand* being alone and unmated, and she ranted and railed against her teaching job (but didn't try to find a good way out of it). So, in spite of her exercising, Nonnie depressed herself.

Nonnie's main Irrational *Beliefs* (IBs) were that she *absolutely must* be permanently mated before she was 37, and that she *must* have a choice of interesting jobs that would require no more training than she already had. As she began to dispute these creeds, she depressed herself much less and tolerated teaching better. When she only partially believed her disputing and the rational coping statements that it helped her formulate, she used an REBT technique invented by British psychologist Windy Dryden, one of the foremost theorists and practitioners of REBT.

Dryden's technique involves two steps:

⬧ vigorously disputing her Irrational *Beliefs*,

⬧ checking on the accuracy of the Rational *Beliefs* that she arrived at through her original disputing.

Thus, Nonnie's main dysfunctional dogma was that she couldn't stand her "boring teaching job." In disputing this dogma, she came up with the coping statement, "I may never like teaching first-grade students, but I definitely *can* stand it and even get some pleasure out of doing it." She only mildly convinced herself of this flexible idea and, therefore, deliberately used the Dryden technique to reinforce and sustain it. Thus, she asked herself, "Where is the evidence that I *can* stand this boring teaching job?" She came up with the answers: "It obviously won't kill me, and I *can* lead a reasonably happy life even if I keep it till my retirement. I still have many things that give me pleasure and that compensate for my job — such as my running and calisthenics, and enjoying my dates with attractive men, even though I haven't yet found a permanent mate. I also distinctly enjoy close friendships with my mother, father, and brother and sister. There are several aspects of my life that are highly pleasing, *if* I stop plaguing myself about being bored with teaching."

Nonnie also then asked herself, "Why *can* I stand my boring teaching job and even get some pleasure from doing it?" She answered, "The job is not by any means *totally* boring. Some of the children are cute and lovable; I could almost eat them up! I also love being of real help to the few handicapped students that I have, and I enjoy aiding them academically and seeing that they lead a happier life. I like speaking with the sophisticated parents of some of my students, and conferring with them as to how they can scholastically and emotionally assist their children. I enjoy my relationships with some of the other teachers, with whom I have a lot in common."

By using this method of questioning her light Rational *Beliefs* and showing herself that they definitely held water, Nonnie was able to believe them more thoroughly, to much better tolerate the hassles of her work, and to overcome much of her self-depressing.

Nonnie still enjoyed and benefited from her exercising. But when she began to acquire anti-depressive, rational philosophizing, she used exercising less to distract herself from her boring job and her failure to find a permanent mate, and more as a satisfaction in its own right. If you use various kinds of exercise to alleviate your self-disturbing, you, too, can continue to benefit, but also, more elegantly, you can get at the main convictions behind upsetting yourself and change them. Exercise as much as you will; but also try to make use of the various cognitive, emotional, and behavioral methods described in this book to help you effect profound changes in your life.

Sports and Athletic Games

Participating in sports and athletic games can be employed as a form of exercise to relieve self-disturbing and to create a more self-fulfilling life, for they have the advantages of independent exercise — and more. They can be particularly useful for several reasons:

+ They require a good deal of training and practice, which are usually healthfully absorbing.

- They often have regular schedules that keep you steadily involved.

- They are sometimes difficult and intriguing — as, for example, playing basketball and hockey are — and therefore keep you mentally preoccupied.

- They often require playing on a team and with other teams, calling for your social involvement.

At the same time, sports may have a number of possible disadvantages.

- They consume much time, energy, and sometimes money.

- You may become involved with people with whom you have little in common, except for the sport itself.

- You may easily over-involve yourself obsessively-compulsively in a sport.

- Certain sports, such as skiing, may be physically dangerous.

As a distraction and relief from anxietizing and self-depressing, sports have pretty much the same limitations noted in the previous section on exercising. They may be even more distracting than simple exercise, and because of your intense involvement, you may keep from getting to and revising the main philosophizing that leads to your self-disturbing.

Bill often erupted violently and had "temper-tantrums," raging against other people that he was utterly convinced were behaving wrongly or unfairly. He was advised by a high school coach to take up boxing, and let all his anger out in the prize-fighting ring. Being well-built and strong, he became a champion fighter in both high school and college, and for awhile he became a professional boxer. His friends and fiancée, however, urged him to give up professional boxing to become a high school gym teacher, which was much safer and more remunerative. But he still did some amount of amateur boxing, and seemed to let off much of his angry steam and to feel good about winning matches with some of the "bad guys."

Unfortunately, the leeway that boxing gave Bill to beat the hell out of some of his opponents helped *increase*, rather than decrease, his aggressiveness. It helped make him more solidly opposed than ever to people who were "damned wrong" and led to his being more determined to angrily show them the error of their ways. He even insisted that his fiancée, Jane, be "right" and "fair," and more than a few times he lost his temper and came close to striking her when, in his eyes, she failed to meet those standards.

Jane put up with Bill's temper tantrums for awhile but then insisted that if he didn't get therapeutic help, she would break off their engagement. Reluctantly he came to see me for, he hoped, a few sessions. Actually, he stayed almost half a year, only gradually beginning to accept and apply some of the virtues of REBT. He still was quite definite in his opinions of what was "right" and what was "wrong" about people's behavior. But he finally saw that he had fascistically demanded that people who were "wrong" must agree with him, change their ways, and behave "rightly" — or else he would damned well see that they did.

In therapy, Bill also saw that his raging at people who behaved "wrongly" was being reinforced by his fighting. Where running or playing golf might serve to distract him and give him a chance to calm down when he enraged himself, boxing — including yelling and screaming at his opponents — made him think that he was "righter" than ever and that other people were inexcusably wrong. Therefore, his boxing encouraged temper tantrums. Once in a while, his loss of temper helped him win a fight, as when he landed a haymaker. But usually it interfered with his more precise boxing skills and contributed to him actually losing matches.

On one occasion, Bill was very angry at his school principal and thought of K-Oing him because he was unfair to Bill and to several other teachers. I showed Bill that he probably was quite right about criticizing this principal — because, by usual standards, he did seem to be acting unfairly and the teachers under him were suffering unduly.

"All right," I said, "let's suppose that he's really unfair and that he's doing a good deal of harm. You're madly contending, 'He should be fair! He has no right to be unfair! He has to be stopped from being that way!' But I say, he *should* be just as unfair as he is. In fact, right now, at this moment, he *has* to be unfair — because he *is*. And there's no evidence that you will make him fair by viciously fighting him. In fact, your anger will most probably engender return anger — and then he will act even more unfairly than usual. But again, he *has* the right to be unfair when he isn't fair. I want you to strongly say after me, 'Damn it! So he's unfair! He has a *perfect right*, a real prerogative, to be just as unfair as he is! In fact, right now, he *can't* very well be otherwise — he can't be fair!' Repeat this, just as strongly as I said it."

Bill was reluctant, but finally agreed to repeat these words — a lot less strongly than I had said them. I got him to repeat them a few more times — each time more strongly. "Now," I said, "how do you honestly feel at this moment?" Bill had to admit that he felt a little better, a little less angry. "All right," I said. "Take this as a homework assignment. Every day for the next few days say these words strongly to yourself — as strongly as you can. And let's see what happens."

Bill did the assignment and began to control his anger. At the end of two weeks, he acknowledged, "You know, I'm really beginning to see it. My principal *should* be unfair because that's the way he usually is. Very unfair! Therefore, he cannot very well, right now, be fair. And I'm foolishly demanding that he be what he, right now, cannot be. And I'm probably encouraging him, with my demands, to be even more unfair. I'm really aiding and encouraging his unfairness! How stupid of me!"

Bill got the point and kept working on accepting, *though never liking*, his principal's unfairness. He lost most of his anger and became more effective in organizing some of the other teachers to discuss issues, fairly calmly, with the principal. He still kept up some of his amateur boxing — but became a better, more adept and less self-angering boxer. He used boxing as a sport, a pastime, and not as a release or distraction from his rage at other people. His tantrums with his fiancée and his friends diminished considerably as well.

If you participate in sports to make yourself feel better when you afflict yourself with anxiety, depression, or rage, you can partly model yourself after Bill. You can interrupt your disturbed feelings by focusing on the sports that you use, by distracting yourself with them, and by deriving real pleasure — which usually is also anti-disturbing — from your participation. But distracting yourself may well not be enough. Suspect that your self-disturbing is also related to your irrational demands on yourself, others, or life conditions.

Especially when you, as Bill did, fill yourself with rage against people and events, look for the grandiose demands you are making — that people absolutely must not be the "bad" way they are, or that adversities must be the "good" way that they aren't. Find your conscious or unconscious demands and turn them into *flexible preferences*. Yes, you can strongly prefer that Aunt Sophie stop her constant bitching, that your brother and sister treat you fairly in the distribution of your parents' assets, that your boss give you due credit for working overtime when you have a nasty cold, and that your children keep the house in fairly good order when you are on vacation. But don't *insist* that these "good" things *must* happen and that "bad" things *must not*. You'll often have enormous trouble changing people's ways when you find them annoying; but you'll have less trouble changing your own reactions to their ways when you can't change them. The less you stress yourself about the unniceties of your life, the fewer stressed-out reactions you'll experience.

So, when unfair and undue hassles befall you and you have little control over them, sports may help you to make profound philosophical changes that will truly improve your present and future life.

Errin, for example, played a great deal of tennis to distract herself from her self-upsetting when she could only keep a low-paying civil service job while most of her friends went on to be successful lawyers, doctors, or other professionals. Eventually she realized that even though she played well, with all her practice she would never excel or win any championships. So she focused on the pleasures of playing, and of occasionally making an excellent shot, rather than on the necessity of winning. She developed a general philosophy of being *joyfully absorbed* in sports and other activities, rather than proving how great a person she was by winning.

Errin's new philosophy enabled her to greatly enjoy several activities at which she hardly excelled, and to unconditionally accept herself even when she failed. She thereafter lived a fairly unaccomplishing life, but an actively enjoyable one. Following her new philosophy, she even thrived on throwing herself into her mundane job and accepting the challenges it sometimes presented.

Participating in sports, then, can lead you to make anti-disturbing philosophical changes, as well as distracting you from your self-upsetting. By thinking about your involvement in sports you can:

- accept yourself fully even with your failures and mediocrities

- enjoy the social aspect and camaraderie with other players

- acquire discipline and tolerate frustration better

- conclude that playing poorly is more enjoyable than not playing at all

- see the health benefits of your participation

- gain additional values and self-changes from your sporting activities

You can, of course, learn to perform a sport better if you keep practicing. But you can also teach yourself to improve your goal-seeking by developing a sensible philosophy of sports participating.

Yoga Exercises

Yoga exercises have been used for many centuries for relaxing purposes and to distract oneself from self-disturbing. Many people have benefited from the exercises, usually consisting of gentle, relaxing movements that demand steady concentration. Therefore, while you are performing Yoga, you interrupt your worrying, depressing, and angering, you relax the various muscles of your body, and you frequently focus on pleasant thoughts. Yoga is also often accompanied by Hindu, Buddhist, Taoist, and other philosophies that may counteract your worrying and help you temporarily, or more permanently, create tension-free actions.

Like all distracting activities, Yoga exercises tend to be palliative in that they do not necessarily change your basic ways of thinking, but give you full permission, as it were, to return to agitating yourself. Therefore they have some of the same limitations as exercise and sports, described above.

Also, though Yoga exercises have been used for many centuries, practically no empirical studies have been done to show which specific exercises are more effective than others, and which may be harming. Reports have noted, for example, that certain head stands— part of some Yoga exercises — have resulted in serious neck injuries that have required medical attention. As a result, Yoga teachers may avoid using particular positions with their pupils. A great many different types of Yoga exercises exist, and much research is necessary to see how effective — or ineffective — they tend to be.

In performing Yoga, you can choose to do it by itself — as millions of people all over the world do — or in conjunction with one of the Eastern philosophies that go with it. Again, these philosophies, though widely used, have by no means been researched. Some of them seem to consist of mystical nonsense. Such notions — such as the Taoist idea that all things in the universe, including inanimate rocks and human life, are equally alive and have equal rights — are almost certainly false when viewed from the perspective of practical "reality." But that doesn't mean that you cannot believe in them and benefit from them. As

I noted in the section on spiritual and religious methods of helping yourself in the previous chapter, ideas that might otherwise appear unrealistic may sometimes help. If you devoutly believe that God or the Devil has personal interest in you and will help you with your specific problems, you may derive benefits from holding this implausible hypothesis.

So if you decide to do Yoga exercises regularly and they seem to be helping you, you can get even more permanent results, and feel better as well as get better, by picking some aspects of the philosophizing that goes with your brand of Yoga; or select some other sensible philosophy that will help you make a profound attitude change. Naturally, I recommend the REBT philosophies that are presented in this book. But you have the choice of other kinds that may work for you.

Business and Other Practical Distractions

Many people save themselves from much anxiety and depression by keeping busy with business or practical affairs. Some do it deliberately, knowing that it will work; others just have so many things to do in life, in order to earn a living or to keep their affairs going, that they are preoccupied with activities much of the time. As long as they keep their nose to the grindstone and do not insist that they *absolutely should and must* beautifully solve business and practical problems, they can nicely use busyness for distracting purposes.

This, as we have been showing, has limited mental health value. It may keep you from worrying excessively, but may also prevent you from recognizing the Irrational *Beliefs* behind your worrying, and then revising them.

Temporarily, however, this distracting technique, like many others, can be useful. For instance, Manny constantly worried about whether he was attractive enough to win the approval of women he wanted to date and develop intimate relationships with. He was sure that he could not succeed in these respects, and consequently avoided social gatherings, hating himself for copping out. Consequently he devoted himself day and night, and weekends, too, to his real-estate business. While he did very well at it, his work left virtually no time to look for suitable romantic partners. He wasn't really getting what he wanted from social relationships, but his very busy life kept him from much self-disturbing.

Manny's best friend insisted that he was largely wasting his life in this one-sided manner, and pushed him into therapy to work on his social-sexual anxietizing and on his phobic withdrawing.

In REBT, Manny learned that he was achieving *conditional self-accepting* by doing so well in his real estate business and patting himself on the back for his success. He saw himself as being very successful, and therefore a *productive and good person*. He tried not to think about his disappointing social life, but still considered himself an inadequate person because of it.

His work in REBT helped Manny decide that he was not a good or a bad *person*, but merely a person who *did some things* very well, such as real estate, and *some things* badly, such as socializing. He worked very hard on rating and evaluating only *what he did* and not *himself as a person*.

When he started seeing this, Manny also saw that failing with women was against his interests, and therefore bad, but that didn't at all make *him* inferior. At worst, it would make him someone who won the favor of fewer attractive women than most men of his age, but it would not mean that he was totally inadequate, and that he couldn't achieve any of his social-sexual goals.

Seeing both sides of the self-rating coin was truly a revelation for Manny. He realized that being great at real estate didn't make *him* a great — or even a good — person. And being deficient at socializing didn't make *him* a bad one. His social performance was inadequate for his goals — but he was far from being an inadequate man! These self-revelations deprived Manny of some of his main reasons for compulsively keeping busy at real estate. He no longer gained human worth by doing so. His business no longer distracted him from his self-downing for failing to socialize. He stayed quite busy (though not compulsively so) because he really enjoyed real estate, and made considerable money at it. He therefore continued doing the right thing — but now for the right reasons. And he made himself take some time to socialize so that his life improved considerably in that area as well.

Busyness, in business and other practical affairs, is a valuable part of life. By all means "indulge" in it — unfrantically and uncompulsively — not to prove your worth— but for various other reasons that are satisfying to you. As with other kinds of distractions that you can use to feel better when you are emotionally out of sorts, try out busyness for its own sake; you may thoroughly enjoy it, and still be able to tackle your self-upsetting by getting at the philosophical underpinnings and restructuring them.

Skill Training Methods

REBT, from its inception, has always favored a good many skill-training techniques in psychotherapy. Thus, REBT has specialized in assertiveness training, communication training, sex, and love relationship training, social skills training, and various other kinds of skill training. Janet Wolfe, Executive Director of the Albert Ellis Institute in New York, and I teach these skills during our therapy sessions with individual and group clients, and we have regular lectures and workshops on this kind of training at the Institute. An important component of Cognitive Behavior Therapy is showing people how to gain and improve key life skills.

Why? Well, obviously if people disturb themselves because they are deficient in certain common skills, helping them to remedy their abilities will often help them to accept the frustration of doing poorly, and to stop putting themselves down. From a therapeutic standpoint, what could be clearer?

Like other therapeutic methods, however, skill training can be palliative, temporary, and can actually block more elegant therapeutic change. For one thing, it is very human to accept oneself conditionally — because one relates well, dances beautifully, is good at sports, and acts in a generally competent manner. Achieving often leads to feelings of self-efficacy; and as I have noted before in this book, self-efficacy encourages *conditional self-accepting, because* one behaves efficiently; while *unconditional self-accepting* means respecting oneself *whether or not* one behaves efficaciously.

Skill training, moreover, is often preoccupying. Some skills take a long time to learn and require steady concentration while you are learning them. Therefore, you have trouble simultaneously worrying and depressing yourself about Adversities in your life.

Moreover, after you have learned a skill — like ballroom dancing or operating a computer — you are likely to spend a good deal of time practicing and enjoying it. Here, again, you may well distract yourself from the troubles with which you may assail yourself if you were not busily occupied. So, like business or engaging in sports, skill training often leads to preoccupying yourself with various endeavors, which, as I have already shown, help take you away from anxiety, depression, and rage.

Once again, however, the time you spend skill training and devoting yourself to practicing these skills may only stop you from disturbing yourself temporarily — and hardly elegantly. As an example, Katie badly tolerated the difficulties of her work as a waitress, her social relationships, and keeping her apartment in order. So she either avoided doing irksome tasks, or else she partially did them. Either way, she kept bitching and complaining about how awful her life was when she had to spend so much time doing things that she hated just to make a living and to get along with her friends and family. She consequently depressed herself much of the time.

Katie's lack of frustration tolerance also kept her away from trying to do what she always wanted to do: to become an actress. She hated taking acting classes, especially doing improvisations. She fought with her acting partners, always accusing them of trying to upstage her. She rarely went for auditions, since they required endless waiting and rarely led to any interesting parts.

When Katie started to go with Ned, also an aspiring actor, he began to push her into taking acting courses, to work on her rage against her acting partners, and to go for a good many auditions. As a result of Ned's encouragement, Katie started to really devote herself to rehearsing and became adept at displaying her talents at auditions and at acting itself. She became so preoccupied with her acting career that, except for the time she spent with Ned, she had little opportunity to build up or display her propensity to poorly tolerate frustration.

This worked out fine as far as Katie's acting was concerned. But it didn't quite generalize to the rest of her life. Katie still complained bitterly about her work as a waitress, was impossibly demanding of her friends and relatives, and kept her apartment a constant mess. In fact, just because she began to tolerate frustration better, she seemed to think that she could get away with giving vent to angering herself in other aspects of her life. If anything, she made these aspects worse.

Katie, at Ned's urging, came to some REBT sessions, read a few of my REBT books, and listened to several tapes. She then realized how she was going for immediate gratification and avoiding the pain required for self-discipline. Her main Irrational *Beliefs* (IBs) were: "I *must* have a *guarantee* that my putting up with the hassles of life will get me what I really want — and quickly! Some things, like acting, are a joy to do, but they require too many other annoyances to make them worthwhile. If I'm really bright and effective, I'll be able to find ways of getting what I want without going through the impossible burdens that are often required for getting there."

As a central feature of her work in therapy, Katie vigorously disputed these convictions and made some progress in giving them up. One of the REBT techniques she used was *forceful Disputing*. So she had Ned role-play herself and rigidly hold these self-defeating ideas and refuse to surrender them when she, playing herself at the same time, argued with him and tried to get him to give them up. Ned really knew her self-defeating convictions and steadily hung on to them when he took her part in their role-playing. But Katie persisted, got practice in actively Disputing them, and ultimately made significant inroads against them. Then she worked on her general inability to tolerate frustrating conditions, as well as to applying herself to her acting career. She began to accept her work as a waitress with few complaints, to give up her impossible demands on her friends and relatives, and to keep her apartment in reasonably good order. She finally faced the fact that her refusal to tolerate frustration was enabling her to "get away with things" in the short run — but immensely bollixing up her life in the long run.

Skill training, such as Katie did with her acting, doesn't always stop you from dawdling in other aspects of your life, from incensing yourself against other people, or from refusing to accept yourself unconditionally, even when your skills improve. Usually, though, it too can be combined with basic philosophizing change.

Dennis put himself down for not being adept on the computer, as was his wife, Davida. She used it much more efficiently in their business than he did, and he was sure that he never would be able to equal her skills. As his therapist, I kept showing him that even if he were correct — that no amount of skill training on the computer would make him as good at using it as Davida — he would not be a deficient person — just someone who had less skill on the computer than his wife. At the same time, I induced him to take a course in operating the computer, which Davida had never taken, having taught herself to become proficient.

After a slow start, Dennis was able to operate the computer almost as well as Davida, and began to enjoy doing so instead of threatening to abandon it and let Davida do all their computer work. He realized that his impatience about learning quickly, and his self-downing for learning less ably than Davida, were seriously getting in his way. So he not only interrupted these two self-defeating behaviors by first working hard to learn the computer, but he also worked ideologically-emotionally against the roots of his self-downing and low frustration tolerance.

Dennis— unlike Katie described above — began to *unconditionally* accept himself — especially when he was not very good at business. He also worked on conquering low frustration tolerance with his in-laws when he saw that they were not going to change their "obnoxious" ways, and realized that angering himself at them was harming his relationship with Davida.

Skill training, as noted above, can provide you with inelegant *and* more elegant therapeutic results. The mere fact that you spend much time and energy learning an important skill may distract you from your self-distressing. It may also show you that aptitude for this skill is important but not sacred, that you can accept yourself without being proficient at it, and that you can increase your self-disciplining by taking the trouble to acquire it. While engaging in skill training, you can think carefully about the advantages of doing so, and can even see that your life is better for accepting the trouble you take to acquire new skills.

You can choose to learn new skills, to change some of your self-defeating attitudes, or both. Naturally, I recommend that you take the latter choice!

7

Getting Better I:
Thinking and Philosophizing Methods

ow that you have taken some time to focus on methods of
feeling better, let us return to the more profound
methods of feeling *and* getting better. These tend to be
harder to achieve for many people — but well worth the effort!

There are a number of thinking or philosophic ways in
which you can not only minimize your emotional-behavioral
dysfunctioning, but also get better and make yourself less
disturbable. I'll cover several of them in this chapter. First, a
reminder: *"Philosophizing" does not only mean simply thinking*. It
also includes — because you are human — emoting and
behaving. In particular, the philosophies that are presented in this
chapter can affect you deeply and intensively if they are just that
— *affective* (emotional). You had better hold them forcefully,
vigorously, persistently, thoroughly and yes, *emotionally*. Also,
you had better hold them actively, energetically, and assiduously
— meaning, *behaviorally*. We will discuss their emotional and
behavioral aspects in more detail later. But let's understand right
now that philosophies, especially those presented in this chapter,

include both *affective* elements and *action* tendencies. That is why they work!

The philosophizings that you can use to get better and stay better are not separate and distinct. They overlap with each other and are often closely connected. By the time I get to each of them, I have already, to some extent, mentioned the previous ones so they will be partially repetitious. But that is an advantage; by repeating them in several forms, you will get used to them — cognitively, emotionally, and behaviorally. If they are useful — as of course I think they are — they bear repeating. Your reflection upon and use of them will help them sink into your thinking, feeling, and doing.

Disputing Core Irrational Believing: Absolutistic Shoulds, Oughts, and Musts

As I have already shown, according to REBT, practically all humans — including Joyce from chapter 2 and other panicky, depressed, and raging people — drive themselves to despair by turning sensible *wishes, desires*, and *goals* into absolutistic internal *demands* and *commands* — that is, into imperative *shoulds, oughts*, and *musts*.

Jules, a 27-year-old graduate student in English literature, had the usual desire to excel in class, write a brilliant thesis, and become, in a few years, an outstanding professor and the author of a critically-acclaimed book on the romantic novel. Nothing wrong with aspiring to do remarkably well; his goal was similar to that of many graduate students. However, Jules had a long history of turning his healthy wishes into extreme demands. Like Joyce, he had three main dogmatic *musts*:

• "I absolutely *must* do remarkably well in my courses and write the best thesis ever turned into my department."

• "My main professor and advisor, Dr. Smith, absolutely *must not* block me in any way, as he is prone to do. He is thoroughly no good if he does block me."

• "Conditions in my department, and the university in general, absolutely *must* not be too difficult, and should make it easy for me to get my degree in record time."

Holding these three imperatives, Jules panicked whenever he thought he would get a mediocre grade in any of his courses. He was often extremely angry at Dr. Smith for giving him a hard time with his thesis. And he suffered from low frustration tolerance (LFT) and from depressing himself when his school changed some of his course requirements and lowered his scholarship stipends.

I first showed Jules that his goals and preferences to do well, get cooperation from Dr. Smith, and have the school administration function better were all healthy aims and values. REBT practically never argues with or disputes people's basic preferences and goals — as long as they are just that, strong *preferences*.

I put Jules' *Beliefs* (IBs) system within the ABCs of REBT and then taught him how to Dispute (D) his dysfunctional *Beliefs* (B) and arrive at E, an Effective New Philosophy that would help him make himself significantly less panicky, raging, and depressing. His Disputing consisted of questioning and challenging his IBs, first realistically or empirically; second, logically; and third, practically, pragmatically, or heuristically. His use of the ABCs of REBT then included:

G (Goal) — to do remarkably well in my graduate courses.

A (Adversity) — "My course in the Nineteenth Century Novel is quite difficult and my professor may give my class a very rough test in which I may do badly."

RB (Rational *Beliefs*) — "I want to do well in this course and win my professor's approval. I'd better work hard to do this."

C (Consequence: Healthy Negative Feeling and Behaving) — Feelings of concern and determining to study and do well in the course.

IB (Irrational *Beliefs*) — "I *absolutely must* get a high mark in this course! If I don't, it will be disastrous! I'll fail to get my Ph.D. and be a complete jerk!"

C (Consequence: Unhealthy Negative Feelings and Behavings) — *Panicking*. Unable to concentrate well on studying for the course.

D (Disputing of Irrational *Beliefs*) — *Realistic Disputing*. "Why *must* I get a high mark in this course? Where is it written that it will be disastrous if I don't?"

E (Effective New *Beliefs*) — "I obviously don't *have to* get a high mark in this course, though that would be highly preferable. A *preference*, however, is not a *necessity*. It will not be disastrous if I don't get a high mark in this course, because my life and the world won't come to an end. It will just be very inconvenient, but I can still survive and get my Ph.D."

D (Disputing of Irrational *Beliefs*) — *Logical Disputing*. "Does it follow that if I do poorly in this course, I will fail to get my Ph.D. and be a complete jerk?"

E (Effective New *Beliefs*) — "No, it doesn't logically follow. Even if I do poorly, I can still get my Ph.D. Even if I fail to finish my doctorate, that will make me, at worst, a person who at times *acts* jerkily, but never a *total jerk*. I may behave poorly, but *I* am no*t* my *behaving*. To think so is to inaccurately over-generalize."

D (Disputing Irrational *Beliefs*) — *Pragmatic or Practical Disputing*. "If I strongly believe that I *absolutely must* get a high mark in this course, that I will *never* get my Ph.D. if I don't (and therefore be a complete jerk), where will this philosophizing get me?"

E (Effective New *Beliefs*) — "It will get me very panicked; because of my panicking I'll probably do poorly in studying for the course. So I'd better change this *believing* (Believing-Emoting-Behaving)!"

When Jules Disputed his Irrational *Beliefs*, that he *absolutely had to* do his course work well, in these realistic, logical, and practical ways, he still *desired* to do well in his course and was *concerned* about doing so, but he didn't *panic* and he studied more effectively. We also Disputed his *Beliefs* that led to his angering himself at Dr. Smith. His ABCDE's were as follows:

G (Goal) — To get along well with Dr. Smith and win his favor.

A (Adversity) — "Dr. Smith is giving me a hard time with my thesis."

RB (Rational *Beliefs*) — "I wish he wouldn't be so difficult and give me such a hard time."

C (Consequence: Healthy Negative Feelings and Behavings) — Feeling disappointing and frustrating. Determining to try to get Dr. Smith to change and favor him.

IB (Irrational *Beliefs*) — "Dr. Smith *absolutely shouldn't* be so difficult and give me such a hard time. How terrible! He's a rotten bastard!"

C (Consequence: Unhealthy Negative Feelings and Behaving) — Strong feelings of raging.

D (Disputing of Irrational *Beliefs*). *Realistic Disputing* — "Is it true that Dr. Smith *absolutely must not* give me such a hard time? Why is it terrible if he does?"

E (Effective New *Beliefs*) — "No, He definitely *should* give me a hard time! That's his way and it *should* be, right now, just because it *is!* It's highly inconvenient that he's giving me such a hard time. But it's not totally bad or terrible; it could be a lot worse. For instance, he could abandon me and my thesis altogether, and get me thrown out of school!"

D (Disputing of Irrational *Beliefs*). *Logical Disputing* — "Even if Dr. Smith gives me a hard time, does it follow that he is a rotten bastard?"

E (Effective New *Beliefs*) — "No. His acting badly to me by giving me a hard time only proves that, in my eyes, some of his *acts* are bad, but not that he as a *whole person* is rotten. That's foolish over-generalizing."

D (Disputing of Irrational *Beliefs*). *Pragmatic or Practical Disputing* — "Where will it get me if I strongly believe that Dr. Smith *absolutely should not* be so difficult when he actually *is* that difficult?"

E (Effective New *Beliefs*) — "It will make me angry at him, which, if he sees my angering, will probably lead to him being more difficult."

With the use of these ABC's and with the Disputing of his Irrational *Beliefs* (IBs), Jules felt himself at point C (Consequence), very *displeased* with Dr. Smith giving him a hard time, but no longer *enraged*.

Finally, Jules used the ABCDEs of REBT in the following manner to work on his low tolerating of his frustrations and his depressing himself:

G (Goal) — To quickly and easily achieve a Ph.D. in English Literature.

A (Adversity) — The school abolishes some of Jules' courses and lowers his scholarship stipends.

RB (Rational *Beliefs*) — "I really wish they would not change these courses and want them to give me the same scholarship funds they gave me last year."

C (Consequence: Healthy Negative Feelings and Behaving) — Feeling and acting distinctly annoyed and frustrated at the school's actions.

IB (Irrational *Beliefs*) — "How *awful!* I *can't stand* their acting this way! They *absolutely must not* be allowed to change things like that. How horribly unfair! What a rotten school!"

D (Disputing Irrational *Beliefs*: *Realistic Disputing*) — "What makes their actions awful? Can I really not stand their behaving this way? Is there any reason why they absolutely *must not* be allowed to act the way they did?"

E (Effective New *Beliefs*) — "Their actions are hardly as bad as they could be. They're just very inconvenient! I obviously *can* stand them, since I haven't died of them yet; and if I *couldn't stand* them, I'd have no happiness whatever. But I do, in spite of them, have things that I enjoy. There is no reason whatever why the school *must not* be allowed to change things. Even though I don't like it, it is clearly their prerogative!"

D (Disputing Irrational *Beliefs*: *Logical Disputing*) — Even if the school is very unfair in changing things and making them worse for me, how does it logically follow that they *absolutely must* be fair? Granted that, at least in my eyes, they are wrong to make these changes, does their wrongness make the school *totally rotten*?"

E (Effective New *Beliefs*) — "No matter how unfair the school's acts may be, it is silly to say that they *must* be fair. Obviously, if they *had to* be fair, they would be! The school's wrongness may indeed be very wrong, but this only proves that some of their actions are wrong, and not that the school is *completely* rotten. Clearly, they do some right and good things, too."

D (Disputing Irrational *Beliefs*: *Practical Disputing*) — "Where will it get me if I say that the school's actions are *awful*, that I *can't stand* them, that it *must not* be allowed to change things the way it has changed them, and that it is a totally rotten school?"

E (Effective New *Beliefs*) — "It will get me nowhere, except very upset. It certainly won't help me change the school and their unfairness to me. Not a bit! Nor will it help me to get my degree!"

When Jules Disputed his Irrational *Beliefs* about his own need to excel, about the iniquity of Professor Smith, and about the horror of the school's changed conditions, he minimized his self-downing, his rage at Professor Smith, his poor tolerating of frustrating conditions, and his depressing himself about his school changes. He then proceeded, more efficiently, to get his Ph.D.

And Now It's Your Turn

In your own case, if you tend to be anxietizing, self-depressing, raging, or tolerate frustration poorly, try the following steps:

♦ Acknowledge your disturbing, unhealthy feelings — such as your severe panicking, self-depressing, or raging and other self-defeating behaving.

♦ Assume that some Adversity (A) exists that opposes your important goals (G) — such as your desire for achieving success, approval, and comfort.

♦ Assume that you are consciously or unconsciously holding some distinct *Beliefs* (B) about the Adversity (A) that you are concerned about.

♦ Assume that you have some *Rational Beliefs* (RBs) about these Adversities (A's), such as: "I wish they didn't exist." "How annoying." "I don't like them and will try to change them." You *prefer* that your A's not exist or that they change.

♦ Assume that you also have *Irrational Beliefs* (IBs) about your A's. Such as, "These Adversities shouldn't exist!" "It's *awful* that I have them!" "I can't stand them!" "I am no good for helping to create them!" These are *demands,* or *insistences,* that your Adversities not exist or be reduced.

• Persist at finding your IBs with your A's — your *shoulds, oughts, musts,* and *awfulizing* about them. Look for them until you clearly see them.

• Actively and vigorously Dispute (D) your IBs *realistically* and *empirically* to prove to yourself that they have no basis in social reality — they are opposed to the facts of life. Typical realistic Disputes are: "Why *must* I perform well?" "Where is the evidence that people *have to* treat me fairly?" "Where is it written that good conditions *certainly must* exist?" "What proof is there that because I failed a few times, I'll *always* fail?"

• Actively and forcefully Dispute (D) your IBs *logically.* Show that they are inconsistent — that your conclusions do not follow from your premises and your factual findings. Typical logical Disputes are: "Because I *want* very much to succeed, does it follow that I *have* to?" "Even if I fail many times, does that really make me a *failure* or an *inadequate person?*" "If people treat me unfairly and badly, does that make them *rotten people?*"

• Actively and forcefully Dispute (D) your IBs *practically, pragmatically,* or *heuristically* — to see what results you get. Typical practical Disputings are: "What results will I get if I think that I *absolutely must* succeed and am a *worthless* person if I don't?" "Will believing that other people *absolutely must* treat me fairly get them to treat me better?"

• Persist in Disputing your IBs until, after awhile, you rarely uphold them and automatically tend to disbelieve them.

• Also, Dispute your IBs by using the emotive-experiential and active methods of working against them that are described later in this book. You might find this difficult. You may tend to persist in your Irrational *Beliefs* steadily and habitually. Instead, strongly persist in *challenging, acting against, feeling against,* and *Disputing* them until you minimize them.

8

Getting Better II: More Thinking and Philosophizing Methods

As I have been demonstrating, you can easily disturb yourself by *catastrophizing* and *awfulizing* about the past, the present, and the future. To "catastrophize" (a word I invented in 1956) is to exaggerate Adversities into something far worse than they actually are — to see them at their worst, when sometimes they are relatively minor. Then, in addition to catastrophizing, you add "awfulizing." This means that you not only see something as very bad — which it may indeed be, in terms of your goals and values — but you also tend to see it as *totally bad,* or as so bad that it *absolutely should not* be that bad. Occasionally, you may even see it as worse than bad — which is of course impossible; but that doesn't mean that you don't see it that way!

Dealing With Catastrophizing Thinking About the Future

As a member of the human race, you think not only about the past and the present, but preventively about the future. This can be very good, since you may thereby ward off unfortunate things that are likely to occur. You may first — sanely — think, "*What if* bad things occur?" "*What if* I act foolishly and produce poor results?" "*What if* people treat me unfairly and I let them get away with it?" Good — to some extent, but easily run into the ground — by you and other people. If you think only about Adversities that have a high probability of occurring — such as failing a test if you don't study for it — fine, then you can preventively do something — such as study sufficiently — to stop this undesirable event from happening. But — ah! — you may have the tendency to think of *low-probability* disasters — such as the airplane you are on crashing, or your instructor unfairly marking down the test you have adequately studied for — and to incessantly worry about these rare occurrences actually happening. Or you may worry about something that could easily occur — such as failing an unusually hard test — and think of the unlikely results that could also occur: such as being thrown out of school for failing the test; never being able to get in to another school; failing to get the degree you need to become an accountant; and being forced to spend the rest of your life in a low-paying, unsatisfactory job.

To catastrophize usually means to turn a relatively small event into a holocaust; awfulizing means to think that horrors will easily occur when normal misfortune befalls you and you are only moderately inconvenienced. Catastrophizing about possible future Adversities usually includes either or both of these forms of exaggerating. You can use a number of thinking or philosophic methods to stop your *What if?* catastrophizing and awfulizing. Such as these:

♦ Arnold Lazarus recommends changing your "What if?" to "So what if?" Not that misfortune is highly unimportant, but your "So what if?" strongly implies that you can deal with it in various ways. For instance: "So what if I fail an impossibly hard test? I can take it over and probably pass it next time." "So what if the teacher marks me unfairly and fails me when I have really passed the test? I can talk to her and probably get her to change it to a fair mark. I can get by and pass other tests. I can take another course if necessary and pass that one. I can make myself only feel sad and regretful, and not enrage and depress myself. I can cope with this unfairness in several other possible ways."

• If you think you can cope with the worst possible "What ifs?" and are convinced that you don't have to be utterly miserable if they occur, you will probably see that there is only a small likelihood of occurrence. But even if a misfortune is great, and damages actually happen because of it, you can be determined, again, to handle the misfortune with some degree of success. First think of the worst possible thing that might occur, and figure out ways to handle and improve the situation. Then calculate the small chances of it actually happening. It is possible to handle a real catastrophe — like the plane you are on falling into the ocean — by accepting your oncoming death as happening earlier than you expected, by using cognitive relaxing methods as the plane goes down, by writing loving words to your loved ones, by helping calm down the person sitting next to you, by thinking philosophical thoughts. You can! Pick one of these methods in advance and have it ready for use in case of a plane crash. (The chances of an actual crash are extremely small, of course!)

• You can face your "What if?" thoughts by understanding that if anything really bad does happen, it most probably has advantages as well as disadvantages. If you are fired from your job, you may have a fine, useful vacation and end up with a better job. If you lose a partner, you may enjoy the adventure of trying to find a new one — and, perhaps, a better one! If you give a public speech poorly, you may learn by your errors and do much better next time. Of course, not every bad happening has advantages — dying in pain has darned few! But many misfortunes have benefits, and you can focus on those possibilities.

• Engaging in "What-if?"-ing will rarely prevent an unfortunate thing from happening, but may also help it to occur because your panicking may lead to poor performance. Most *possible* disasters do not actually occur, and millions of minor mistakes hardly lead to disastrous results. Remember the wise statement of Mark Twain, "My life has been filled with terrible misfortunes — most of which never happened!"

◆ You can learn about many — yes, a great many — individuals who've suffered from "terrible" events and who nonetheless have led productive and enjoyable lives. People have been afflicted with serious diseases, bankruptcy, the loss of several loved ones, rejection by someone they dearly love, and numerous other Adversities, and have gone on to lead useful and happy existences. If this kind of grim fate befalls you, why not use these individuals as models and similarly lead a good existence? When confronted with dire troubles you're not likely to lead *as* happy a life as you would have without them, but you can still get by if you *think* you can and *resolve* to do so.

◆ One of the worst forms of "What ifs?" is to imagine something bad lasting forever and getting worse and worse. Such probabilities, again, are unusually low. Skin cancer will normally not develop into pancreatic cancer. A bankruptcy probably will not lead to a whole series of bankruptcies, prolonged poverty, and ostracism by your friends. If one of your children becomes gravely ill — or even dies — the others most likely will not.

◆ Don't believe the superstition that because things are going well for you, fate will surely put a halt to that and give you trouble. It is statistically true that if things keep going well, something may turn sour and go badly. But it is not true that some unkind fate is watching you, spying on your good fortune, and arranging to disrupt it. Fate is often statistically but not intentionally grim. Even if you do foolish and wrong acts, you will not necessarily suffer — though there is a good chance that you eventually will. You may also suffer from doing a good deed, for example, being robbed by someone you stop to help on the street. But not because the universe doesn't allow you good results and punishes you *because* you experience them.

◆ Superstitions are rife with "What ifs?" What if you meet a black cat? What if you fail to knock on wood and have bad luck? What if you lose your cross or mezuzah and cease to have good luck? What if? What if? Stop narcissistically attributing special interest in you to the universe. It most probably isn't interested!

◆ Live in and enjoy the present by being concerned — but not overconcerned — about the future. Plot and scheme to ward off Adversities, but don't obsess yourself about their possible occurrence. If you focus thoroughly on enjoying the present, you will have less chance of catastrophizing and awfulizing about the future. If you wish for and work for a pleasant future, but not demand that it absolutely must occur, you will have a much better chance of experiencing it.

♦ One of the thinking, feeling, and behaving techniques of REBT is to make fun of your self-defeating beliefs and to use rational humorous songs to see how ironic these beliefs are. Here's a song that I wrote to help you humorously rip up some of your overly serious "What ifs?"

♦ ♦ ♦ ♦ ♦ ♦ ♦ ♦ ♦ ♦ ♦ ♦ ♦ ♦ ♦ ♦ ♦ ♦ ♦ ♦

What If, What If...!

Music by Johann Strauss, Jr. "The Beautiful Blue Danube"
(New lyrics by Albert Ellis)

I think of what if, what if!
And scare myself stiff, yes, stiff, quite stiff!
When things are as certain as can be,
I ask for a perfect guarantee.
I've got to strike out with solid biffs
At all of my sick what ifs, what ifs,
But what if I fail to prevail —
Oh, my God, what if I fail!

(Copyright by Albert Ellis Institute, 1999.)

♦ ♦ ♦ ♦ ♦ ♦ ♦ ♦ ♦ ♦ ♦ ♦ ♦ ♦ ♦ ♦ ♦ ♦ ♦

Applying a Cost-Benefit Analysis to What You Do and What Happens to You

As we keep noting in this book, practically everything in your life has advantages — such as getting what you desire — and disadvantages — such as getting what you don't desire. Your goals, preferences, desires, and purposes are crucial to getting what you want and how you evaluate it. It's normal to rate what you want as "good" and what you don't want as "bad." But if you forget your basic goals, invent the necessity of getting them fulfilled, or exaggerate the disadvantages of not achieving them, you'll get more of what you don't want and less of what you do want.

There probably is always something of a cost-benefit ratio for fulfilling or not fulfilling your desires. Even if you get something without effort — such as winning the lottery with a ticket someone has given you — you almost always have some disadvantages of doing so. Thus, other people may become jealous and hostile toward you. You may develop bad spending habits and lose the money you have won. You may quit working at an enjoyable job and be bored to death. You may fight with your mate over how to spend the money you won. The person who gave you the ticket may file a lawsuit and claim the winnings...

Your time and energy are almost always limited — especially since you live a certain number of years and no more. So to get what you desire, you have to expend some effort, and evaluate how much to give in order to attain your desires. You also may have certain wants fulfilled without too much effort — like being loved by someone who is naturally attracted to you. But even that has its disadvantages and drawbacks. You may have to spend time and energy attending to the person who loves you. You may lose out on other people's love by choosing to benefit from one person's affection. You risk gaining — and later losing — this person's attention, especially when you are used to getting it.

Most of us fairly automatically calculate the cost-benefit ratio for many of the things we do. You may spend time and energy going to a movie, but consider it worth it. You go to the trouble of preparing good food, and again hardly consciously consider the money and time you spend shopping for and preparing it. You let yourself love and care for someone — which gives you distinct pleasure — but consciously (and unconsciously) perceive the trouble you take to satisfy this person. So you naturally weigh the costs and benefits of much of your behavior and often come to quick, almost automatic conclusions about it.

Unfortunately, you probably do a couple of things to bollix up your cost-benefit calculating. First, you forget about the hidden costs of many benefits and pleasures. You smoke, and push out of mind the potential dangers. You procrastinate on paying taxes, and forget about the fines you may incur. You hastily shop for food, badly prepare it, and ignore the results — indigestion, nutritional harm, and disappointment — that you may easily experience.

Secondly, you do things that are needlessly troublesome, rather than figuring out less bothersome ways of doing them. Thus, you perfectionistically take too much pain to study for a test or a presentation. You compulsively dot every "i" and cross every "t" in a term paper, and take needless time and trouble to finish it. You slave away to get the eternal love of people who are not capable of loving you in return.

Watch it! And I really mean watch it — but not compulsively or perfectionistically. For if you take too much time to weigh all the advantages and disadvantages of doing something, you may never do it. By endlessly calculating the cost-benefit ratio of a project, your calculation itself has a cost-benefit ratio, and is not necessarily all to the good. It all depends on how and to what extent you do it. As usual, moderation or balance is the thing, and extreme mulling rarely works. If you are too finicky, and take the cost-benefit ratio too much into account, your doing so becomes too costly! If you consider it too carelessly, that again becomes too costly. It's a difficult balancing exercise!

Here are some of the things to consider about the cost-benefit ratio of what you do and what you refrain from doing:

♦ Carefully, and with some degree of concern and caution, consider the benefits and the harm of your important doings, and do your best to be duly vigilant and concerned, but not panicking or overconcerned. If you make yourself worry excessively, you may withdraw from doing "good" things, do them carelessly and impatiently, do them "badly," or ruminate about them endlessly, thereby increasing the cost and decreasing the benefits.

♦ Making yourself underconcerned, forgetful, and careless is perhaps just as harmful as frantically worrying. If you do not consider things carefully, you may ignore the benefits of self-discipline (like quitting smoking), disregard the future bad results of doing something (like eating badly), focus only on the benefits of avoiding difficulties (like not going to the trouble of installing a good fire alarm system), and otherwise court needless self-victimizing. If you are underconcerned, you often don't "look before you leap," refusing to see the foolishness of certain risks and ignoring the disadvantages of immediate gratification. Consider the ill effects of putting your head in the sand, and routinely force yourself to see both sides of what you're doing — the benefits and the downsides.

♦ Watch your panicking about the possible "disbenefits" — costs, negative results, downside risks — of what you are about to do or what you have done. Your awfulizing won't help you to think straight about these possibilities and will cloud your mind and cause you to see the disbenefits in an extremely gruesome light. It may also freeze you and prevent you from reacting appropriately to bad decisions — those that have more disbenefits than benefits — and to correct them. Panicking will frequently "help" you make things much worse than they actually are.

♦ Your panicking usually stems from your musts and demands: "I absolutely *must* make the right decision — meaning, one that has few disbenefits and many benefits. If I don't do as I must, I am inadequate and worthless, will never do my cost-benefit calculating correctly, and will consequently suffer the torments of the damned. I cannot bear the results of making the wrong decisions — but I really deserve to get bad results because I am such a clod for not doing a proper cost-benefit analysis." Look for these interfering musts, change them to preferences, then proceed to sensible cost-benefit calculating.

Overcoming the Need for Perfectionizing

I campaigned against my own perfectionizing in my adolescence, presented forceful arguments against it in *Reason and Emotion in Psychotherapy* (1962), and influenced Aaron Beck, David Burns, Gordon L. Flett and other therapists to take a dim view of it in later years. Self-congratulations!

Fairly obviously, real perfectionism won't work. Witness:

• You can *do* a few things perfectly — at least for a while. Like adding figures, for example. But forever?

• You can't *be* a perfect human. No chance! You would then have to do perfectly well under all conditions at all times. Well?!!

• To *prefer* and to *try* to do something perfectly is fine: producing some works of genius. But to *insist* on doing so? You'll produce "perfect" anxiety!

• When you "have to" do something perfectly well, you will incessantly keep at it, reject several good and workable solutions to the problem you are trying to solve, and become so anxious that you may well do poorly, or give up and settle for poor solutions.

• Perfectionists almost always put *themselves,* and not merely their imperfect behavior, down. As a real perfectionist, you will tend to equate perfect behavior with your whole *self* being an adequate person. And you will equate imperfection with your wormhood. Distinctly conditional — not unconditional — self-acceptance!

• Even if you occasionally do perfectly well at an important task, what about next time? Anxietizing, anxietizing, anxietizing!

You may have a high degree of probability that certain things will happen for you — for example, that you will often feel hungry, will work at some kind of a job, and will be asked by the IRS to pay taxes each year. But just about the only thing you are absolutely certain of is your eventual death. You may *desire* to eat regularly, hold a good job, and have enough money to pay your taxes, but your *absolutely demanding* them brings trouble. At the bottom of most of your worrying and making yourself insecure is your unrealistic need for a guarantee — which, even if sincerely promised to you, may not easily be realized. The road to hell is paved with unrealistic expectations — especially that your expectations *absolutely have to*, with certainty, be fulfilled.

Your *desire* for perfectionism may also be legitimate — to be perfectly achieving, lovable, and comfortable. Go desire — but don't insist. Certainty hardly ever exists, and perfection almost never. All humans — you included — are highly fallible; therefore, by demanding perfection you risk almost certain failure.

You can let go of your need for certainty and perfection in the following ways:

◆ Accept the law of probability. With work and effort — not to mention ability — you will probably succeed at many tasks and projects. But you don't have to! And not perfectly! With time and trouble, you can often arrange good conditions. But not certainly. And not perfectly. Give yourself leeway. Try for *your* best — not *the* best.

◆ Expect considerable uncertainty — in love, definitely; but even in friendship. People who guarantee benefits are often liars or super-optimists. Take them *unseriously*.

◆ Don't attach your worth as a person — your essential goodness — to any of your traits or doings. Certainly, not to perfect doings! Leave yourself room for error — plenty of error!

◆ Uncertainty, ambiguity, and imperfection are sometimes a drag. But you can also choose to view them as challenging and adventurous. If your life were truly absolutely certain and safe, that might be really boring!

◆ The more certain you imagine you have to be, and the more you insist on doing things perfectly, the less risks you will take and the less you will do. Not only will you thereby deny yourself adventure and novelty, but you will restrict your life considerably and wind up practically always doing routine and boring things. Since creative pursuits are usually novel and risk-taking, you will also tend to make yourself distinctly less creative. You will not be able to practice what Harvard psychologist Ellen Langer and others call *mindfulness*, which requires the process of drawing novel distinctions.

◆ If you rigidly keep insisting on perfect and sure answers to problems, you will not find them, and may give up trying for reasonably good ones.

◆ Your need for perfection and certainty will probably lead to your panicking. Your need to be certain that your panicking *absolutely must stop* will lead to still more panicking.

◆ Often *try* to do a task perfectly well — if it is not too long and complicated!

◆ Recognize — once again — your human fallibility.

♦ *Absolutely perfect* solutions to any problem are, at best, rare and short-lived. Will you screw them up *later?*

♦ Choose solutions to difficulties that will work, but not necessarily work perfectly. Try them out. *Later*, perhaps, revise them.

♦ Use perfecting as a goal, a *process* — not as an end result. As Nebraska counselor Kevin FitzMaurice says, "Shoot for the stars, but be happy if you land on the moon!"

Using Modeling Methods to Overcome Handicapping and Disturbing Yourself

When you face serious Adversities and manage to emote healthily instead of unhealthily, you either ward off "upsetting" problems or, more elegantly, you refuse to disturb yourself about them. Both of these solutions to Adversities may be hard to achieve. But you can *model* yourself, as Stanford psychologist Albert Bandura has shown, after other individuals who solve such problems effectively. Your models can be someone you actually know or people you hear about.

Jim suffered from diabetes and at first angered himself about being afflicted and refused to stay with a good nutritional regimen. When he encountered an eight-year-old boy and a twelve-year-old girl who took their diabetes stoically and followed their regimens carefully, he gave up his angry rebelling and began to take care of himself properly.

Martha was severely depressed after her teacher treated her unfairly, made her submit two difficult term papers, and gave her a C in history. After reading about a group of holocaust survivors who refused to depress themselves and who led reasonably happy lives — one of these survivors had worked for years as a clown and enjoyed making handicapped children laugh — Martha changed her depression to keen disappointment. From those powerful models, Martha recognized that Adversity could be grim without necessarily being depressing.

You can use modeling to overcome your Adversities and needlessly disturbing yourself about them. Try these methods:

♦ Find some people who have conquered some unusual handicaps — physical or mental — by working hard to overcome them. See that if you have handicaps and Adversities, you are capable of coping as well as some others. Do so for your own good, not to best others who have done so.

♦ Find people who still have handicaps or Adversities — like blindness or poverty — and who refuse to depress, anxietize, or anger themselves about them. Copy their refusal to disturb themselves and their ability to find enjoyable pursuits in spite of limitations.

♦ Experiment with modeling various kinds of thinking and behavior of handicapped people. Some may be good for them, but not for you. Try them and see for yourself.

♦ If you find it almost impossible to model the good thinking and behavior of some handicapped people, don't give up. Try some more. If your modeling still does not work, admit your failure, but never put yourself down for not succeeding at it.

Using Problem-Solving Methods

REBT shows you how to use problem-solving methods in the usual ways, because often you may have a practical problem — such as how to get a good job, how to pass a course, or how to win other people's approval — and you may frequently depress yourself about this practical difficulty. Thus, if you fail to solve your practical problems, you panic or depress yourself.

REBT, however, first shows you how to deal with your emotional problems *about* your practical problems. Then, when you reduce your self-disturbing, you can more easily find better solutions to your practical problems — and have less chance of recreating them in the future.

Sonny angered himself at his overly critical boss — and his angering, as you might expect, got him into trouble with this boss. So I first showed him that he was creating his rage by demanding, "My boss is unfair! He must not be so critical, as he damned well is, and treat me so unjustly!" I induced Sonny to believe, "Yes, my boss treats me unfairly! But that is his nature, to overly criticize; and he really has to, at least right now, follow that nature."

Sonny reduced his angering immensely and merely made himself displeased with his boss's undue criticism. Then he was able, unangrily, to do more things his boss's way, to praise the boss for being so "helpful" with his criticism, and to follow work rules even when he thought they were stupid. These practical solutions worked and Sonny's boss became less critical and more cooperative. So we first tackled Sonny's angering himself and making himself so vulnerable to criticism, and then we were able to figure out some practical problem-solving. He finally got another job — and was able to anger himself much less than he did on the first job when some of his co-workers, he was convinced, treated him unfairly.

Well and good. But solving practical problems may lead you to *feel better* and not necessarily *get better*, for it reduces or eliminates the Adversities you may encounter, and thus gives you little to upset yourself about. With your problems reduced, you actually may feel good instead of self-disturbing.

However, there are troubles with this kind of "solution." First, the solution to your practical problem may later prove to be partial or poor. Second, you may solve it only temporarily. Third, you stop distressing yourself *because* you solved your practical problem and you only know *that* kind of resolution. You may still not know how you disturbed yourself, and what *you* can do to un-create your self-disturbance if for any reason you bring it on again.

So practical problem-solving, as many therapies have shown, is useful, and may even indirectly reduce your disturbed reacting. But it mainly makes you *feel* better and not really *get* better.

You can use a different kind of problem-solving to help yourself get better when you upset yourself. You can figure out your specific *Beliefs* with which you encourage your emotional dysfunction. You can Dispute your unrealistic and illogical philosophizing and can realistically and logically change it. You can try out several rational coping statements, derived from your Effective New Philosophies (E), to substitute for your Irrational *Beliefs* (IBs).

These and other thinking methods are indeed problem-solving — and we can call them profound or ultimate problem-solving techniques, since they help you figure out your core dysfunctional *Beliefs* and change them. So this special kind of philosophically oriented problem solving can help you feel better as well as get better. Specifically you can use it as follows:

♦ Recognize that your disturbance is partly self-created and doesn't *just* stem from your encountering practical problems and Adversities.

♦ Search for the *Beliefs* that you use to create your serious upsetting, particularly for the absolutistic shoulding, musting, and demanding that accompany it.

♦ Acknowledge that you naturally think irrationally, that you also learn to do so from your family and culture, and that you are prone to make a habit of doing so. Realize, therefore, that it will probably take much time and energy, much force and effort, to do your elegant problem solving — or perhaps we should call it "disturbance-dissolving" — methods.

♦ Use several effective coping techniques of working against your Irrational *Beliefs* (IBs), especially empirical and logical Disputing of the accompanying irrationalities. Concertedly and vigorously think against your dysfunctional philosophizing; be determined — and solidly *choose* — to correct it.

♦ Problem-solving consists of looking open-mindedly for alternative solutions to difficulties, and not rigidly sticking to poor solutions. Therefore, think of several ways in which you can change your unconstructive *Beliefs* and experiment with them, then check on the results and revise and add to them accordingly. Think more about them. You don't have to come up with a *perfect* disturbance-dissolving method. A *better* one will do!

Minimizing Overgeneralizing and Absolutistic Thinking

It is difficult to know what is the basic cause of irrational thinking that leads you to disturb yourself emotionally — if, indeed, there is any basic cause. Psychoanalyst Karen Horney implied that it was the "tyranny of the shoulds," and REBT has gone even beyond her views and stated that if you were able to remain with only your preferring and desiring, and never escalate them into absolutistic shoulds, oughts, and musts, you would have great difficulty in upsetting yourself. Even when you are biologically predisposed to making yourself panicky or depressed, your biological imbalances may lead you to think irrationally, so that you resort more frequently to absolutistic shoulds, oughts, and musts than you do when you are not biochemically afflicted. So *musturbating* seems to be basic to much — though I am not contending all — human disturbance.

Alfred Korzybski, in *Science and Sanity*, stressed the place of overgeneralizing and absolutistic thinking in helping to make humans "unsane." He particularly stressed the danger of the *"is* of identity" — labeling yourself as a bad or a good *person* when you do important bad or good *deeds*. Your *"is* of identity" is, of course, a form of overgeneralizing. But so are your absolutistic musts. When you hold them, you contend that under all conditions at all times, you must perform well or must be approved by other people — and then, of course, you overgeneralize.

Counselor Kevin FitzMaurice has been campaigning for years against the human habit of turning thoughts into things and constructing misleading "thought-things." Thus, as I pointed out in my section on Unconditional Self-Accepting (USA) in chapter 2, we frequently have a thought such as, "I shall unconditionally accept myself and other people" — where *accept* is a verb — and we turn it into a noun, *acceptance*. Then we think that *acceptance* really exists as an entity in itself, a thought-thing. Accepting is something we *do* — an action — but we confuse it with a *thing* that has an external embodiment.

When you do something well, you may think, "I am acting well." *Acting well* is a verb and an adverb describing what you are *doing*. But if you say, "My *act* is good," you are changing your *behavior* into a thing, a *good act*. You thereby have confused your behavior (acting) with your evaluation of it (a thought). You see the *act* as *good* rather than an act that you *viewed* as good.

When you view one of your *actions* (a thing) as bad, you may also think that *you* (a person) are bad. Crooked thinking indeed! REBT can help you to see the difference: you may be *doing* well or badly, but your *actions* (things) and *personhood* (self) are not good or bad. Learn to measure and evaluate your *behaving* and not *yourself.* Try not to create thought-things.

Scientists tend to be flexible, nondogmatic, and unabsolutistic. They set up hypotheses and then they corral evidence to "prove" that these hypotheses are tentatively true — but they don't *have to* be true or correct under all conditions at all times. Standards of *probability* are acceptable in science: "It is 99.999% probable that this is true." So scientists generalize — set up theories — but do their best not to overgeneralize. We could say, therefore, that if you were strictly scientific about viewing yourself, other people, and the world, you would again have a hard time emotionally disturbing yourself.

When you tolerate difficulties badly and wail about them instead of constructively dealing with them, you afflict yourself with low frustration tolerance (LFT), which includes overgeneralizing. You insist that doing painful things is *too* hard, that it is *horrible* and *awful* that you have to do them, that you *can't stand* doing them, and that you can't be happy *at all* if you have to do them. These are all forms of overgeneralizing because they imply that bad things are always, completely, and universally bad. Very unlikely!

In one way or another, therefore, when you disturb yourself you almost always think in overgeneralized, "musturbatory," all-inclusive ways. REBT helps you to see that you are doing this, to realize that it significantly affects your disturbing thinking, feeling, and acting, and shows you how to minimize your overgeneralizing and "musturbating," and thereby make yourself less disturbed. In particular, it shows you how to be aware, when you act against your interests and against social interests, that you are most probably using absolutistic, dogmatic, demanding ways of thinking, and it gives you a number of methods of disputing your demanding and arriving at more sensible, practical concluding. Here are some techniques you can use in this respect:

• When you depress, panic, or enrage yourself, suspect that you are doing some unconditional, absolutistic *shoulding* and *musting*, find it, and change it into realistic *preferring*. See that when you are self-downing you are probably believing something like this: "Because I would very much like to do well and to be approved of by significant others, I *have to do so* or else I am a pretty worthless person." If so, change that to, "I would distinctly *like to* do well and be approved of by significant others, but there are no reasons why I *have to* do so. I don't have to make my worth as a person dependent on succeeding at important tasks or being favored by significant people." Also, when you engage in low frustration tolerance, look for your beliefs: "I absolutely *have to* get what I want or it is *awful.* Then I can't be happy *at all!*" If so, change that to, "I would greatly prefer to get what I want, but I never have to get it. I can still be happy — though not as happy — if I am deprived of some of the things that I desire."

   • Watch your overgeneralizing; your use of "all" and "never." "If I fail at important tasks, that means that I will *never* succeed and *never* achieve what I really want to achieve." Change this to: "If I fail at important tasks, I can frequently learn by my failure and succeed next time. It is most unlikely that I will always fail and never succeed. But if I do, I do. *I am not a failure for failing* and I can live reasonably happily, though admittedly not as happily, as if I succeed." Also change, "Because I very much want significant people to love me, this means that they have to do so and it is *absolutely terrible* if they don't," to, "No matter how much I want significant people to love me, it doesn't follow that they have to do so. It is quite unfortunate if they don't, but it isn't *awful* — it's not the end of the world!"

   • Monitor your awfulizing. As I noted before, awfulizing makes you think things like, "This failure is totally bad!" "This loss is the end of the world!" These are absolute, over-generalized self-statements. You can change them to, "This failure may indeed be very bad, but it obviously could be worse and could lead to worse results." "This rejection is indeed a great loss, but it's hardly the end of my life, and I can go on to get other acceptances." Awfulizing follows from insisting that your preferring *absolutely must* be fulfilled. Go back to simply preferring and you will feel and act much better.

◆ Watch your emotional reasoning. The fact that you *feel* like a loser when you fail, or *feel* that *you* are personally rejected when only your *request* is refused, only proves that you are creating these overgeneralizing feelings. It doesn't prove anything about you as a total person or prove that you are the only one in the world who fails or gets rejected. Your emotions do not make you anything but a person who has strong feelings.

◆ Watch out for going from one extreme to another. Winning a campaign doesn't make you a noble, glorious person or an all-time winner. And losing the campaign doesn't mean that you're a total loser or a failure. Both extreme assessments, and your feelings that go with them, are inaccurate and hardly last for all time — unless you keep working hard to make them last!

◆ Failing at an important project doesn't mean that you will always fail and never succeed. Did all other people withdraw after a failure and make themselves feel hopeless? Or did many of them go on to succeed later? University of Pennsylvania psychologist Martin Seligman and his associates have shown that rats who are forced to keep endlessly failing by an experimenter give up, feel helpless, and acquire learned helplessness. Humans, like you and me may do so after just a few trials that end as failures. We "learn" that failure is inevitable when it is only occasional. We invent hopelessness from a few defeats. Resist jumping to this kind of overgeneralized concluding.

◆ By all means theorize and generalize — and then check to see if your generalizing follows from the facts. But firmly resist overgeneralizing. Thus, refuse to think that you *are* what you *do*. Don't label people by a few of their acts or traits. Avoid thinking of your thoughts as entities in their own right. They are aspects of you — only aspects that exist within you. To help you think clearly about them, try not to make nouns of your adjectives. If you procrastinate, you *are* a person who engages in procrastination. But your procrastination doesn't exist by itself and is not an entity in its own right.

◆ As semanticist Alfred Korzybski pointed out many years ago, watch your labeling things as either/or, black or white. Try to see them as *both/and* and *et cetera*. You have good traits, neutral traits, and bad traits — meaning that they are good, bad, or neutral for certain purposes and goals. You are never really a good or a bad *person*. If you label and overgeneralize yourself, you tend to do the same thing about other people; and if you consistently label them, you tend to augment your own self-labeling.

   ♦ Try to be open-minded, skeptical, and experimental. "Final answers" to your own, to others', and to the world's problems are highly suspect, since later evidence may arise to make them inaccurate. Even the "evidence" that you use to "prove" your hypotheses may be influenced by your (and others') views, desires, and prejudices. Absolute and final truths do not seem to exist.

How to Stop Disturbing Yourself About Disturbing Yourself

One of the most common things that people do when they disturb themselves — make themselves panicked, depressed, enraged, or self-pitying, and bring on dysfunctional compulsions and phobias — is to disturb themselves about their self-disturbing. In REBT terms, they frequently command, "I absolutely must not depress myself," and then they depress themselves about their depressing. They healthily *prefer* not to disturb themselves and then turn their preferences into unrealistic commands. They thereby tend to be ego-disturbing: "If I depress myself, as I absolutely *must not*, I am an inadequate, worthless person!" Or they tend to have low frustration tolerance: "If I depress myself, as I absolutely *must not*, my depressing is *awful* and *unbearable*, and life is much *too* hard for me, and therefore I can justifiably be miserable about my misery!"

   Disturbing yourself about disturbing yourself makes you, if anything, twice as dysfunctional; your secondary distress often becomes so intense that it stops you from dealing effectively with your primary distress. Consequently, you had better recognize it and deal with it first — and then go on to deal with your primary self-defeating *Beliefs*.

   Here are some of REBT's main methods of counteracting your tendency to disturb yourself about your dysfunctioning:

◆ Recognize that, as a human, you are probably quite prone to bring on both primary and secondary distress. Whenever you make yourself upset, assume that you may also disturb yourself (secondary) about your disturbance (primary). You may be whining and moaning about your original panicking or depressing. Perhaps you're demanding that it *absolutely must not* exist and that if it does it makes you an inadequate person. Or maybe it is "too much to bear" and because of your unwillingness to tolerate it, you tend to horrify yourself about it. Stop! Let yourself be human! You are disturbing yourself (primary). Enough!

◆ If you find that you are secondarily disturbing yourself, look for your insistence that you *absolutely must not* suffer from your primary disturbance. Take a real good look to see what *musts* and *demands* lead to your abysmal suffering about your suffering!

◆ Realistically dispute your secondary self-disturbing if you discover it. Ask yourself these kinds of questions: "Where is it *written* that I *must not* feel horribly about my dysfunctioning? *Prove* that my 'horror' *must not* exist!" "If I disturb myself about feeling distressed, why is it *awful?*" Persist at answering these questions until you clearly see that your self-disturbing *has to* exist right now — because it *does*. Too bad, but it does! Now, how can you deal with it?

◆ Logically dispute your demand that your secondary disturbance not exist. "How does it follow that because I do not want to disturb myself about depressing myself, I *absolutely must not?*" Answer: "It doesn't!" "Yes, my original disturbance is quite debilitating, but does that prove that I should also not be afflicted with a secondary one?" Answer: "No. If I am afflicted, I am!" "Is it logical to conclude that, if I disturb myself about my panicking, I am a thoroughly incompetent, worthless person for doing so?" Answer: "No, I am a person with an unfortunate feeling!"

◆ Pragmatically dispute your insistence that you *should not* and *must not* upset yourself about upsetting yourself: "Where will it get me if I insist that I absolutely must not disturb myself?" Answer: "Doubly disturbed!" "How will making myself disturbed about my self-upsetting help me to deal with my original distress?" Answer: "Not at all! It may well lead to my exacerbating it."

Constructivist Solution-Focused Methods of Helping Yourself

Over the years, a good many therapists have pointed out that diagnosing and "therapizing" tends to label and pathologize people with problems. Thomas Szasz, Dorothy Becvar, Jerome Frank, Allen Ivey, Abe Maslow, Richard Nelson, Michael Mahoney, Jefferson Fish, and especially Steven deShazer, are among the psychotherapist-authors who have made this point. Their works have suggested various forms of constructivist and solution-focused therapy that emphasize beneficial and self-helping tendencies, and play down self-destructive ones. Sometimes, of course, these thinkers are super-optimistic and gloss over people's *natural* defeating tendencies — and thereby give a one-sided view of human functioning — unrealistically!

The constructivist solution-focused view of people's potential propensity for self-help has become very popular in recent years and, without being super-optimistic about it, you can use it to great advantage. Here are several useful views from this perspective:

♦ When you have emotional-behavioral problems, you very likely have already applied your self-actualizing tendencies to solve them. Good! So you can recall the successful methods you used and replay them again to help resolve your present difficulties.

♦ You — as I keep repeating in this book — are an *innate* as well as a *learned* problem-solver. You create and *un*create your troublings. So you can construct *new* solutions to recurring anxietizing and self-depressing.

♦ As part of your constructive devising, you can investigate other people's ways of resolving your type of distress, and become a benign copycat and see if that works for you.

♦ You can explore and experiment, try several potential solutions to your catastrophizing and awfulizing, see which work better, and keep experimenting with new ones. You, like virtually all humans, have built-in capabilities for such "scientific" sleuthing. Use them.

♦ Like other animals, you can think. Like other humans, you can think, think about your thinking, and even think about thinking about your thinking. Let the dolphin imitate that propensity! You consciously *and* unconsciously can change your thinking, feeling, and behaving. As stressed in this book, you can *choose* to do so far more than any other animal (as far as is now known). If you work at doing so, and if you use the power — the potential *action* — that goes with your will, you can aid constructive and solution-focused self-help by asking yourself some of the following questions:

♦ What kind of emotional and practical problems did I previously solve?

♦ What exactly did I think, feel, and do to solve them?

♦ Which of my experiments worked best?

♦ What were the times that I anxietized and depressed myself less, and what did I do to help myself?

♦ What did I do to overcome depressing myself about my depressing, and anxietizing about my anxietizing?

♦ If my past self-helping did not work too well or last too long, how can I figure out new procedures and use them today?

♦ Did I persist with my self-helping efforts, or carelessly and too quickly give them up before they worked? If so, how can I go back to the drawing board?

For many reasons such as these, you, like other humans, can be creative, constructive, problem-solving, experimental, inventive, visionary, capable of changing — well, you name it. Not only, of course, about your mental-emotional functioning, but also in regard to work, art, music, science, physical health, and so forth. You have much ability to change external situations — and yourself.

Self-Help Has Limits

Let's not exaggerate your constructive tendencies and, as some thinkers and therapists do, neglect their limitations. In your efforts to improve yourself, you may find that constructivist and solution-focusing techniques of self-help — and of psychotherapy, too — have some limitations, for several reasons:

♦ Your past solutions to emotional-behavioral problems may not have worked too well if you have the same difficulty again.

◆ You may not have devised good solutions in the past, and even if you did, you may not remember or be able to effectively use them today.

◆ You may be so self-upsetting at present that you cannot think, feel, and behave well and use your previously effective problem-solving.

◆ Okay, your previous neurosis-solving efforts were *somewhat* good at changing. You may have overvalued them and kept yourself from doing them *better*.

◆ Your anxietizing and depressing today may be quite different from that which you suffered before. So your previous solutions may not be relevant today.

◆ Your methods of overcoming anxiety in the past may have been *palliative* rather than *curative*. Thus, you may have "overcome" your elevator phobia by taking an apartment and offices on the first floor. Now you have to work on the 20th floor to keep your excellent job. Some "solution"!

For reasons such as these, seeking constructive and solution-focused self-help procedures may help you (temporarily!) feel better, but not (more permanently) get better. Use your constructivist, experimental potentials to see if this is likely. If it is, try some of the getting-better methods described in this book *together with* the solution-focused ones you have been using.

Maury, for example, used the solution-focusing technique of making a long list of the sports, social, and business participations he was *not* anxietizing about in order to overcome damning himself for panicking about public speaking. For a while, he was much less anxious about his panicking, and also was somewhat less terrified about public speaking. When his job required him to give more public presentations, he still refused to damn himself for anxietizing about these presentations. But his original panicking returned full blast and he could not reduce it. "I *absolutely must not* miserably fail at public speaking, thereby making an ass of myself, and allowing people to defame me forever!"

So he started to Dispute his Irrational *Beliefs*. After doing this vigorously for two months, and exposing himself to anxiety by making public talks, Maury rarely terrorized himself any more about "making an ass" of himself while speaking. His previous solution-focused self-help technique still partially helped him, but combining it with more profound REBT methods worked much better.

Maury's successful blend of methods could work for you, too. Consider using constructivist and solution-focused methods *along with* some specific REBT techniques if you want to try a self-help approach to profound change.

Although constructivist and solution-focusing methods often concentrate on your present thinking, feeling, and acting, and gloss over the past — which is forever gone — you can still, of course, creatively use your past to help change your present and future. REBT holds that in the past you upset yourself with *Beliefs* that were dysfunctional, and that you still carry some of these *Beliefs* today (and perhaps tomorrow). You can creatively explore, investigate, and reflect on your past *today*. You could use psychoanalytic methods to do so, but they are usually too long, too side-tracking, and too misleading.

REBT reflecting about your past is different. It *un*obsessively investigates what others did to you — *and* how you choose to react to the Adversities they partly created. Yes, how you reacted well ("rationally"), and how you reacted badly ("irrationally"). Using a constructivist outlook, you can discover the functional *and* dysfunctional *Beliefs* of your past *and* present. As you work at keeping the best and discarding the worst of your past and present responses, you can use the questions outlined in this section to help yourself understand and change.

Solution-focused self-help techniques you've used to resolve *past* emotional problems, together with your general constructivist tendencies, may serve you well *today*. Dovetailing this method with other elegant REBT may help you, once again, feel *and* get better. Try it and see!

Imaging Techniques

For many years, Rutgers University psychologist and author Arnold Lazarus has encouraged the use of imaging techniques in therapy. When you vividly imagine a good or a bad thing happening to you, you are using your cognitive faculties. Imagining is a *cognitive* process, but you also get *emotionally* in touch with events and their impact on you (and others), and you set in motion your *action* tendencies to deal with the event. Therefore, when you use exposure, as REBT recommends, to *desensitize* yourself to traumatic events or to *sensitize* yourself to pleasures, you can do so either *in vivo* (in the actual life situation) or *imaginatively* (in your mind). Both approaches have considerable research evidence to show that they work.

Like everything else, you can use your imagining palliatively and distractingly — or can link it up with more profound philosophizing methods to effect more permanent and pervasive change. Take, for example, Lazarus's "time-tripping" technique. Using this method, you can take an event that you remember with anxiety and depression and imagine it and its results taking place, say, a year from now. Or you can imagine it occurring five years ago. You will then likely tend to view it with relative indifference or detachment — and figure out how to resolve or live with it. Why? Because distance may lend perspective and safety. Using this imaginative distancing technique may give you leeway or encouragement for changing your catastrophizing attitudes toward Adversities, and therefore may lead to *getting* better as well as *feeling* better.

Imagery methods may be combined with other REBT techniques — as in rational emotive imagery, which I previously described. You can use it to *cognitively* picture "disasters," to get in touch with your disturbing *feelings*, and to change them *behaviorally* to healthy negative emoting.

Various kinds of imaging, then, can be combined with "elegant" REBT thinking-feeling-behaving methods to bring about your profound getting-better personality changes.

Writing About Past Or Present Feelings Or Experiences

Writing some of the detail of your present or past feelings may help you release these feelings, help you feel better, and help you bring up emotions that you've not dealt with. Many story writers and novelists — for example, Marcel Proust and James Joyce — have helped themselves with this detailed and honest type of expression. Author Ira Progoff for many years espoused journal writing to help people express, desensitize themselves to, and deal with their deep-seated feelings. As Brian A. Esterling and his associates have shown, this kind of therapeutic writing may help you to log your anxietizing and self-depressing, clearly expose traumatic events until you desensitize yourself to them, figure out ways to cope with them philosophically, and apply several of the cognitive, experiential, and behavioral methods described in this book.

Writing from day to day the ABCDE's of REBT (as outlined in the REBT Self-Help form originated by Windy Dryden and Jane Walker, and slightly revised by me) has been found by the clients at the Albert Ellis Institute psychological clinic in New York to be very helpful. You can also use it regularly on your own.

Expressing yourself in writing has the advantages of intense *abreactive* self-help therapy, which focuses on recall and confrontation of strong emotions. Without thinking and behaving components, however, such feeling-centered therapies may *increase* your dysfunctional feelings. Combining feelings approaches with rational philosophizing and functional behavior methods can help you feel better *and* get better.

Reframing and Checking Your Negative Perceptions of Adversities

Many people have found that if they *reframe* their negative perceiving of Adversities in a different light, they quickly and "magically" stop their upsetting. Many therapists — such as Maxie Maultsby, Jr., Rian McMullin, and Susan Walen, Ray DiGiuseppe, and Windy Dryden —have advocated a reframing method when their clients distress themselves. If you enrage yourself against

REBT Self-help Form

A (ACTIVATING EVENT)

- Briefly summarize the situation you are disturbed about (what would a camera see?)
- An A can be *internal* or *external, real or imagined.*
- An A can be an event in the *past, present,* or *future.*

IB's (IRRATIONAL BELIEFS)

To identify IB's, look for:

- DOGMATIC DEMANDS
  (musts, absolutes, shoulds)

- AWFULIZING
  (It's awful, terrible, horrible)

- LOW FRUSTRATION TOLERANCE
  (I can't stand it)

- SELF/OTHER RATING
  (I'm / he / she is bad, worthless)

C (CONSEQUENCES)

Major unhealthy negative **emotions:**

Major self-defeating **behaviors:**

Unhealthy negative emotions include:

- Anxiety　• Depression　• Rage　• Low Frustration Tolerance
- Shame/Embarrassment　• Hurt　• Jealousy　• Guilt

RB's (RATIONAL BELIEFS)

To think more rationally, strive for:

- NON-DOGMATIC PREFERENCES
  (wishes, wants, desires)

- EVALUATING BADNESS
  (it's bad, unfortunate)

- HIGH FRUSTRATION TOLERANCE
  (I don't like it, but I can stand it)

- NOT GLOBALLY RATING SELF OR OTHERS (I—and others—are fallible human beings)

D (DISPUTING IB'S)

To dispute ask yourself:

- Where is holding this belief getting me? Is it *helpful* or *self-defeating?*
- Where is the evidence to support the existence of my irrational belief? Is it *consistent with reality?*
- Is my belief *logical?* Does it follow from my preferences?
- Is it *really awful* (as bad as it could be?)
- Can I really not *stand it?*

E (NEW EFFECT)

New healthy **negative emotions:**

New constructive **behaviors:**

Healthy negative emotions include:

- Disappointment
- Concern
- Annoyance
- Sadness
- Regret
- Frustration

© Windy Dryden & Jane Walker 1992. Revised by Albert Ellis Institute, 1996. *Reproduced by permission.*

some people who have "deliberately" treated you "unfairly," you can look at this Adversity in several ways that may quickly reduce your rage. Thus:

- ◆ You can perceive that they "accidentally," not "deliberately," treated you "unfairly."

- ◆ You can perceive that they really tried to treat you "fairly," but unfortunately failed.

- ◆ You can see that you *thought* their treatment was "unfair" but, on second thought, you realize it was "fair."

- ◆ You can see that, by ordinary standards, they treated you "unfairly" (say, sold you on a "bad" stock), but that actually you benefited by their "unfairness" (say, the stock went up considerably).

- ◆ You can perceive that, indeed, they treated you unfairly, but that other people saw this, came to your rescue, and arranged a "wonderful" deal for you.

Adversities or Activating Events (A's), then, truly exist for you, but you can view the very same A's as "good," "bad," or "indifferent." If you exaggeratedly *evaluate* or *define* them as "awful" when they are merely "very bad," REBT shows you that you are telling yourself something like, "It *must not be* as bad as it is!" and that your *Belief* about them is something of a fiction. *You* are needlessly depressing yourself about it when you could make yourself healthfully sorry and disappointed.

You can therefore have two views of Adversities: One, they are factual, and most people would see them as such and deplore them — murder or terrorism, for example. Two, they would be "bad" if they were factual but, while some people see them as existing, others — including you — may not. Therefore, when you upset yourself about some Adversities, you can minimize your anguish by first questioning whether they *really* occurred as you — perhaps erroneously — perceived them as happening. Second, assuming that you really "saw" the Adversity actually happen, you can question your absolutistic musts and demands about the Adversity, thereby reducing your upset. Thus, you can Dispute your *perception* of Adversities — or Dispute your *evaluation* of them when you "really" perceive them. Better, you can question *both* your perception and your evaluation.

Disputing or checking your perception of Adversity is also called *reframing*. Jillian was convinced that her friend, Ariel, was having an affair with their tennis coach, Manfred, and that the coach favored Ariel, teaching her better, giving her extra time on the court, and inducing some of his proficient friends to spend time practicing tennis with her. Jillian convinced herself that this was very unfair and hated both Ariel and Manfred (not to mention Manfred's friends).

When Jillian checked out her conviction, and actually got some of her friends to spy on Ariel to discover if it was true, she found it to be quite false. Both Ariel and Manfred were monogamously devoted to their own jealous lovers, and went out of the way to be with each other only in public. Ariel cared for Manfred as a coach, but not as a romantic partner.

Learning this, Jillian undid her rage, and was then able to see that Manfred favored Ariel somewhat because she was exceptionally nice and flattering to him; and that he disfavored Jillian because she was so angry and critical of him. When she began to perceive the "facts" behind her negative convictions, Jillian dropped her anger, treated Manfred more favorably, and actually got him to sometimes favor her over Ariel.

All that's well did not end too well, however. Jillian remained panicked about Ariel because her friend might still part from her *present* lover, end up in Manfred's arms, and *then* be favored by him. What an awful thought!

I saw Jillian for six therapy sessions and had her tackle her "what ifs?" now that she saw that her *present* jealousy was unfounded. Ariel *could* possibly have an affair with Manfred, be favored by him for other reasons, have his tennis friends practice with her, and so on. None of these "unfairnesses" probably *would* happen; but any and all of them *could*. She could have no way of knowing that these "terrible" things could *not* happen; it was always *possible* that they would.

So I helped Jillian use the ultimate elegant Disputing of REBT. She imagined that the worst *did* happen — that Manfred definitely and unfairly favored Ariel, giving Ariel the chance to greatly excel at tennis. Yes, she assumed the *worst*, saw the Irrational *Beliefs* that were *awful*, and then responded with the following forceful rational coping statements:

"Well, this disaster *may* occur, but it most likely *won't*. But suppose it does! Suppose Ariel decidedly beats me at tennis. Too damned bad! If it happens, it *must* happen. If Manfred is, for any reason, unfair to me, he *has* to be. Tough! Shitty! But hardly the end of the world! I can wind up being a worse — even much worse — tennis player than Ariel, but still a fairly good one. I can make myself an *un*miserable, happy person, if I *think* I can be, and work hard at being so. So get over it! Get back to being nice to Manfred and playing tennis as well as I can play it!"

Jillian first Disputed and reframed her negative *perceptions* about Ariel and Manfred and *felt* much better. But then, seeing her terrifying *evaluations* of possible factual perceptions, she nicely used REBT and Disputed them. Although she didn't altogether *get* better by *completely* overcoming her jealousy — who ever does? — she *appreciably* overcame it.

Checking and reframing your perceived "grim" Adversities is one way of Disputing them, but additionally Disputing your awful evaluation of them — if and when they do occur — is even better. You can then see them, at worst, as highly frustrating and inconvenient — but not "terrible" and "disastrous."

By training yourself to see that some of the worst and most unlikely misfortunes *may* occur, and accepting the challenge that, if they do, you will greatly *disappoint* — but not *horrify* — yourself about them, you will be working on the adventure of *achieving minimal upsetting*. You will then philosophically-emotionally-behaviorally prepare yourself for the worst possible eventualities. If there is such a thing as minimizing your self-inflicted terror in advance, you can preventively REBT-ize yourself to think, feel, and behave in the least upsetting way. What a constructivist invitation and path you can accept and take!

Using Anti-catastrophizing and Anti-awfulizing

I was the first major therapist to emphasize *catastrophizing* as a prime element in emotional dysfunctioning. Later, I saw that real catastrophes — such as terrorism, war, and floods — do exist, whether or not you view them as *awful* and *terrible*. So I invented the terms *awfulizing* and *terribilizing* to describe what you and other people often put yourself through.

To catastrophize or awfulize is to take some aspect of your environment that you dislike — and healthily would view as "bad" or even "very bad" — and then greatly exaggerate its frequency and/or its danger. Thus, you may utterly convince yourself that the slightest cut on your finger will definitely lead to a deadly infection. Or that a noisy airplane overhead is about to crash into your home, killing you and all the members of your family. Or that bad economic news means the end of the world is in sight and will surely happen tomorrow. You may try to Dispute these catastrophizing and awfulizing convictions, but have trouble doing so.

Rian McMullin suggests an anti-catastrophizing and anti-awfulizing method that you can use to reduce your worrying. Write down a way that you frequently catastrophize — for example, "If I eat a hot-dog, I will surely die of botulism." Estimate on a scale of one to ten how likely this "disaster" is to happen, then picture the *best* possible outcome in this situation. Reflect in general on the chances of this event occurring, how many people suffer from a similar catastrophe, and what could happen if your imagined "horror" actually occurs. Based on your actual experience, estimate how probable it is that this "catastrophe" will ensue and, if it does, what is the worst thing that is likely to happen? By facing this imagined catastrophe and consciously reflecting on it and its worst possible consequences, you will be able to anti-awfulize about it and sensibly accept the outcome.

Using Cognitive Flooding Methods

Most humans are born with a talent for avoiding "terrible" feelings, like anxiety and depression. This is probably a useful and life-preserving tendency — since, if you always faced them and they didn't go away, you might make yourself exceptionally disturbed about them and might not be motivated to go on living. So avoiding such feelings — including denying them, rationalizing about them, and addicting yourself to alcohol, drugs, gambling, or some other pleasure that will cover your "horrible" feelings — is probably built into the human race. But not entirely to your advantage! Unless you *feel* your feelings, assess some of them as self-defeating, and use harmless methods — such as those described in this book — to reduce or eradicate them, you may be stuck — painfully stuck — with them. Again, you have a choice of two evils: you may acutely *feel* your anxiety and depression while working to minimize them; or, you may attempt to avoid those feelings, allowing them to stay beneath the surface and painfully break through from time to time. Which plan shall you consciously choose when you find that you are — usually unconsciously — picking the avoidance strategy?

Let's suppose you try to get in touch with your feelings of anxiety, depression, and rage, no matter how painful they are, and try to minimize them, instead of covering them up with different kinds of avoiding. In chapter 11, I describe active behaving methods — especially, *in vivo* desensitization or exposure — that enable you to face your worst feelings and irrational anxieties and to work through them. These exposure procedures, as Edna Foa and other psychologists have shown, have a good record and have helped many panicking and self-enraging people. By all means try them.

In addition to actively exposing yourself to some of your worst feelings, you can use some of the imaginal or cognitive methods described by Rian McMullin in his book, *The New Handbook of Cognitive Therapy*. With these imaginal techniques you can head off your natural tendency to avoid experiencing some of your intense, painful feelings, and thereby avoid perpetuating this kind of dysfunctioning.

Here is one way of imaginally facing your feelings that you can practice:

Imagine, in vivid detail, the "terrifying" experience that you actually keep thinking about and dreading, and imagine having an exaggerated Irrational *Beliefs* that often goes along with this imagined experience. Thus, you can imagine driving on a thruway behind an erratic, possibly drunken driver, and you can imagine your telling yourself, "Oh, my God! He's insane! Maybe he's hopelessly drunk! I can't get away from his car! I'm stuck! And my own panic makes me feel even more stuck! Oh, hell, there's no escape!" Let yourself feel, really feel, your panic, and don't let yourself escape from it — until you become satiated and bored with it, desire to once and for all conquer it, and actually turn it into feelings of real concern and determination to figure a way out of this "horrifying" situation.

If you use this imaginal "flooding" method, you obviously will experience your catastrophizing thinking and the "terrible" feelings of panicking that accompany it. But you can actively *force* yourself to face these cognitions and emotions, and use the method to Dispute Irrational *Beliefs* (IBs). Finally, you can add actual *in vivo* desensitization or exposure to a real-life situation — for example, practice riding on the "dangerous" highways you have been avoiding, thus adding *action* flooding to your *imaginal* flooding.

Try verbal flooding about past or historical "traumas" by vividly imagining their details many times — until you get fed up with the repetition and become desensitized to their "horrors." You can do the same kind of monotonous and desensitizing repetition of the Irrational *Beliefs* you had when these traumatic events occurred is the past. This exercise will make it less likely that you will obsessively hold on to these IBs in the future.

As you may have guessed by now, I like the Thinking and Philosophizing methods, and consider them among the most valuable for getting better. So much so that the next two chapters are devoted to even more of them! Keep working on your thinking and philosophizing — and remember to accentuate the Rational!

9

Getting Better III: Still More Thinking and Philosophizing Methods

Windy Dryden, professor of counseling at Goldsmith's College in London, is a pioneering practitioner of Rational Emotive Behavior Therapy (REBT) who has made many outstanding contributions to its theory and practice. Dryden has observed something interesting among people who Dispute their Irrational *Beliefs* and come up with Rational convictions to replace them. Many of these folks cavalierly repeat their new Rational ideas and truly think that they subscribe to them, while underneath they more vigorously and forcefully hold on to their Irrational ones. They acknowledge that their Disputing of Irrational Believing-Emoting-Behavings is "correct" or "accurate," but they only lightly hold the "true" answers that they give themselves. Professor Dryden gives several methods of questioning and challenging Rational as well as Irrational *Beliefs* in his recent books, *How To Accept Yourself* and *Thinking, Feeling, and Behaving Rationally and Healthily*. With his permission, I'll summarize some of his ideas, but I'd recommend reading his writings for more details.

One of the main things you can do in order to question your *light* Rational *Beliefs* (RBs) as you Dispute your *strong* Irrational ones is to distinguish clearly between your *rational preferences,* with their desires and wishes, and your *irrational demands,* with their shoulds, oughts, musts, and other insistences. Don't forget that one of the most important theories of REBT holds that if you strongly and consistently stay with your *preferences*, and rarely escalate them into grandiose *demands*, you will have great difficulty in making yourself disturbed or dysfunctional.

What are the basic differences between preferring and demanding? Let me describe these again. Preferences, as used in REBT, are wishes, wants, desires — and they are flexible, undogmatic, and unabsolutistic. Demands are preferences raised to commands and insistences — and they tend to be inflexible, dogmatic, and absolutistic. For the purpose of this discussion, we shall use a basic and common *preference* that you, as well as others, are likely to have:

> *I would very much like to keep succeeding at important goals (such as work, school, relating to others, sex, or sports), and I would very much like to find other people approving and not disapproving of me.*

When you raise this preference to an insistent, dogmatic, absolutistic *demand*, you change it to something like this:

> *Because I would very much like to succeed at important goals and find other people approving rather than disapproving of me, I absolutely must, at all times and under all conditions, succeed and garner the approval of others.*

For greater clarity, we can divide your preferring and your demanding into several aspects or factors, such as the following:

Preferable shoulding and wishing: "It would be preferable (more advantageous for me) if I keep succeeding at important goals and gain the approval of other people, but it is not necessary for me to do so."

Inflexible shoulding and musting: "Because I would very much like to keep succeeding at important goals and gain the approval of other people, I *absolutely must* do so at all times and under all conditions!"

Absolutistic demanding: "Because I very much want to succeed at important goals and gain the approval of other people, I have to totally, at all times and under all conditions, do so!" "I can't be happy if I am not achieving all this!" "I can't enjoy succeeding at other goals if I am not perfectly achieving my main ones!"

Unconditionally accepting others and external conditions: "I very much want to succeed at important goals and to gain the approval of other people, but I can fully accept myself as a person if I fail at my goal or do not gain the approval of others." "I can fully accept other people if they block me from succeeding or they are disapproving." "I can accept, but not like, external conditions that block me from succeeding or cause people to disapprove of me."

Conditional accepting: "I very much want to succeed at important goals and gain the approval of other people, and I can accept myself as a person and consider myself worthwhile only if I achieve these goals!" "I can accept other people only if they never block me from succeeding or are never disapproving!" "I cannot accept external conditions at all when they block me from succeeding or cause people to disapprove of me!"

High frustration tolerating wishing and preferring: "I very much want to keep succeeding at important goals and to gain the approval of other people, but when conditions and people keep blocking and frustrating my goals, I can make myself feel disappointed and regretful but not depressed and angry." "I can stand frustrating conditions and people blocking me and still find enjoyable pursuits." "It's not the end of the world; I can find alternative things to do that will provide me with reasonable happiness."

Low frustration tolerating wishing and preferring: "When I want very much to succeed at important goals and gain the approval of other people, but conditions and people keep blocking and frustrating me, it's very upsetting, but *not* awful and terrible; I *can* stand it, and I *can* be somewhat happy!" "The world's not treating me well, but it's *not* a rotten place that *should not* exist as it does."

As you can see, there are wide differences between the rational and self-helping *preferring* attitude — that you do well, be approved of by others, and have good things happen to you — and the irrational and self-defeating *demanding* attitude — that you absolutely must do well, must have other people's approval and cooperation, and must have external conditions that wholly favor and never seriously block you. Arriving at Rational *Beliefs*, and Disputing and minimizing Irrational ones, is more than likely to bring you benefits and to minimize your disbenefits. In previous chapters, I have already shown how you can strongly Dispute and act against your Irrational *Beliefs* (IBs). Now, for review purposes, I'll describe Disputing of some of your irrational convictions again. I'll also show how you can do some of the questioning and challenging of your Rational Believing-Emoting-Behavings so that you can come to hold them more solidly, as Windy Dryden importantly suggests.

Three-Way Disputes
The three main ways of Disputing both your Irrational and Rational *Beliefs* are:

(1) *Realistic questioning* — Determine if your IBs and RBs are factual, and whether they hold up to scrutiny in your everyday life and in your specific culture.

(2) *Logical questioning* — Check to see if your conclusions about your self-helping preferring and self-defeating demanding follow from your assumptions about them.

(3) *Practical or healthy Disputing* — Question your philosophies to see if they are likely to lead to beneficial or harmful results for you and other people.

Let's now apply these three major ways of Disputing to some of the Irrational *Beliefs* that are listed above, and then to some of the Rational *Beliefs*.

Disputing Inflexible Shoulding and Musting
"Because I would very much like to keep succeeding at important goals and gaining the approval of other people, I *absolutely must* do so at all times and under all conditions!"

Realistic Disputing: "Why must I absolutely keep succeeding at important goals and keep gaining the approval of other people? Where is it written that I always have to do so? What law of the universe says that I must? What social law states that I have to? Is it factual that I absolutely must do so at all times under all conditions?"

Realistic answer: "There is no reason why I absolutely must keep succeeding at important goals and must keep gaining the approval of other people. It is only written that I must in my mistaken head, not in the universe and not in social reality. It is not a fact that I must, only an assumption. It would be highly preferable if I always kept succeeding at important goals and kept gaining the approval of other people, but this is most unlikely, considering my fallibility and the prejudices of others. I'd better stick to my preferring to achieve these ends, and not make them into an unrealistic necessity!"

Logical Disputing: "Does it follow that because I would very much like to keep succeeding at important goals and winning the approval of other people that therefore I absolutely have to do so? Must I get what I want, because I strongly desire it?"

Logical answer: "Of course it doesn't follow that because I want something, I must get what I want. If it did follow, that would be lovely! But it doesn't in the least!"

Practical and healthy Disputing: "Where will I be if I think and feel that I absolutely must succeed at important goals and keep winning the approval of other people? What results am I likely to get? Will my insisting on this actually help me get what I very much want?"

Rational and healthy answer: "My insisting on getting what I want will very likely make me anxietize about the possibility of not getting it and depress myself when I actually do not get it. My anxietizing about possibly not getting what I think I must get — achieving my important goals and winning the approving of others — will interfere with my actually getting what I want, since my anxietizing and self-depressing will make me less efficient in gaining what I want. When people see my anxiety, see how needy I am, they will likely turn away from me and not approve of me or help me get what I want."

Preferable Shoulding and Wishing

"It would be preferable (more advantageous to me) if I kept succeeding at important goals and gaining the approval of other people, but it is not necessary for me to do so."

Realistic Disputing: "Why is it just *preferable* for me to keep succeeding at my goals and keep gaining the approval of other people? Why is it not *necessary* for me to do so?"

Realistic answer: "It is preferable for me to want to achieve these goals just because I decide on these preferences. As a human, I am entitled to any preferences I make — though I am not entitled to get them fulfilled. My desires are legitimate just because I have them, and I always have the right to have them and to change them. It is not necessary for me to achieve my goals or to keep gaining the approval of others, because if it were absolutely necessary, then the laws of the universe would arrange that I do so. Obviously, I often do not get what I want, and that demonstrates that it is not necessary that I get it."

Logical Disputing: "Is it logical for me to keep trying to get what I want — to try to achieve my goals and gain the approval of other people? Does it follow that I sometimes will probably succeed at achieving these goals?"

Logical answer: "Yes, it is logical for me to keep trying to get what I want, as long as I don't anxietize by demanding that I get it. I can even logically wish for the sky without expecting or demanding that I will get it. Does it follow that if I very much want to achieve my goals and win the approval of other people, I may be able to actually do so? Yes, in some instances, especially if my wishing for these things motivates me to keep trying for them and to work at getting them. Statistically, it follows that if I keep trying hard to achieve them, I will increase my chances of doing so, even though I can't guarantee that I will get the results that I want."

Practical and healthy Disputing: "If I continue my preferable and rational shoulding and wishing to achieve important goals and to win the approval of others, what practical results will I get?"

Practical and healthy answer: "I'll resist anxietizing about getting these goals, as long as I keep preferably desiring and not musturbatorily demanding them. If I don't get them fulfilled, I'll only be sorry and disappointed, not depressed. Preferring to achieve them will most likely help me get some part, if not all, of them."

Disputing Unconditional Self-Accepting, Unconditional Other-Accepting, and Unconditional Condition-Accepting

"I very much want to keep succeeding at important goals and gaining the approval of other people, but I can fully accept myself as a person if I fail at my goals or do not gain the approval of others. I can also fully accept other people if they block me from succeeding or are unjustly disapproving of me. I can also accept, but not like, external conditions if they block me from succeeding or cause people to be unfairly disapproving of me."

Realistic Disputing: "Why can I unconditionally accept myself, other people, and conditions in spite of my poor and their unfair behavior? Is it really possible for me to fully accept myself when I foolishly act badly, and to accept other people when they act badly and immorally?"

Realistic answer: "Yes, I have the choice of accepting or nonaccepting myself and other people, and I can simply take that choice, of accepting rather than nonaccepting. That is my human prerogative. Realistically, if I don't take the choice of fully accepting myself and others, no matter what we do, I will have to keep wavering from unconditional to conditional accepting, because I and others continually do good and bad deeds. So, realistically, I will often keep utterly accepting and utterly damning myself and others —acting quite contradictorily in that respect."

Logical Disputing: "Is it logical for me to totally accept myself and others even though we all perform quite badly at times? Can I consider myself a worthwhile person in spite of my many social and personal mistakes, and can I do the same for other people?"

Answer to logical Disputing: "Yes, it is logical for me to accept myself and others even though we all perform quite badly at times, because we are born and reared to be fallible humans, and therefore can be considered worthy of continuing our lives in a fallible human manner. If we damn ourselves for our failings, we could hardly continue to live happily, since these failings are realistically inevitable. If we accept ourselves unconditionally, in spite of our failings, we can survive and see ourselves as capable of correcting some of these failings. Although unconditional self- and other-accepting may be definitional and essentially unprovable, they are realistically self-preservative; unless we survive, we cannot accomplish anything. Besides, unconditionally accepting ourselves, though definitional, leads to our behaving consistently in this important aspect of our lives. Nonaccepting ourselves and others is inconsistent and therefore illogical. It is based on total ratings of humans for their ever-changing acts, an overgeneralization that will not logically work out well."

Practical and healthy Disputing: "What results will I likely get if I accept myself and other people unconditionally instead of conditionally accepting them on the basis that they inconsistently act 'good' and 'bad'?"

Practical and healthy answer: "I will get, in all probability, much better results with unconditional rather than conditional accepting. Thus:

I will encourage myself and allow myself to behave both 'good' and 'bad' and, by not damning myself for my 'bad' acts, I will aid myself in correcting them and doing better in the future.

I will stop terrifying myself about my failings (and thereby very likely making them worse).

I will give myself a chance to live a relatively happy, long life, instead of interfering with it by behaving badly or choosing to commit suicide.

If I accept other people unconditionally, in spite of their intermittent 'good' and 'bad' activities, I will get along with them better and there will be less risk of them interfering with my life or being hostile toward me."

High Frustration Tolerating Wishing and Preferring

"I very much want to keep succeeding at important goals and being approved of by other people who are important to me. However, when people and conditions keep blocking and frustrating my wishing, I can make myself feel disappointed and regretful, rather than depressed and angry.

Realistic Disputing: "Why do I have the choice of making myself disappointed and regretful, rather than depressed and angry when people and conditions keep blocking and frustrating my wishes? Is it realistic to make myself have the healthy negative feelings of anger and depression when people and conditions keep blocking and frustrating my wishes? Doesn't the fact that people who feel angry and depressed about other people and conditions blocking and frustrating them mean that I have to feel this way, too?"

Realistic answer: "I, as a human, have considerable choice in choosing my emotional reactions when people and conditions frustrate and block me, and therefore I can choose, at least much of the time, to feel disappointed and regretful about this frustration, rather than angry and depressed about it. Because I, like other humans, am able to pick my kind of emotional reacting to frustrating people and conditions, I can work at choosing to feel disappointed and regretful rather than angry and depressed when I actually encounter any kind of frustration. Even though *most* people feel angry and depressed about people and conditions that keep frustrating and blocking them, there are some people who do not feel this way. All people are different in their reactions to frustrating stimuli, and I can model myself after those people who react in a disappointed and regretful manner, rather than model myself after those who react in an angry and depressed manner. Even if I, like many others, have strong innate and acquired tendencies to enrage and depress myself when I face frustration and blocking, I also have the ability to fight against these tendencies and, with some hard work, frequently make myself disappointed and regretful, instead of angry and depressed."

Logical Disputing: "When people and conditions keep blocking and frustrating my wishing, do I have to jump to the conclusion that they will *always* do so and that I will therefore always suffer from severe blocking and frustrating? Although this kind of blocking and frustrating is against my wishes, and therefore I can legitimately consider it bad or unfortunate, do I have to jump to the illogical conclusion that it is awful or terrible, that I can't stand it, and that I can't have any pleasure in life at all?"

Logical answer: "No. Even though people and conditions keep blocking and frustrating my wishing, it is illogical to conclude that they will always do so. 'Always' is illogical overgeneralizing! People and conditions may well change and not block or frustrate me; I may encounter people and conditions that are not frustrating and blocking. Although I can legitimately view the blocking and frustrating of my wishes as unfortunate, I cannot logically jump to concluding that it is 'awful' because it *must* not exist, when it *does* exist, nor conclude that it is 'awful' because it is 'totally' bad. Nor can I logically conclude that I can't stand it, when I obviously will not die of it. Nor can I logically conclude that I can't have any pleasure at all in life because people and conditions are frustrating. My 'logical' conclusions — which I now see are not logical — are contradicted by the facts of my life and existence."

Practical and healthy Disputing: "What kind of practical results will I get if I keep reacting with high frustration tolerating to not fulfilling my strong wishes?"

Practical and healthy answer: "I will most probably get several good results:

♦ I will stop whining and complaining about my unfortunate conditions and, as a result, will have more time and energy to improve them.

♦ I will refuse to depress and anger myself about my unfortunate conditions, and will suffer the much milder discomforts of disappointment and regret about them.

♦ I will see that I really am in distinct control of my emotional destiny and that I can continue to exert good control over it."

The ideas presented in this chapter are at the same time simple and complex. I urge you to review them — several times! — to be sure you have learned how to use them in dealing with your own Irrational *Beliefs! Push your ass* (PYA)!

10

Getting Better IV: Emotive, Evocative, and Experiential Methods

The most elegant way of getting better, instead of merely feeling better, is to acknowledge that you partly create or construct your dysfunctional feeling and behaving. Recognize that you do so by insisting that you *absolutely must* perform well, be treated considerately, and encounter favorable living conditions, and then see that you really can give up these irrational, self-defeating, musturbatory *Beliefs*.

The crux of the matter here is the word *really*. For humans, including you, have a powerful tendency to *lightly* see their self-sabotaging philosophizing and behaving — and then to *strongly* still hold them. That is, *when* they see them. As Sigmund Freud and his daughter Anna clearly pointed out, humans often act defensively and dishonestly, and beautifully manage not to see the harmful things that they are doing to themselves — or to see them and ignore doing much about them. As Aesop (centuries ago!) pointed out in the story of *The Fox and the Grapes*, they brilliantly look away from their destructive ideas and motives, rationalize about them, and make up foolish excuses for not changing them.

Using Forceful Disputing of Irrational Beliefs

At 27, Tanya was a very practical and straight-thinking graduate student of philosophy who did very well in school and at her part-time job as a computer analyst. Socially, however, she only dated men she considered "inferior" because she was sure that she was not attractive or stable enough to keep a "good" one. Actually, she was distinctly attractive and had many other qualities that the kind of a man she really wanted would welcome. Because of her severe feelings of inadequacy, however, she only went with partners who in some way did not quite measure up, and who would presumably forgive and forget her failings — if they indeed saw them.

Tanya took to REBT quickly because it followed many of her own philosophical leanings. She agreed that she might have some inferior traits, but that she was not an inferior person. Agreed, that is, in theory. She "proved" to herself, using REBT principles, that some terrific men might well reject her for one reason or another, but that she had enough "good" traits to succeed with one of them if she stopped taking rejections too seriously and kept trying to date. She also agreed with the REBT principle that she could view herself as a valuable person in her own right, even when she had real failings and had been rejected by several men she viewed as "superior."

Theoretically Tanya's new REBT philosophy should have helped her to go after some better-than-average males, but she didn't. She had no trouble dating "insignificant" men, but panicked herself whenever she met an outstanding one. She *agreed lightly* with the REBT philosophy that her *failings* didn't make her a *failure,* but she much more *strongly believed* that they really *did*, and that as a failure, she was barred from winning a first-class man.

I urged Tanya to do some very vigorous disputing of her irrational thinking by using a cassette player to record her main irrational beliefs: "I am really not attractive enough to get a man I truly like, and my unattractiveness makes me an inept, failing person. What's the use? No matter how much I try, I'll never get what I really want, so I might as well settle for a man who is inferior to what I want. At least he will forgive my looks and accept me." Tanya then recorded her vigorous disputing on the same tape.

At first, she disputed this IB rather lightly and ineffectively, and didn't even realize that she was doing so. Because the content of her disputing was correct, she assumed that her vigor was, too. But as several of her close friends and I listened in, we all seemed to agree that it wasn't vigorous enough. So she went over her disputing several times and kept retaping it, until she came up with some strong and forceful disputations. Among her strong disputes were these:

"Am I *really* not attractive enough to get a man I would truly like to be with? Well, I'm no great beauty, but women far less attractive seem to wind up with someone I would find really desirable. Even if it could be shown that I am less attractive than the average woman my age, this only proves that I might lose some men, but I would hardly turn ALL of them off. That's ridiculous! Not all good men are hung up on looks, and some don't even seem to care — especially if I am nice to them and good in bed. It may be difficult to find the kind of man I want, but *difficult* doesn't mean *impossible!* I *can* get one I really want if I keep risking rejection. And rejection isn't *awful*, and it certainly doesn't prove anything about me as a person. I *am not* my behavior; I only *do* it. Damn it all, I'll really keep trying, trying, trying!"

This kind of forceful disputing finally worked with Tanya. She not only saw that her beliefs about men were exaggerated and false, she *felt* their falsity, and she strongly replaced them with Rational *Beliefs*. She still had difficulty permanently seeing and feeling that she had a reasonably good chance of getting the kind of man she wanted, but she finally achieved this solid kind of emotional insight. As she noted in her recorded tape, she kept trying, trying, trying. About a year after she overcame her basic feelings of inadequacy, she did meet and become engaged to what seemed to her to be a "superior" man. Or, as she herself more accurately noted, "a man *with* some superior traits."

Disputing (D) your Irrational *Beliefs* (IBs), and arriving at E, your Effective New Philosophizing, had better often be vigorous.

Like many other people, you may easily create and strongly hold on to your dysfunctional viewing, so that light disputing will help make you temporarily feel better. But it will not really sink into your *being* and remain there.

Using a cassette recorder, as Tanya did, record some of your self-defeating ideas, and then dispute them as vigorously as you can — realistically, logically, and pragmatically (as I described in chapter 2 and chapter 3). Listen to the tape to see if your disputing is sufficiently forceful, and then revise it to make it still more vigorous. Ask some close friends or relatives to listen to it and appraise not only its content, but its style. Keep revising your taped presentation until your listeners agree that it is strong enough. See if this method works for you, and also try some of the other emotive-evocative methods of REBT described in this chapter.

Using Forceful Coping Self-Statements

The purpose of disputing in REBT is to arrive at E, your Effective New Philosophies, which turns your grandiose demands into reasonable desires and helps you achieve more of what you want and less of what you don't want. These self-statements, or philosophies, can then be written down or put on a tape and repeated many times until you really see that they are self-helping. But repetition is not enough! As you repeat them to yourself, keep thinking about them — why they are accurate and potentially effective. Don't merely parrot them to yourself in an unthinking manner.

Joseph began using rational coping statements within a few weeks after learning how he could apply them to his problem of being hypochondriacal. All his life he had been terribly afraid of catching various diseases, even though he had nothing more serious than chicken pox as a child. At the slightest sign of a cough, cold, or any mild infection, he ran to his doctor to make sure he did not have some horrible disease. Although doctors assured him he had no serious health problems, that did no good, and he kept returning for more medical checkups. Some of his doctors actually got rid of him as a patient.

As is the case with many hypochondriacs, Joseph tolerated frustration poorly and believed that all diseases and infections were *horrible*, that he absolutely *couldn't stand* them, and that his life was *completely in danger* if he were to suffer from one. He was somewhat "allergic" to directly disputing these irrational convictions, but he did manage to make up a number of rational coping statements that contradicted and, in a sense, disputed them. "My doctors are quite reliable, and when they say I don't have any diseases, they are almost certainly right. Worrying about getting a disease and constantly checking with my doctors won't ward it off if it is going to afflict me anyway. By panicking about diseases I am likely to upset my physical system and perhaps even my immune system, which could help bring on rather than ward off disease. If I do get a disease, I can take care of it medically. If I come down with a disease, it probably won't last long, and although it may be *inconvenient*, it probably won't be *absolutely horrible and debilitating*."

These were good coping statements but, like his medical exams, helped Joseph only temporarily live with the possibility of ailments, for he believed them only lightly — and with very strong ifs and buts. He lightly agreed with his coping statement, that worrying about getting a disease wouldn't ward it off, since it might well occur anyway. But he then strongly added, "But if I worry, I'll be more cautious and less likely to get a disease, and if I keep checking with my doctors about it they might find it earlier and treat it more effectively."

No matter what good coping statements he used, Joseph always came up with a powerful *but* to cancel them out, so they naturally proved ineffective. I helped him think seriously about his self-statements, to prove that they were accurate, and that his ifs and buts were unrealistic. This helped a little, but not enough; Joseph kept running to doctors and worrying about possible afflictions.

Finally, I helped Joseph take his rational coping statements and repeat them to himself several times very, very strongly until they sank into his head and heart. He wrote down and repeated them over and over with great emphasis, especially this one: "Worrying about a disease and constantly checking with my doctors won't ward it off if it is going to come anyway. It WON'T, it WON'T, it WON'T! Not in any darned way will it! If I am doomed to get a disease, NOTHING will stop me from having it! Worry will NEVER, NEVER work! It can ONLY make it worse! It has NO positive effect!" When Joseph emphasized his coping statements in this manner, and kept at it until they sank into his head and heart, he was then able to resist calling his doctors. By forcing himself not to call his doctors, combined with his vigorous coping self-statements, he was able to see that nothing actually happened to him, and he gradually became less anxious.

If you use coping statements to combat your irrational beliefs about disease — or anything else — use them regularly and lightly at first. But if that doesn't work, increase the force and vigor with which you use them. Thinking includes an emotional as well as cognitive element. You can aid this emotional factor by forcefully repeating your coping statements and emphasizing them in a highly ardent manner. You naturally think and feel at the same time, but you can focus on the feeling element and make it stronger. Your rational coping statements will be much more effective if you think *and feel* them.

Rational Emotive Imagery

In the 1960s I realized that REBT can be enhanced by employing a good many experiential exercises, such as those that were introduced to psychotherapy by Fritz Perls, Will Schutz, and other therapists. Many of these exercises were introduced for the wrong reasons: their creators thought that by getting in touch with your feelings and really and truly experiencing them, instead of denying and inhibiting them, you would automatically change and release yourself from their ravages.

This point, like practically all therapeutic techniques, has some truth to it. For one thing, it is a form of *in vivo* desensitization. Thus, when you hate someone and uninhibitedly say, "I hate you! I could really kill you!" instead of holding your anger in or denying that you really feel it, you sometimes get desensitized to it and feel it less strongly. Facing it honestly somehow may inure you to it; while, on the other hand, denying it or suppressing it gives you no chance to experience it fully, and may block you from getting in touch with it and giving it up.

Moreover, if you express your anger fully, either to the people you are angry at or to yourself, you may see several things that help you give it up:

♦ You may see how silly it is — for you are condemning a whole person completely for a few of the things she did, and your damning is inaccurate and childish.

♦ You may realize that the person you are angry at does many good and beneficial things, as well as a few wrong ones.

♦ You may see that you, too, are hardly a noble person who never acts badly.

♦ You may observe that your anger is obsessive and stirs up your own body quite badly, and therefore you may work at reducing it.

As I continue to note in this book, thoughts and feelings are tightly connected, each leading to the other. Therefore, when you give vent to your emoting and do so fully, you can get a host of possible ideas — some of which may be beneficial and may induce you to curb the very emoting you are feeling.

On the other hand, it has been found in many experiments, and *in vivo,* that fully expressing your feelings — especially your feelings of anger — may increase the strength of the feelings. Seymour Feshbach, Jerry Deffenbacher, Howard Kassinove, and Raymond DiGiuseppe have pioneered in showing that the expression of anger, either directly or indirectly, can magnify it, and may lead you to "punish" the target of your anger more severely. (This is further detailed in my book with Chip Tafrate, *How to Control Your Anger Before It Controls You.*)

Nonetheless, although they may have distinct dangers, and may possibly do more harm than good — as, indeed, may any therapeutic technique — methods that encourage you to express your feelings directly and fully are often helpful. If wisely selected, they will help you to become aware of and change the dysfunctional philosophies that accompany these feelings. So, when used properly, emotionally expressive techniques can prove to be therapeutic.

One of the best emotive-evocative techniques frequently used in REBT is an adaptation of Maxie Maultsby's Rational Emotive Imagery. Maxie came to study with me in 1968, and spent a great deal of time observing me in individual and group therapy with my clients, as well as reading the REBT literature published at that time. After returning to Madison, Wisconsin, he practiced psychiatry and founded a variation on REBT called Rational Behavior Therapy (RBT), and developed several useful therapy techniques, especially Rational Emotive Imagery (REI).

REI is, in some ways, the opposite of positive thinking or positive visualization. For to do REI, you vividly imagine one of the worst things that might happen to you — failing miserably at a job, for example, or being lied to and duped by another person — and let yourself spontaneously feel anger, panic, and/or depression about this imagined event. You let yourself feel very upset for a short while, get fully in touch with this feeling, and even exaggerate or implode it until you feel exceptionally distressed.

REBT encourages you to prescribe for yourself a healthy negative feeling — such as sorrow, regret, disappointment, or frustration, instead of the unhealthy one you feel. Keeping the same dreadful image in mind, you work for a few minutes at producing a healthy feeling, and not your unhealthy one.

When you have succeeded in doing so, you determine exactly what you did to change your unhealthy feelings to healthy negative feelings, and you use this philosophy again and again to keep training yourself, using the same grim imagery, to feel healthy instead of unhealthy negative feelings. You essentially do this, by consciously changing your philosophizing — your Irrational *Beliefs* — about your negative image to a new effective, rational, or functional philosophizing. You then practice Rational Emotive Imagery for at least once a day for thirty days until you automatically react with healthy instead of unhealthy negative feelings about the grim event you are imagining.

I used Rational Emotive Imagery with Mary, a woman who was practically crippled with anger at her parents, her husband, and even at her ten-year-old son, Tommy, whenever they acted "badly" and presumably upset her. I showed her how she was crazily demanding that they act well, when they were often incapable of doing so, and was needlessly upsetting herself — not with their behavior, as she supposed, but with her exaggerated and self-defeating reactions.

I showed Mary how to become aware of her Irrational *Beliefs* behind her rage at her family members — "They absolutely *must not* act the way they do and upset me with their wrong actions!" — and I helped her dispute these self-sabotaging ideas. At times she was able to do so — especially when she saw that the family members were not really trying to upset her, but were just acting the way they did because that was their natural tendency and they would have great difficulty not behaving in that "wrong" manner. But she frequently lapsed back into extreme rage, especially at her father and mother for not rearing her "properly" and for interfering with her raising her son.

"Close your eyes," I said to Mary, "and think of some of the worst things that your parents have done and are doing. Think of how they unfairly criticized you when you were a child, and even physically abused you; how they are constantly criticizing you for not being very strict and punitive with your son, Tommy.

"Visualize how they kept after you, time and time again, both in the past and the present, and told you what a worm you are for not following their dictates. See them acting most unfairly and badly. Visualize it very, very clearly. Can you do this? Can you see them acting unfairly and cruelly?"

"Oh, very easily!" Mary said. "I can see them doing it steadily, both in the past and in the present. Very definitely!"

"And how do you feel, in your heart and in your gut, as you strongly visualize them acting this way? What is your honest feeling?"

"I feel furious. Enraged. I could kill them! Just as I have always felt toward them. Practically homicidal!"

"Good. Feel that feeling. Let yourself really feel quite raging, quite furious, almost homicidal. Feel it, feel it. Get in touch with that feeling. Let your fury take over. Let it control you. Feel it, feel it!"

"Oh, I do! I'm really enraged. I could just about kill them!"

"Fine. Feel it a little longer. Let your rage take over. Feel it to the hilt."

"I do, I do!"

"Good. Now, keep the same image, keep imagining that they are treating you unfairly and berating you fiercely about your son, about your failings, and about everything else. Feel as enraged as you can feel. Then, keeping the same image — don't change it at all or improve it — work on your feeling, change your feeling, make yourself feel very sorrowful and disappointed with the *way they're behaving*, but not angry at *them*. Just sorry and disappointed with what they're doing. But not enraged, not angry at them, only sorrowful and disappointed. Tell me when you're able to feel — which you definitely are able to do — only sorrow and regret about their behavior, but not anger at them. Only sorrow and regret."

Mary at first had trouble working on changing her feeling, and thought that she could not do so. But I encouraged her to keep trying, and assured her that she definitely could change her enraged feelings to those of sorrow and disappointment. After about two minutes she said that she had done so.

"You're now only feeling sorrow and disappointment with your parents' behavior, and not rage at them? Is that so? Do you really feel that way?"

"Yes, I really do. I feel released. I have let go of the anger and now feel only sorry."

"Okay. What did you do to change your feeling? How did you change it from extreme anger to just feeling sorrow and disappointment with your parents' behavior?"

"Well, let me see. I just — well, I just reminded myself that their unfair treatment of me, both in the past and today, is not *all* that they did. They also were nice to me in many ways; they really helped me at times with my son. So I saw that although their acts were bad — bad behavior, as you called it — they weren't really bad people. Their deeds were vile — but *they* weren't total villains. So I felt very sorrowful and disappointed with some of their behavior, but was able to let go, really let go, of the rage at them. I just dropped it."

"Fine. Very good. You really did it — as I said you could. You control your feelings — even though you don't control the behavior of your parents and of others. You can feel as you want to feel — healthily sorrowful and regretful, or unhealthily enraged and upset. See?"

"Yes, I do see. I control my feelings — not the acts of others."

"Right. Now what I want you to do is to repeat this same Rational Emotive Imagery exercise for 30 days. It only takes a couple of minutes, as you saw. So every day, at least once a day, imagine the worst, imagine your parents really acting cruelly and unjustly. Let yourself feel as you actually feel — probably enraged. Feel it, really feel it. Then, after a couple of minutes, change your feeling, as you just did, to one of sorrow and regret and not rage. Really change it — as you are able to do. Do this at least once a day.

"Then you'll really train yourself to automatically, unconsciously, and spontaneously feel sorrow and regret about your parents' behavior, but not feel rage at them. You'll train yourself, if you use Rational Emotive Imagery, to automatically feel the healthy feelings of sorrow and regret, rather than the unhealthy ones of rage. You'll see that it becomes automatic. And even when your parents, in real life, actually act cruelly and unfairly, you'll notice that you will automatically be able to feel just sorrow and regret, not furious and enraged."

"You really think I can train myself to do this?"

"Yes. I have used Rational Emotive Imagery with literally thousands of people, and if they really keep it up, they tend to train themselves to automatically and unconsciously feel healthy rather than unhealthy emoting. We don't want you — or anyone — not to feel. REBT encourages you to have feelings — strong feelings. But it encourages healthy and not unhealthy negative feelings — those that help you get more of what you want and less of what you don't want.

"Now, will you try it for 30 days and train yourself to feel in a healthier manner?"

"Yes," said Mary. "I will certainly try."

"Okay. And if you have any trouble doing so, if you tend to forget to do the Rational Emotive Imagery or find it too difficult to do, let me add reinforcement or operant conditioning to it."

"Reinforcement?"

"Yes, what do you like to do — what pleasure — that you do practically every day in the week? Something you really enjoy."

"Let me see. Oh, yes. Listen to music; I do that every day."

"Fine. For the next 30 days only do it contingently — *after* you have done the Rational Emotive Imagery and changed your feeling from an unhealthy to a healthy one. See?"

"Yes, only after I do the Rational Emotive Imagery and change my feeling, then I listen to music."

"Right. And if that somehow doesn't work too well, you can also use a penalty."

"A penalty?"

"What do you hate to do, some chore or task that you really abhor, and therefore you rarely do it unless you have to?"

"Cleaning the toilet," said Mary.

"Fine. For the next 30 days when bedtime arrives, if you still haven't done Rational Emotive Imagery, then stay up for an hour and clean the toilet. And if it gets too clean, clean your neighbors' toilets!"

Mary laughed. She practiced Rational Emotive Imagery and, as I predicted, she made herself automatically sorrowful and regretful, and not enraged, when she thought of her parents treating her cruelly and unfairly in the past or the present. She became much less hating toward them in real life, and then she began working on her anger at her son, which at times also had gone beyond bounds.

You, too, can use Rational Emotive Imagery (REI) on any serious emotional problem — rage, depression, or panic. Imagine one of the worst possible scenes. Let yourself feel very upset about it. Then work on changing your feeling to a healthy negative one — sorrow, regret, or frustration. Keep doing this, for several days in a row, until you automatically start feeling the healthy instead of the unhealthy negative feelings. Whenever you imagine a really bad scene — or even when it actually occurs — you not only bring on and get in touch with your destructive feelings — which many therapies encourage — but REBT shows you how to change them to healthy negative emotions. You can do it. You construct your unhealthy feelings, and you can reconstruct healthy ones again.

Shame-Attacking Exercises

In the 1960's I realized that feelings of shame or embarrassment is the essence of much human disturbance. For when you really feel self-shaming, you are usually not putting down just your behavior, but also yourself. Philip, for example, shamed himself about innumerable things that he did — or didn't — do. If he farted in public — which at times he could not avoid doing — he made himself strongly ashamed and embarrassed. But also, if he didn't tell a joke well, was ignorant of the Yankees' standing in baseball, missed an easy play at tennis, or you name it, he felt shamed about not doing it well, not doing it well enough, or not doing it perfectly well.

Naturally, Philip suffered from one of the worst cases of reactive depression I ever saw. For he was continually failing to do well at something or other, then defaming himself for his failure — and then defaming himself for depressing himself. In just about all cases, I was able to show him that he was demanding and commanding success and competency, was often unable to achieve these goals, and was beating himself mercilessly! Actually, he was a highly competent physician, helped many of his patients recover from injuries and illnesses, but felt he *absolutely should* always do better than he did, and therefore was self-deprecating.

That's what shame almost always is: self-deprecating. You want to do something well or perfectly well and you don't fulfill your expectations. You also see — or think you see — that others observe your incompetency. So you berate yourself for your "poor" performance and for others supposedly seeing it and putting you down for it.

Philip rarely did poorly as a physician; virtually no patients criticized him. He was so obviously competent and eager to do his best, at a sacrifice of his own time and energy, that he never had a malpractice suit against him and was busier than he really wanted to be. No matter! Whenever he made what he considered a mistake, or didn't do absolutely as well as he supposedly *should* have done, he felt desperately ashamed, ruminated about his "error" for days or weeks, and actually deprived himself of some enjoyments, such as going to the theatre, because a no-goodnik like him didn't "deserve" it.

I had no trouble showing Philip how impossibly demanding he was, and how his shamed and inadequate feelings stemmed from his perfectionistic demands on himself. At times, I helped him to accept himself with his "errors" — but not when others observed and presumably despised him for them. When he neglected to insist that one of his older patients get a flu shot one year, and this patient ended up with a serious case of the flu and berated Philip for his neglect, he damned himself completely and almost felt suicidal.

Philip did REBT disputing *lightly* and usually came to the "right" conclusions: that his behavior was occasionally neglectful, but that he wasn't a shameful person for perpetrating it. At the same time, he *strongly* insisted that not only his act was shameful, but that he was a really rotten person for committing it. So REBT disputing helped, but not enough. He still frequently felt like a bad, shameful person for committing a "bad" deed.

I explained to Philip the rationale behind my famous shame-attacking exercises — which I invented in the 1960's. I saw then that shaming was at the heart of much disturbance, and that it usually consisted of:

+ doing a "stupid" or "wrong" thing

+ being observed doing it by significant people

+ acknowledging that the act was "bad" and "shameful"

+ putting oneself severely down as an "idiot" or an "incompetent" for doing it.

The shaming person rates *himself* and not merely his action as "shameful," and frequently feels that everyone would be unforgiving for the "horrible mistake" — as they "rightfully" *should* be!

Assuming that you behave foolishly or ineptly, and that others know this, you can rationally acknowledge your behavior and still see that you, a whole human, are never a *bad person*. If you were a truly bad person, then it would be hopeless — since you would hardly be able to do better in the future and would be condemned to a lifetime of "unforgivable" acts. So the REBT answer to shame is USA — unconditional self-accepting, no matter how foolish your act is and how many people (wrongly) condemn you for it.

Easier said than done. Disputing your "rottenness," and doing it very strongly, will usually partially work. In addition, however, you had better *practice* doing "stupid" and "wrong" acts and giving yourself the opportunity to admit them, while never, never putting your entire being down. The shame-attacking exercise gives you ample opportunity to do this.

Here are the instructions I gave Philip in using this exercise: "I want you to be able to strongly and forcefully see that a foolish or incompetent *act* never makes you a fool or an incompetent *person*. It just makes you a person who has done this act, and who has the ability to stop doing it. So in REBT we often persuade self-downing people, like yourself, to go out in public and deliberately do some asinine, wrong act, and let other people see you do it. Do something that you really feel ashamed of doing — and not something you would do as a lark or a joke. Take the risk that, by doing it, other people will look down on you and think you're an utter idiot."

"You mean," asked Philip, "something like panhandling, or walking naked in the street?"

"No, not exactly, because you may not be able to get away with that. Actually, you can be arrested for panhandling. And, of course, you could go to jail for walking down the street naked. So nothing like that — that would harm you. And nothing that would harm someone else, like slapping someone in the face or trying to steal his wallet. Something foolish, silly, and ridiculous — but not that would harm you or someone else."

"Like singing in the street at the top of my lungs?" asked Philip.

"Yes, that's one of the common ones that we use in the shame-attacking exercises," I said. "Singing in the street. Or wearing some outlandish clothing. Or walking with a big black umbrella over your head on a sunny day. Or yelling out the stops in the subway and staying on the train. Or any number of other things that you would feel embarrassed to do."

"And the purpose of this exercise, if I do it, is what?"

"The purpose is to see that nothing is really shameful; that you merely define it as such. Many things are socially wrong, and some things are actually immoral — such as stealing, for example. But making yourself feel unashamed means to do something that you and others think is wrong without putting yourself down for it. You may rate and evaluate your *behavior*, but don't give *yourself* a global rating, and never think that *you* are bad because your *act* may be wrong. Also, recognize that others may think you silly, and may actually penalize you for acting in a certain way. But don't take their view of yourself too seriously, and don't *agree* with it."

"But won't people think I'm no good if I do something they think is foolish?"

"Yes, they often will. But, again, you don't have to agree with them. So don't do a shame-attacking exercise when you may be penalized for doing it — at work, for example, or in a class at school. Do it among strangers, people you don't know and are not likely to meet again. And show yourself that you don't have to feel down, low, or ashamed if they do think you're acting foolishly and look askance at you. Preferably do it several times, until you see that you may act stupidly — but you are never a stupid or rotten person for behaving that way."

"What about doing something I would feel guilty about — like, as you noted before, stealing? Should I do that?"

"No, don't do anything immoral or that really hurts people or bothers them too much, such as playing your radio very loud and bothering your neighbors. When you're guilty, you're usually acting immorally and telling yourself that it is wrong — which it may well be — and that you are a bad person for doing it. Even then, you could acknowledge fully that you are behaving wrongly, but that you are a person who is doing a *bad act*; you are not a *bad person*. But don't do anything immoral — just something silly, ridiculous, foolish, that doesn't harm you or another person. Let's see if you can really do this — which of course you can — and not feel like a fool. Then, your downing yourself for your so-called errors and mistakes will tend to be reduced. By all means keep rating what you do, to see if it is wrong or hurtful, but stop rating yourself, your essence, your being. The shame-attacking exercise gives you a good deal of practice in doing that."

Philip was at first really reluctant to do a shame-attacking exercise, but finally did one of our common ones: Yell out the time — "10:00 a.m." — in a department store. He first yelled it very mildly and was hardly even heard. But he forced himself to yell quite loudly several other times and felt very self-shaming — especially when he thought that one of his friends or patients might be in the store and might hear him. But then he saw, in action, that nothing terrible happened. Even the department store guard merely smiled and walked away. So he yelled out the time several more times and was able to feel little shame.

Finally, Philip volunteered to do even more relevant —and risky — shame-attacking exercises. He told a few of his medical colleagues that he had misdiagnosed some of his patients. He confessed to one of his patients that he had forgotten to urge her to take a flu shot and now belatedly urged her to do so. He allowed his nurse to see some of his mistakes that he would have previously shamefully kept from her. By doing the shame-attacking exercises, he saw more and more that his mistakes were human and quite allowable, and that he could legitimately feel sorry and regretful about them, but that he did not have to put himself down. He began to see this so well that he taught some of the elements of REBT to his nurse, to his wife, and to several of his patients, and he was able to increase his own unconditional self-accepting (USA) by repetitively teaching it to them. He helped himself greatly in this respect and soon was automatically criticizing some of his acts, but hardly ever berating himself for them. Then he tackled his "shame of shame." He eventually became able to accept himself when he occasionally brought on feelings of shaming. He saw that he was wrong in bringing these feelings on himself, but stopped putting himself down further for feeling them.

Rational Role-Playing

Role-playing, or psychodrama, was created by J. Moreno in the 1920s and is a very useful method of therapy. As Moreno himself did it — and I saw him give demonstrations several times — he usually let the client play himself, while he might play the client's alter ego and enact various other aspects of the client's personality. Sometimes the client played himself and perhaps other intimates, such as his mother and father, and enacted a dramatic dialogue among them. Often old traumatic scenes were played again and again, and the client would be enabled to face past injuries and hurts and work through them.

Fritz Perls' "empty chair" technique is a form of role-playing whereby the client talks to a significant person in her life represented by an empty chair, then takes the empty chair herself, and becomes that person. An impassioned dialogue may then ensue, and the client is able to see things from the other person's frame of reference and to work through some conflicts with this person.

This kind of role-playing is usually an emotive-evocative technique and can lead to expressions of feelings by the client and other members whose role he takes, can bring out important hidden feelings, and can help resolve various emotion-laden issues. Like most expressive techniques, however, it has its limitations in that emotions may be revealed and by no means resolved; in fact, the mere expression of them may further exaggerate them. Thus, when you play a family member who has supposedly treated you badly, you may wind up hating her even more than you normally do, and may make your life worse than it is. So this form of role-playing may be dangerous when you play it alone, and is usually better done with a trained therapist who leads you and your "partners" into sensible, conflict-resolving pathways. Even when you let your feelings out during role-playing and feel much better because of your honest expression of them, your relief can easily be temporary, since you have not explored the basic philosophizing that led to these feelings, nor have you significantly changed them.

Raymond Corsini, Robert Alberti, Michael Emmons, and other therapists have promoted a form of role-playing which is largely used for skill training purposes. Thus, if you have trouble encountering a desirable member of the other sex — or, if you are gay, a desirable member of your own sex — you arrange for someone to role-play this other person with you and engage in a "suitable" conversation with him. Some observers watch you and your role-playing partner and later tell you how you were doing in your approach and how to improve it. You then role-play the situation again to see how you can better your performance.

This can be a very useful form of role-playing because it is instructive, shows you how well you are doing, and how to perform better. Also, by playing the role of the approacher, which you may at first anxietize about doing, you get used to playing it, lose your awkwardness, and frequently make yourself less anxious. The role-playing shows you that you can actually make a "fearful" approach, that nothing terrible happens if you bollix it up, and that you can accept yourself as a fallible human who by no means always makes "good" approaches. So, like *in vivo* desensitization, this kind of role-playing may lead to philosophic changes, and may considerably reduce your disturbed feelings — as well as enable you to acquire approaching skills.

In REBT, we have a special kind of rational role-playing, which is a variation on the two kinds I just described. We may use dramatic-expressive role-playing, and arrange for you to enact conflicts with people with whom you are intimate and thereby help to reveal your profound feelings — such as hostility. You are then instructed to look for your dysfunctional *Beliefs* — the shoulds, oughts, and musts — by which you are creating those feelings and work at changing them.

Or you can arrange, in REBT, to role-play a fearful situation — such as a job interview — with a chosen partner who plays the role of the interviewer. Onlookers not only critique your role-playing and show you how to do it better — thus increasing your skill training — but they also watch to see if you panic, depress, or otherwise upset yourself in the course of it. If so, they temporarily stop your role-playing and ask, "What are you telling yourself right now to make yourself panicky or depressed?" They help you find your Irrational *Beliefs*, to fully acknowledge them, and to dispute them right then and there. This helps you see that you are upsetting yourself when you are in a live situation, to discover what you are saying to create your upset, and then to work at changing your Irrational *Beliefs*.

After your role-playing has been interrupted for a short time and you are in touch with your upsetting and have done some work to reduce it, the role-playing can resume with its important skill training aspects.

You can do this rational form of role-playing with a friend or associate — preferably with a few onlookers — and can use it to bring out your self-disturbing feelings and employ REBT disputing to deal with them. This emotive-evocative technique then uncovers your dysfunctional emoting, but also importantly zeroes in on the philosophies behind it, and shows you how to change these philosophies for less disturbing ideas.

Similarly, you can engage in other kinds of self-disturbing performances — such as improvisations or acting in a play with other people — to help to bring out feelings that you are only slightly aware of having. When you discover these panicky and depressed feelings, you can interrupt your acting and deal with them rationally, as shown in the last two paragraphs, or you can review them a little later by yourself or with others. Either way, find the self-statements behind these panicky and depressed feelings aroused during your acting and deal with the Irrational *Beliefs* that lead to them.

Using Humor to Interrupt and Dispute Disturbing

When people disturb themselves, they usually lose their sense of humor and take things seriously — much too seriously. Naturally, you want to deal appropriately with problems that arise in your social relations, your job, and even your recreations. But when you take them too seriously, and especially exaggerate the grim consequences — not to mention the likelihood — of your failing at any important project, you tend to upset yourself. Moreover, you frequently see no way out of it. You are mired down by your catastrophizing and awfulizing, stuck in their muddy sediment, and can hardly figure how to get loose.

On the contrary, deliberately taking things lightly when you are beset with problems is hardly a cure-all — in fact, it may distract you from solving them if you take them too lightly — but it has great advantages. For example, seeing things, even difficulties, in a humorous light:

+ prevents you from self-depressing

+ challenges you to see alternatives instead of grim results

+ blocks your tendencies to view things only as black or white

+ adds a sense of play to your life

+ helps you laugh at the behavior of yourself and others, instead of seeing only the dark side

+ punctures your and other people's grandiosity

+ shows you that you have some real control over your feelings

+ dramatically interrupts some of your dysfunctional patterns

+ lets you relate better to people, including some difficult ones

+ shows you that human foibles are universal.

You can, however, run humor into the ground by trying to be compulsively funny, and not giving enough attention to actually solving your practical and philosophic problems.

I have always used a good deal of humor in my REBT sessions, particularly in group therapy, where I lighten things up by making humorous remarks about some of the "ridiculous" problems that people invent for themselves. I find that the results are good, and that many of my clients start seeing their foibles in a less grim light.

In 1976 my colleague, Robert A. Harper, asked me to appear on a symposium on humor at the American Psychological Association Convention in Washington, where I gave a paper showing how I used humor in REBT. For many years one of my hobbies has been to take popular songs — especially those with "slushy" lyrics — and rewrite them, composing new lyrics that satirized people's tendency to take things too seriously. Alas, as I prepared to sing a few, my musical accompaniment — a cassette recorder — made a miserable noise and then conked out! On the spur of the moment, however, I decided to sing the songs *a' capella.* I did so, to great acclaim — probably because no singing had ever been done before at an APA conference — and partly because I had the guts to sing, in my god awful baritone, without accompaniment.

My songs went over so well — because of or in spite of my singing! — that thereafter I included some of them in practically every workshop I gave. Moreover, we printed up a song sheet of several of them and passed them out to all our clients so that they can sing an anti-panicking song when they make themselves anxious, an anti-depressing song when they depress themselves, and so on. We have had excellent results with these humorous songs, and many clients have told me that when all else fails, singing these songs can sometimes pull them out of despair.

Here are some of the rational humorous songs that you can try for yourself when you indulge in disturbing moods.

First, try these songs if you mire yourself down in a dire need for love and approval and create misery:

  Love Me, Love Me, Only Me!
(Tune:"Yankee Doodle Dandy")

> *Love me, love me, only me*
> *Or I will die without you!*
> *O, make your love a guarantee*
> *So I can never doubt you!*
> *Love me, love me totally — really, really try dear;*
> *But if you demand love, too*
> *I'll hate you till I die, dear!*
>
> *Love me, love me all the time*
> *Thoroughly and wholly!*

My life turns into slushy slime
Unless you love me solely!
Love me with great tenderness
With no ifs or buts, dear.
If you love me somewhat less,
I'll hate your goddamned guts, dear!

You For Me And Me For Me
(Tune:"Tea for Two," by Vincent Youmans)

Picture you upon my knee
Just you for me, and me for me!
And then you'll see
How happy I will be!
Though you beseech me
You never will reach me —
For I am autistic
As any real mystic!
And only relate to
Myself with a great to-do, dear!
If you dare to try to care
You'll see my caring soon will wear,
For I can't pair and make our sharing fair!
If you want a family,
We'll both agree you'll baby me —
Then you'll see how happy I will be!

If you have trouble tolerating frustration and foolishly think
that you always *need* some of the things that you really *want*, try
these songs:

Whine, Whine, Whine
(Tune:"Yale Whiffenpoof Song,"
composed in 1896 by a Harvard man!)

I cannot have all my wishes filled —
Whine, whine, whine!
I cannot have every frustration stilled —
Whine, whine, whine!

Life really owes me the things that I miss,
Fate has to grant me eternal bliss!
And since I must settle for less than this —
Whine, whine, whine!

 Beautiful Hang-Up
(Tune:"Beautiful Dreamer," by Stephen Foster)

Beautiful hang-up, why should we part
When we have shared our whole lives from the start?
We are so used to taking one course,
Oh, what a crime it would be to divorce!
Beautiful hang-up, don't go away!
Who will befriend me if you do not stay?
Though you still make me look like a jerk,
Living without you would take too much work!
Living without you would take too much work!

If you hang on to perfectionism — and perhaps a bit of narcissism and take yourself and things too seriously — you can try these two songs, both to the tune of *Funiculi, Funicula* by Luigi Denza:

 Perfect Rationality

Some think the world must have a right direction
And so do I — and so do I!
Some think that, with the slightest imperfection
They can't get by — and so do I!
For I, I have to prove I'm superhuman,
And better far than people are!
To show I have miraculous acumen —
And always rate among the Great!
Perfect, perfect rationality
Is, of course, the only thing for me!
How can I ever think of being
If I must live fallibly?
Rationality must be a perfect thing for me!

You Are Not The Greatest!

Some think that you are not the goddamned greatest —
    and so do I, and so do I!
Some think that you come in the very latest —
    and so do I, and so do I!
For I, I really hate your self-inflation
And find it odd that you are God!
I try to pry apart each indication
That you suggest still makes you best!

I can't stand your grandiosity!
I demand that you more humble be!
How can I ever think you're godly
When it's clear as clear can be
All the earth and sun is really run
By me, me, me!

If you consume yourself with raging at certain people you think you can't stand, try this anti-angering song:

Glory, Glory Hallelujah!
(Tune:"Battle Hymn of the Republic")

Mine eyes have seen the glory of relationships that glow
And then falter by the wayside as love passions come —
and go!
I've heard of great romances where there is no slightest
lull —
But I am skeptical!
Glory, glory hallelujah!
People love ya till they screw ya!
If you'd lessen how they do ya
Then don't expect they won't!
Glory, glory hallelujah!
People cheer ya — then pooh-pooh ya!
If you'd soften how they screw ya!
Then don't expect they won't!

If you often make yourself anxietizing, try this anti-anxietizing song:

 I'm Just Wild About Worry
(Tune:"I'm Just Wild About Harry," by Eubie Blake)

> *Oh, I'm just wild about worry*
> *And worry's wild about me!*
> *We're quite a twosome to make life gruesome*
> *And filled with anxiety!*
> *Oh, worry's anguish I curry*
> *And look for its guarantee!*
> *Oh, I'm just wild about worry*
> *And worry's wild about*
> *Never mild about,*
> *Most beguiled about me!*

When you depress yourself and want to humorously interrupt your depressing and work against it, you can try this song:

 I'm Depressed, Depressed!
(Tune:"The Band Played On," by Charles E. Ward)

> *When anything slightly goes wrong with my life,*
> *I'm depressed, depressed!*
> *Whenever I'm stricken with chickenshit strife,*
> *I feel most distressed!*
> *When life isn't fated to be consecrated*
> *I can't tolerate it at all!*
> *When anything slightly goes wrong with my life,*
> *I just bawl, bawl, bawl!*

If you are a general musturbator and want to interfere with your tendency to think in terms of absolutistic shoulds, oughts, and musts, try this anti-musturbatory song:

I Like Musturbation
(Tune:"Yankee Doodle Dandy")

> Some folks like a happy state
> And strive for elation,
> Some folks like to masturbate
> But I like MUSTurbation!
> MUSTurbation keep it up!
> MUSTurbation dandy!
> Mind the got-to's, yup, yup, yup!
> And with the shoulds be handy!
>
> Yes, I know I could create
> Greater satisfaction
> But I would rather MUSTurbate
> And keep my mind in traction!
> MUSTurbation, keep it up!
> Let its message fit good!
> Mind the got-to's, yup, yup, yup!
> As shouldhood leads to shithood!

If you create secondary symptoms of disturbance and tend to upset yourself seriously about your panicking, depressing, or raging, try this rational humorous song:

 I Wish I Were Not Crazy
(Tune:"Dixie," by Dan Emmet)

> Oh, I wish I were really put together —
> Smooth and fine as patent leather!
> Oh, how great to be rated innately sedate!
> But I'm afraid that I was fated
> To be rather aberrated —
> Oh, how sad to be mad as my Mom and my Dad!
>
> Oh, I wish I were not crazy! Hooray! Hooray!
> I wish my mind were less inclined
> To be the kind that's hazy!

I could, you see, agree to be less crazy —
But I, alas, am just too goddamned lazy!

(Song lyrics by Albert Ellis, copyrighted by the
Albert Ellis Institute, 1977 to 1999.)

These, then, are some of the rational humorous songs you can use to combat, dispute, and interrupt your disturbances. If you keep using them, you may see how practically all serious emotional upset includes musturbatory *Beliefs*, and that you can view them as irrational and self-sabotaging. You can then replace your IBs with sensible preferences, and help yourself considerably — sometimes in a brief period of time.

There are various other techniques that you can use to put a little humor in your life and dispel your overly serious irrational thinking. Let me list a few of them:

Irony. Let yourself see how ironic it is that you think you absolutely need others' approval at the cost of your own wants and pleasure. You may insist that you can't change your feelings or behaviors — at the same time you demand that, somehow, others change theirs. You avoid — and perhaps phobicize about — some harmless pursuits, like speaking in public or trying a new sport, and you refuse to do the one thing that would make you adept at this performance: practicing. You don't let yourself enjoy a game, such as tennis, by frantically insisting that you *absolutely must* win. You tend to piss away the one life you'll ever have by doing very safe and dull things. You call yourself a jerk for acting badly — and then interfere with your acting less jerkily.

Seeing humorous paradoxes. See that it is *good* to be rejected by people you prefer — for then you can identify and get rid of — fast! — the people who dislike you. Recognize that "self-esteem" is a great sickness, and not an asset, for it means that you only esteem yourself when you do well or when others rate you highly, and then horrify yourself because you may not do so well or others may not see you as great next time. Agree with Oscar Wilde's rule: "Anything that's worth doing is worth doing badly." And what would happen if you convinced yourself that "The best way to get people to like me is to show them what worms they really are!"

Reduce your irrational beliefs to absurdity. Convince yourself that you must be super-perfect, else you are a perfect idiot. Point out to yourself, "Of course no one else in the whole world procrastinates, so I'd better kill myself!" Show yourself, "The next time I get caught in a traffic jam and start screaming about it, I'd better commit hari-kari." Tell yourself, "Now that I've lost out on two love affairs, I'll always be rejected and therefore should become a monk or a nun."

Puns and evocative language. "Musturbation is self-abuse." "Shouldhood leads to shithood." "I must do what my family tells me to do, since blood is sicker than water." "Life is spelled H-A-S-S-L-E for me and other humans." "I'll always be a FFH — fallible, f——- -up human."

Humorous self-mocking. "Poor me, poor me! I only got an A in the course when I should have got an A-plus." "I can't stand doing reasonably well in tennis. I shouldn't have missed a single stroke!"

Disputing extreme musturbation. "I must do perfectly well and be approved by all other people because everyone else does beautifully and is completely loved and approved for doing so." "Everyone will hate me for failing, except those who will love me for being a bigger schnook than they are."

Stopping extreme I-can't-stand-it-itis. "I *can't stand not getting exactly* what I want all the time because my parents took care of me when I was two years old, so everyone else has to make things easy for me now!"

Disputing extreme awfulizing. "It's *awful* when people treat me unkindly and inconsiderately because I run the universe and everyone should know it and treat me accordingly." "It's *horrible* to be treated unfairly because no one else in the world ever gets treated that way — only itty bitty shitty little me!"

Stopping extreme shithoodizing. "I'm really a total shit because I should have an I.Q. of 200 and I only have 199!" I'm a horribly ugly person because I have a mole on my thigh that can be seen with a powerful microscope on a clear day."

In addition, you can devise and use humorous rational coping statements, such as these: "People are talented at treating me poorly. Tough!" "I have a perfect right to be wrong, and goddamn it I'll keep using it." "How can people treat me shabbily and unfairly. Very easily!"

You can also put REBT insights into humorous form and enable yourself to see them more clearly: "Yes, I sneak into your gut and churn it up and make you miserable. And you do the same to me. We really are great magicians!"

Realistic Optimism and Self-Encouragement

Martin Seligman and his associates have done many psychological studies that show mice and men who are pessimistic, and keep predicting that they will never get what they really want lead much more miserable lives than optimists, who take a favorable view of the future even when the present is fairly grim. Rats and humans who are subjected to consistently frustrating experiences frequently suffer from learned helplessness. They predict that their situation is hopeless and they often become — or make themselves — depressed.

Studies have also shown that having an optimistic attitude tends to appreciably help people to be productive, to eventually succeed in important tasks, to look forward to the future, and to live healthier and happier lives. Optimism can, especially when it is extreme, have its disadvantages. Thinking over-optimistically about the present and future may make you disillusioned when the great things that you predict will happen do not actually occur. Unless you are rigidly optimistic — which is difficult! — you may tend to become shocked at misfortunes, to predict that bad things will always occur and, as a result, end up in the pessimistic class.

What to do? Be realistically optimistic and self-encouraging. Recognize some of the main principles of human living:

- You have great potential for learning and changing.
- Bad things and situations shall pass.
- You control your emotional destiny; you can bring on healthy instead of unhealthy negative feelings about Adversities.
- Work and practice will get you somewhere much of the time, in spite of their setbacks and limitations.
- You can plan and plot for both short-term and long-term enjoyments when things are presently rough.

If you keep these points in mind, your life may often be difficult, but not "hopeless." You can use encouragement from others — if it is indeed not *too* optimistic — but you can always rely on yourself for self-encouragement. No, there is no pie in the sky. No, your fairy godmother will not come down and help you. No, you probably won't win the lottery. But you can take a realistically optimistic view of your future, even when afflicted by present Adversities. See that you often can change bad conditions and create good ones. As we say in REBT, then "PYA" — push your ass!

Why not try super-optimism, and always predict that your future will be rosy? Unrealistic optimists, as some studies have shown, are happier than pessimists. Because they are sure they can make things turn out all right, they frequently do so. When they can't actually change things for the better, they still unrealistically think that they can — so they "suffer" happily! Why not, therefore, stoutly believe in kind providence, even when the chances are it will not exist?

That's okay, if you can really do so. But, as noted above, dismal events will definitely occur, and you will be subject to abject disillusionment. You will have a hard time "knowing" that you will win the lottery after you have bought a thousand tickets and failed to do so. You will wait for good things to occur and probably do little to make them occur. When bad events still happen, in spite of your optimism, you may take them too seriously and see them as worse than they are. You may well alienate realistic people who are much less optimistic than you are.

Unfortunately, unrealistic optimism does work — in a few cases. Some people, in spite of steady hassles, forge ahead and accomplish more or remain happy without getting much of what they want. But you are probably not naturally this way and will have to work hard to get there and maintain your unrealistic optimism. Therefore, realism is usually safer and better.

With realism, you see that you can improve things — but don't *have to*. You can do better than you are doing, though there may be distinct limitations. You can see grim reality — and still accept it and enjoy yourself considerably. You may not be unrealistically joyous and happy in the face of adversity — but you almost certainly can be unmiserable and find some pleasures. You may well miss some of the pie-in-the-sky highs — but you'll also forestall most of the real lows. You will focus on being as happy as you can be when bad things happen to you and you can often ultimately change them for the better. You can be almost certain, with a realistic attitude, that you will run your own life. While with a super-optimistic attitude, you can feel certain that things will turn out well — but probably always suspect, underneath, that they may not, and thereby create underlying anxiety. Realistic optimism is something like playing it safer by taking out life or fire insurance. It's hard, but you can almost always keep achieving it.

Let us, however, not put down unrealistic optimism. It may work for you and work consistently, in spite of life's pains and misfortunes. But if you are not naturally inclined to it — as most of the human race only partly seems to be — it is going to be a strain, and take much time and effort to maintain it. REBT hypothesizes that since realistic optimism accords with what we often call reality — WIGO or *What Is Going On* in the world — it is usually easier and better to achieve than unrealistic optimism. So you have a choice, and if you recognize the principles of human living noted above, you can take that choice and most probably achieve and benefit from it.

Seeking Fun and Pleasure

Seeking fun and pleasure — and really focusing on finding them and experiencing them — is, of course, one of the best things you can do to distract yourself from the pains and concentrate on the gains of life. True, fun may not last, it may eventually satiate and bore you, distract you from *real* problem-solving, interfere with a *vital* absorbing interest, and have other shortcomings. But what a great preoccupation!

Though usually offering only temporary relief from depression and anxiety, seeking fun and pleasure may actually *aid* your philosophic and purposive changing — and that will last. D. L. Peters, a counselor, shows how seeking fun, as prevention or treatment for troubling yourself, can keep you in *action*, offer you opportunities for *discovery* and *learning*, foster feelings of *relating* and *belonging*, give you a thorough-going *voice* in what you do, help you *look ahead* to avoid serious problems, and lead you to worthwhile things to come. Seeking fun can encourage and enhance profound self-help.

Multiple-Chair Role-Playing

J. L. Moreno and Fritz Perls pioneered using role-playing to explore and play out the different parts of people's personality. As adapted by Kevin Everett FitzMaurice in *REBT Three Chair Work*, and revised by me into *REBT Four-Chair Work*, you can choose four chairs: Chair Number 1 to represent your functioning or Rational *Beliefs* (RBs); Chair Number 2 to represent your dysfunctional Irrational *Beliefs* (IBs); Chair Number 3 to represent your Disputing of your IBs; and Chair Number 4 to represent your dysfunctional Consequences (C), such as anxietizing, self-depressing, avoiding and acting compulsively.

You can use many variations of this role-playing game. For example, you can first sit in Chair 4 and talk about (and preferably experience) your dysfunctional feelings and (in)actions. Thus: "I frequently anxietize about competing at sports." You can then sit in Chair 1 and role-play your RBs, such as: "I really prefer to compete successfully and dislike failing at sports." Then you can sit in Chair 2 and role-play your IBs, such as: "I have to do well in every important match, and am a lousy player and a loser if I don't." Then you can sit in Chair Number 3 and actively and vigorously dispute your IBs. For example: "It is great to do well in sports, but why must I? How do I become a total *loser* when I do poorly?" You can then, if you wish, use Chair 1 again to firmly replay your RBs, or come up with E, your New Effective Philosophizing: "Failing at sports I enjoy is *fine*, but never, never necessary for accepting myself!"

Kevin and I have found that the more forcefully and vigorously you shift from your role-playing chairs, the more you replace your self-defeating musturbating with unassuming — but often strong — preferring.

The *emotive and evocative* strategies we've explored in this chapter offer powerful methods to help you dispute your IBs and replace them with RBs. Along with the *thinking and philosophizing* methods of chapters 7, 8, and 9, they should move you well along the path to a healthier emotional life.

In the next two chapters, we'll explore still more tools for getting better: *behavioral and activity* methods, and *realistic, logical, and pragmatic* methods. Are you ready to push your tush onward?

11

Getting Better V:
Behavioral and Activity Methods

REBT is famous for some of its activity-behavioral methods. I incorporated them into my therapy before I created REBT, largely because I had used them successfully on myself at the age of 19, long before I even was interested in becoming a therapist. I started *phobicizing* myself in early childhood and continued frightening myself all through my adolescence.

First, I was scared witless of public speaking, and brilliantly avoided doing it. I could speak well privately and finally managed to speak before my class when called upon by my teacher. But in front of a large audience — hell no! At 19, I was the youth leader of a political group and was supposed to speak steadily for it. Not me! I only spoke to my own small chapter — friends I knew I could trust.

Determined to earn my keep as a leader, I read much psychology and philosophy to get over my extreme fear. Freud didn't help at all, nor did Jung. Adler helped a little ideologically, but he had no good behavioral methods. Where was I to find help?

Introducing... In Vivo Desensitization

Fortunately, John B. Watson, the first behaviorist, inspired me. Around 1918, he and his assistants began using *in vivo* desensitization to help young children overcome their terrors of mice, rabbits, and other harmless animals. Within twenty minutes of putting the feared animal at one end of a long table and gradually moving it closer, they deconditioned the anxiety of most kids and had them actually petting it. Beautiful. "If," I said to myself, "it is good enough for little kiddies, it's good enough for me! I'll risk it!"

So, with great discomfort, I forced myself once or twice a week to speak in public for my political group. I actually spoke on some street corners! Well, as I sort of expected from my reading, after six or seven grueling times, I became familiar with public speaking, got used to it, relaxed about it — and finally enjoyed it. What do you know? I made a 180-degree change, completely got over my public speaking phobia — and now you can't keep me away from the platform! I discovered, to my surprise, I had a real hidden — very hidden! — talent for public speaking.

Nothing daunted, I tackled my second major phobia — my great fear of approaching and opening a conversation with girls and women in whom I was interested (and with whom I was sometimes madly in love!). Not me! I often flirted with them from a distance — but always copped out about talking to them. Always!

So, spurred on by the experiments of John B. Watson, and by my own success in exposure to public speaking, I gave myself, at the age of 19, a fascinating homework assignment. I would go to the Bronx Botanical Gardens every day in August — when I was on vacation from college — and whenever I saw a suitable woman sitting on a park bench alone, I would sit next to her on the same bench (not in her lap!) and give myself one lousy minute to talk to her (no more!) — which I never had done before in my entire life. "If I die, I die! One minute!"

I found 130 women sitting alone on benches in the park that month — and I sat next to all of them. No debating with myself! Whereupon 30 immediately got up and waltzed away. But that left me with an even sample of a hundred — good for research purposes.

So I did it! No nonsense! I opened a conversation with all of the women I sat next to — again for the *first* time. What about? Anything. About the birds and the bees, the flowers and the trees, the weather, the book they were reading. Yes, anything. My goal, of course, was to date all of these women — of whom I lusted after about 101 out of a hundred — to go to bed with them, and perhaps to marry a few. Alas! If B. F. Skinner, the famous behaviorist who was then teaching psychology at Indiana University, had known about my venture, he would have thought I would have been extinguished. For out of the hundred women I talked to and tried to date, I actually made only one date — and she didn't show up! She eagerly kissed me in the park, made a date for that very night — and disappeared from my life forever. I never found out what happened to her, since I foolishly forgot to take her telephone number — which taught me a lesson for the future!

No dice. Zero. All my efforts were in vain. Except for my horrorizing about approaching women. As in the case of my fear of public speaking, I completely got over this phobicizing, had no trouble approaching them thereafter, and in my second hundred attempts, which I tried in the park during the next two months, I actually made several dates.

Well, that was a great lesson in self-improvement. Exposure or *in vivo* desensitization, I found, really worked. So in my first several years as a psychotherapist, I largely ignored the training I received in graduate school in Carl Rogers' person-centered therapy and used a great deal of *in vivo* desensitization with my clients — particularly with those who acted phobically. Unfortunately, I toned down on this form of behavior therapy in 1947 and for the next six years I largely practiced psychoanalysis, until I stopped doing it in 1953.

When I started doing REBT in January, 1955, I went back to heavily using exposure and other forms of activity-oriented behavior therapy, with excellent results. So REBT makes great use of behavior therapy on both practical and theoretical grounds.

Once again: The theory of REBT holds that thinking, feeling, and behaving are far from separate but include and are integrated with each other. So when you want to significantly change your dysfunctional *Beliefs*, you *work* at changing them, as I have been showing. Thus, I used rational philosophizing to convince myself that speaking poorly in public wasn't "dangerous" and wouldn't kill me. Forcing myself to speak — and often speaking badly — thoroughly *convinced* me that I could do it without some catastrophe occurring.

Before that, I used rational philosophizing to tell myself a thousand times, "If I approach women and they all reject me, nothing terrible will happen to me. I won't be maimed for life." But I never approached them.

When I finally forced myself — painfully! — to get rejected by 100 women within a month, I *convinced* myself that I could do it, that I could enjoy the "futile" talks I had, that I became more adept at conversing, and that rejection wasn't fatal.

So! *Acting* against Irrational *Beliefs* can often be one of the best ways to give them up. Act against insisting that you *can't* do harmless acts. Act against convincing yourself that you *can't stand* people who "make" you angry. Act against your philosophizing that trying for a job and failing to get it *has to* depress you. If you actively dispute these irrationalities, and also act against them as part of the disputing process, you will be much more likely to give them up — and sometimes to give them up for good. Act, dammit, and see for yourself.

You can employ practically all the REBT behavioral techniques that have been found effective in regular individual and group psychotherapy for self-help procedures. In this chapter, I am going to describe several of them that have been commonly found to help people feel better and also enable you, as active behavioral methods often do, to get better.

Using In Vivo Desensitizing:
Exposure to Irrationally Feared Events

You may have a number of irrational fears — such as anxietizing about flying, or about winning someone's approval. These kinds of anxietizing are often groundless and needlessly restricting because flying is not that dangerous and failing to win someone's approval, while uncomfortable, is survivable.

To handle such irrational fears and reduce them, try these procedures along with *in vivo* desensitizing or exposing:

Determine whether your anxietizing or phobicizing is truly self-defeating. Maybe you'd better stay away from dangerous mountain climbing, playing tennis when you have a bad back, or away from taking a job at which you have no skill. Some fears are rational and avoiding certain risks will protect you from needless harm. Consider your chances of benefit and harm in dealing with them.

♦ Decide that some of your anxietizing is senseless and handicapping. It may interfere with your pleasures — flying to Europe, for example, for a pleasant vacation. Some interfere with future pleasures — for example, fear of playing the piano badly for a while as you learn, and therefore never managing to play it at all. Some fears stop your growth potential — such as fear of taking a computer course keeping you on a dull, low-paying job. Yes, you will derive certain advantages from maintaining some phobias — save time and energy, avoid hard work, indulge in comfortable loafing, avoid stress and strain. But is your phobia worth keeping? What is the cost-benefit ratio? Look for the obvious *and* hidden costs.

♦ Focus on the costs and disadvantages of your fears, not just their quick benefits and comforts. Make a list of them. Strongly — yes, strongly — review this list several times a day. Sink the disadvantages into your awareness.

♦ Resolve that your phobicizing is not worth it. See that it is too costly. Focus and refocus on its losses, restrictions, frustrations, displeasures. Be determined — at real cost, though not necessarily at all cost — to work to stop it.

⬥ Get all relevant information on how to stop or reduce your phobicizing. Read this book thoroughly, and use other relevant cognitive-behavioral books, pamphlets, cassettes, and video cassettes. Learn a variety of techniques. Figure out which might work for you. See if you are willing to use them.

⬥ Use these techniques. Keep using them. See how they work. Revise them. See how they then work. Don't give up. Persist. Act, act, act.

Look over the procedures just listed. They are basically the same as the REBT procedures for getting and using will power:

⬥ Decide to change.

⬥ Be determined to change.

⬥ Get the knowledge that will help you change.

⬥ Plot, scheme, and plan to change.

⬥ Act — force yourself to *act* — to implement the change.

⬥ Keep deciding, determining, getting relevant knowledge, plotting and scheming, and — above all — *acting* to change.

In other words, what we call *will* involves several kinds of thinking — especially, deciding, resolving, determining, and planning to change. But *will power* has all of these thinking elements — and *action*. Its main *power* is in its *action*. Of course the action goes with — usually results from — determining and deciding. But it also seems to provide will *power*. Without the action, you create little actual change.

Let's be specific. Harold, one of my clients, was exceptionally afraid of closed spaces — such as elevators, tunnels, and intimate relationships. He was terrified lest he be "trapped" forever in any of these situations. Being very intelligent — he realized that this was a silly fear and he did his best, using some of the REBT he learned in the first few sessions with me, to give it up. He at first made some inroads against his claustrophobicizng in his head, but failed to get up enough courage to act against it.

I recommended exposing or *in vivo* desensitizing. At my suggestion, Harold first tried going in elevators, since they were relatively safe and he could take very short rides in them. Instead of avoiding the elevator and walking up and down four flights of stairs to his fifth floor apartment every day, Harold deliberately practiced going up and down in the elevator one floor at a time for several weeks. He at first was terrified even to take this series of short rides. But after two weeks he got used to them and then started trying to ride two floors at a time despite his pronounced panic. In another week, he got to used to riding two floors. Soon he felt familiar and relaxed with the "long distance" of two floors. Within two months, to his real surprise, everything got "easy," and he rode the elevator up and down to the fifth floor every day, at least once a day. No qualms! He then deliberately went in very high buildings, including the Empire State Building, and used the elevators for long rides. Again, no sweat. One day, one of the elevators he was in got stuck for fifteen minutes between floors. Harold, who was alone in the elevator at the time, remained fairly calm as he talked over the phone to the maintenance men, and was soon released. He saw the incident as a real adventure instead of the disaster he had always dreamed would happen if he were stuck in an elevator for a while.

With his fear of elevators almost entirely gone, Harold tackled his panic about being in other "trapped" situations, as well as his panic about his occasional panic. He convinced himself pretty thoroughly that closed spaces were merely uncomfortable, and that feelings of panic were even more uncomfortable — but that uncomfortable never meant *awful* or *horrible*. really

It took Harold almost a full year to get over his fear of being "trapped" in close relationships — as he had been "trapped," when he was eighteen, with a girlfriend he was afraid to "hurt" by leaving when he wanted to break off their relationship. But by risking relationships with women again — for the first time in ten years — and seeing that he could disentangle himself whenever he wanted to do so, Harold realized that he really had been trapping himself and that the women were not — and could not — trap him. From then on, Harold was, as he put it, "free, really free!"

Whatever you are irrationally frightened of, such as being rejected socially, take these steps to think, feel, and act against your fearing!

♦ Determine that your horror (e.g., of being rejected socially) is irrational, and that it limits you considerably.

♦ Do a specific cost-benefit analysis to see how restrictive and costly it is. Make a list of all its disadvantages, and go over them until you make yourself quite conscious of them.

♦ See that your phobicizing is needlessly expensive and that it is well worth the trouble of overcoming. Focus on the advantages of making yourself free from it.

♦ Get relevant information on how to overcome it — for example, by temporarily making yourself uncomfortable and risking rejection by people who have little power over you.

♦ Act on this information. Make social approaches and connections you are deathly afraid of. Make them, if you will, first in your imagination. But then, more importantly, make them *in vivo*, in real situations. Act, act, act!

In vivo desensitization — steady exposing to any thing or event that you irrationally fear — is a fine example of the conquering of *short-range hedonism* — the avoidance of immediate discomfort at all costs — by *long-range hedonism* — deliberately courting some discomfort to ward off greater discomfort for the rest of your life. You will find it no miracle cure for phobicizing, but when used as part of the REBT network of thinking, emoting, and behaving methods, you can change your needlessly frightening yourself.

Using Risk-Taking Methods

Usually when you phobicize — such as making a "horror" of riding on elevators or escalators — the activity you are afraid of is harmless and there is little to fear about it. Therefore, using *in vivo* desensitization or exposing will show you that you are needlessly panicking.

Some of your fearing, however, may be exaggerated but still real — meaning, you have something to risk or to lose by bringing it on. Thus, you may make yourself enormously fearful of investing even small sums in the stock market because you might lose them. Or you may fear meeting new people — especially on a date — because they may criticize you or reject you. Or you may make participating in a sport scary — because you might do poorly and be laughed at. Of course, you won't die of these "great losses," but you may lose something you really prefer. You may elevate *preferring* success into *needing* it, so you may always avoid these "enormous risks."

Blanche, one of my clients who had little fear of rough sports, like boxing and wrestling, nevertheless enormously scared herself of dating and socializing. If she found a man attractive she ran from him — before he had a chance to reject her. If she saw an available job better than hers, she found every excuse to avoid going for an interview. She avoided playing basketball or soccer, for fear she would be rejected in choosing up sides. Aside from her computer keyboarding job (which was safe because it paid poorly) and her wrestling and boxing interests, she led a very restricted and boring life. Whatever Blanche really wanted to do, she found too "risky."

As a therapist, I quickly showed Blanche that her strong desires to date an attractive man, to get a better job, and to play in some team sports were quite legitimate — simply because she preferred to do so. She continued to make success in dating, job interviews, and being chosen for team sports so *necessary* that she made participating in these competitions *too* risky.

With my help, it took Blanche only a few REBT sessions to see, and partly to *get*, these *rational* beliefs: "I don't *have to* succeed at competitions. I'm not a *loser*, if I fail — just a person who failed this time and could well succeed next time. It's damned unpleasant and depriving to fail at what I want to get — but it's hardly devastating, unless I arbitrarily *make* it so."

Nice! Blanche was well on her rational, somewhat risk-taking way. She made eyes at a few attractive men and had some dates with them. She went for a job interview. She risked lining up for a basketball game and was delighted to be accepted for playing.

Still better. But she never quite rid herself of her feelings of shaming. She flirted with attractive men — but made herself ashamed that they'd think her too forward. She got an interview for a good job — but embarrassingly admitted that she had spent five years on a low-level one. She played basketball with one of the teams — but felt humiliated when she missed a relatively easy shot.

Blanche tracked down her feelings of shame to specific Irrational *Beliefs* (IBs): (1) "No attractive man must think I'm too forward in flirting with him and therefore turn away from me." (2) "I shouldn't have stayed so long at my low-level job and this interviewer will put me down and despise me when he finds out about this!" (3) "What an easy shot I missed in that last basketball game. How humiliating! They'll all see I am really lousy at this game. I'd better quit playing before they reject me!"

Blanche's rational coping statements helped to reduce her feelings of shaming. But not quite enough. She was determined to minimize these feelings.

First, she did several shame-attacking exercises in front of strangers and showed herself that she did not have to feel self-shaming, but only sorry and regretful, when they laughed at her. A few people really seemed to think her "a nut" when she openly read *Screw* Magazine while sitting in the subway and when she wore a fur coat on a warm sunny day in August. When she did these shame-attacking exercises the first few times, she had embarrassing feelings. But when she kept doing them several more times, she felt unashamed and even enjoyed some onlookers' startled reactions.

Then Blanche took several real risks with people she knew. She did her best to get an interview for a job she greatly wanted, and honestly told the interviewer several things about herself that she thought might jeopardize her getting the job but would lead to her feeling freer if she actually got it. She did get it. Then she not only did a lot of flirting with attractive men, but openly approached and talked to them before they approached her. When several of them soon broke off the conversation and turned away, she at first felt very depressed. But she worked on her feelings, refused to reject herself, and went on to approach several more attractive men. One was so taken with her courageousness that he started dating her regularly.

Blanche also risked confiding in the members of her now-steady basketball team, told the other women how self-embarrassed she was and how she was doing risk-taking and shame-attacking exercises to conquer her self-downing feelings.

She induced two of them to acknowledge their own shaming feelings, and to do their own risk-taking to get over them. She also volunteered to teach a class of teen-age girls at the YWCA how to overcome their shyness-creating problems. By teaching them, she did less withdrawing herself. Her social panic only occasionally reared its ugly head — then she killed it again with more REBT.

OK, you're afraid of social, job, or other situations where you may screw up, get rejected, and put yourself down. If you keep avoiding risk-taking situations, what usually happens is that you'll make yourself *more* afraid and *less* risking. Watch it! Do shame-attacking and other "dangerous" acts. Try for jobs, friends, dates, and other participations where you truly may fail and lose something you want. Figure out that your possible losses are really not *that* awful but acknowledge that they are real and frustrating. See that an outside chance is still usually worth taking — if you view the failure as *bad* but not *horrible*. Yes, you may lose — but may also appreciably gain. If you keep risking, the one thing you will almost always gain is freedom — the freedom to be yourself, the freedom to try, the freedom to get over your years — maybe many years — of frightened inhibiting. What have you got to lose but your chains!

Staying in Difficult Situations

When you are stuck in a bad situation — such as a poor partnership, poor marriage, or poor job — you have a natural tendency to get a divorce and leave it for a better situation. Okay, go — if separating is not too costly or if you do not upset yourself too much about your predicament. Having a rotten partner may be bad — but leaving a thriving business may be worse. Staying married to a messy husband may be annoying, but divorcing him when you have no independent income and two young children may even be decidedly more so.

Your raging at your "treacherous" partner or "impossible" mate may easily help you to exaggerate his or her "horrors." Or you may have such a strong tendency to erupt with anger that you may take it to the next partner or mate, and help ruin that relationship. So don't only look at the "rottenness" of the people with whom you are relating. Look — quite penetratingly — at your *own* raging and at *your* low frustration tolerating for your "terrible" situation.

Ron did just that. He looked long and hard at the cost-benefit ratio of staying with his wife, Edna. After ten years of marriage, she seemed to be making herself angrier, meaner, and less sexy every day — and not only nasty to him, but to their three children, to his parents and her own, and to most of their friends. She was severely depressing herself but refused to take any medication or to go for psychotherapy. She insisted that if Ron would only treat her lovingly — which meant catering to her every whim — she would not be depressing and raging so. But his best efforts to do her bidding, which everyone told him were too much, helped her lighten her mood for, at most, a few hours.

Ron began to anger and depress himself about Edna's problems and discussed with his lawyers the possibility of a separation agreement. What he learned from this discussion was grim. Parting from Edna would be very expensive, would mean that she would probably get custody of their children; and without Ron around to pacify her, she would be likely to ride herd on them more than ever. Ron himself was raised by a divorced mother who bitterly hated him and his brother because they resembled his father, who had fled from his unruly wife and moved a thousand miles away. Ron wanted to make sure that this kind of history wasn't repeated. He cursed himself for marrying a woman similar to his mother but he thought that, as a penance for this and other mistakes he had made with Edna, he had to stay.

What to do?

Ron opted for REBT. When he did so, I showed him that Edna was contributing significantly to his angering-depressing himself — but so was he. Yes, she acted unreasonably — but he was demanding, in his head and heart, that she *had to* be reasonable. Yes, she was unfair to their children — but he was *insisting* (and not merely *preferring*) that she be fair. Yes, she was avoiding having sex with him — not because she didn't like having it but because he ("that bastard!") didn't deserve it. But he was telling himself that he *couldn't tolerate* such "horrible!" deprivation and that she was a *lousy bitch* for thwarting him.

Ron, with the help of REBT, told himself that Edna had a perfect right to choose to keep upsetting herself; that she didn't *have to be* fair to their children; and that she was *acting bitchily* but was not a *total bitch* for deliberately punishing him sexually. After a few weeks of convincing himself of his REBT-oriented philosophizing, Ron gave up his angering-depressing. He then *un*angrily decided to divorce Edna!

To solidify his unangry feelings and to help him work more on his depressing, I had Ron put off his divorce, stay with Edna several months more, and give himself practice at putting up with her outrageous behaving. Deliberately not upsetting himself under very difficult conditions worked. When Edna went off the wall and savagely beat and broke the finger of their eight-year-old son, Ron, Jr., for promising to do his homework and then playing ball instead, Ron Sr. forcefully convinced himself that she was a very self-disturbing woman. Ron felt extremely frustrated about her temper tantrums, but did not anger or depress himself about them. He reported her to the child protective services and to the police. He was then able to help Ron, Jr. deal with his raving mother and at least partly accept her as a very unhappy person.

Ron's homework assignment of deliberately staying with Edna awhile to practice working on his remaining angering and depressing himself about her unfair behaving was benefiting to him and his children. After trying the assignment for a few weeks, he determinedly went ahead with divorcing Edna, with much regret but little rage and despair.

You, too, can at times use the method of deciding to stay in an almost impossible situation and practicing not upsetting yourself about it. But not forever! When you are conquering much of your own upsetting *about* this situation, by all means consider leaving it. Sometimes you can actually welcome it, Yes, welcome staying with relatives or friends who — fortunately! — give you the chance to work on your own "intolerable" feelings. Most probably, you won't appreciably change your "tormentors." But they may give you a not-so-rare opportunity to significantly change yourself. You may create a fork in your self-inflicted road to hell by using the hassles of your journey to work on your own low frustration tolerance.

Using Activity Homework

REBT includes thinking, feeling, and acting homework — for, as noted above, your will has little or no power unless you *act* on deciding and determining to change. Tom's strong determination to stop procrastinating on his business reports did not, by itself, stop him from delaying doing them week after week — until his excellent job was in jeopardy. Only when he set himself the goal of working on them two hours a day — including Saturday and Sunday — and forced himself, painfully, to keep to this schedule with no excuses did he, for the first time in three years, get a major report in on time for a board meeting. How did he force himself to do the two hours a day? By following the REBT rule of PYA — *push your ass*. No matter how hard it was for him to do so!

Doing your activity homework is not only crucial when you indulge in procrastinating and depressing — when you won't get going until you literally get going. It also helps to habituate you to Rational instead of Irrational Believing-Emoting-Behaving.

Suzie did not surrender her conviction that it was *too hard* and *too awful* to visit her cranky father-in-law, Ted (who might soon die and leave her and her husband a sizable inheritance), even when she told herself how bad it would be if Ted angrily disinherited them. When she forced herself, mainly to increase her self-discipline, to visit and be pleasant to him once a week, she clearly saw that visiting him was much less *hard* and *awful* than she thought it was, and she actually enjoyed having interesting discussions with him at times when she ignored his critical tone. *Thinking* about visiting Ted was "frightening." Actually *doing* it was moderately annoying — and sometimes enjoyable.

Marilyn depressed herself so on weekends that she stayed in bed and moped most of the day. My telling her that doing something active would make her less depressing was not in the least convincing. Finally, I refused to see her for an hour of therapy and said I would only see her for a half hour a week if she didn't do some activity on Saturday and Sunday. She really wanted the hour-long session (to complain volubly how miserable her life was), so she forced herself to go shopping every Saturday and Sunday. To her surprise, she began to feel less depressing the whole week. Her conviction that she *couldn't* get up on weekends was replaced by the Rational *Belief* that she *could* and that she was much more capable of doing so than she thought she was.

Activity homework will also, when you are avoiding doing things, make you *feel better.* For one thing, stop your self-blaming for being inactive. To *get better*, push your ass to do what you are afraid of doing or find it "too hard" to do. But also, while doing it, work to change your philosophizing. Give up the irrational beliefs that you *can't* get going, that it's *awful* to move when you don't *feel* like it, that incompetent acting makes you a no-goodnik, and that stopping your phobicizing is "terribly dangerous." *Getting better* involves sensible philosophizing *and* activity. Your Rational *Beliefs* (RBs) enable you to act — and your acting reinforces your RBs. Do both!

Using Paradoxical Activity Homework

As I noted previously, sometimes paradoxical homework will help you think quite differently — and more self-helpingly — than you previously did. This is particularly true of paradoxical activity homework. Victor Frankl noted this over fifty years ago, and many therapists, such as Steven Hayes, have used paradoxical assignments since that time.

Jeri studied compulsively. In fact, she did little else but study for upcoming tests in her college classes. She received mostly A's in her courses — but had little time in her young life for social activities. She thought she had to do remarkably well in her courses — or else was just an ordinary, dull person — a fate worse than death! Jeri and I kept Disputing (D) her Irrational *Beliefs* (IBs) for a few sessions, and she improved a little.

Jeri gave herself the activity homework assignment of only studying two hours a day and no more — which was still a lot — for a week before an important test, to cut down her compulsive studying. It did, but then she anxietized and found that this interfered with her learning the studied material.

So we selected one of Jeri's less important courses — music appreciation — and paradoxically gave her the homework assignment of studying for an upcoming test very little — only a half hour a day — and using her extra time for deliberately socializing. Jeri had a hard time carrying out this assignment, since it was so foreign to her "nature," but she made herself do much less studying for the test than she had ever done before in her life. At the same time she tried to paradoxically convince herself that it wasn't important at all how she did in the test. She almost succeeded in her paradoxical assignments — and even somewhat paradoxically enjoyed the half hour she allowed herself. She got an 83 in the test, distinctly worse than she normally would have done, but was delighted to see that she didn't have to study compulsively and still could do reasonably well on a test. She also saw that it wasn't sacred — all-important — to get 90 or more in every test and that her worth as a person (which we had been working on) didn't depend on her high marks. By forcing herself to socialize, she made one good male friend, and was delighted with that.

You, too, can give yourself paradoxical homework assignments if your regular ones don't seem to be working. You can be quite critical of a friend's behaving — when normally you would be scared stiff to even slightly criticize him or her. Or you can apply for a job that you are really not qualified for when you are afraid to apply for jobs for which you are qualified.

When you do this paradoxical homework assignment you may *feel better* because you see you can do it and optimistically think that it will work to relieve your irrational fears or enhance your frustration tolerance. But you can also *get better* by realizing that you can control your disturbed feelings in several paradoxical and nonparadoxical ways and that you have the ability to *think* and *act* against your disturbances. You're in the saddle, one way or the other.

You can acquire the philosophy that you can practically always change for the better, maintain your new functional behavior, and keep changing over the years. And you can be reasonably happy in spite of unusual Adversities! You can paradoxically come to enjoy some of the things that you hate. You can paradoxically accept you, yourself, with your poor behaving — and thereby better enable yourself to change it. And you can paradoxically unconditionally accept yourself and others even if you and they refuse to change their undesirable ways.

Using Reinforcing and Penalizing

The early behaviorists, Ivan Pavlov, John B. Watson, and B. F. Skinner, all found that people and animals can change their (good and bad) behavior through rewards (reinforcements) and penalties (punishments). Thus, you can help yourself keep to a low calorie diet by rewarding yourself with some pleasure (such as socializing or watching TV) *after* you restrict your calories; and you can penalize yourself (do a boring task or burn a fifty-dollar bill) every day you eat, say, more than 2000 calories.

Reinforcing and penalizing are behavioral activities, but they also include thinking and emoting aspects. Thus, you *know* that socializing or watching TV is enjoyable and you *feel* pleasure when engaging in it. So you tell yourself something like, "It's *worth* restricting my calories for this pleasure." You *desire* more pleasure (from socializing or TV watching) when you experience it. So you are motivated, by your thinking and desiring, to restrict your calories.

Gloria drank too much. Even when she got in serious trouble with her job and her friends, she persisted in drinking. She *lightly* "knew" that drinking was self-defeating but she *strongly* "knew" that her life was *too* inhibiting and boring when she was not high and that she *couldn't stand* it. She kept terrifying herself about socializing when sober, so she normally consumed a six-pack of beer every day. Then she was much less self-inhibiting. She made some progress when she toned down her Irrational *Belief*, "I absolutely need the approval of other people or else I'm totally unlovable!" She became somewhat less socially anxietizing but still drank too much — quite against her doctor's recommendations.

So Gloria, with my help, arranged to reinforce herself by allowing herself to read romantic novels only if she had no more than two drinks the day before. She also penalized herself, by sending a hundred dollars to a cult that she thoroughly hated, every day she had more than two drinks.

That worked — particularly her penalty, which she actually invoked once. Gloria only had three drinks or more twice in sixty days, and was very happy with that record. But she realized that she still inhibited herself too much socially, so she was something of a "dry drunk." She therefore used some forceful Disputing and rational coping statements, such as, "I very much would like other people's approval but I NEVER, NEVER *need* it! I can take social chances and NOT put myself down if I'm failing! Too, too bad if people reject me, but I *refuse to reject myself*!"

When she tended to be lax about her forceful Disputing and her rational coping statements, Gloria used the same rewards and penalties she used to cut down her drinking: only allowed herself to read romantic novels when she Disputed, and made herself contribute a hundred dollars to the cult she hated every time she spent less than twenty minutes a day on her Disputing and rational coping statements. Again the penalizing and reinforcing worked, and in a few months she was much less socially inhibiting. Her reduced anxiety made Gloria drink even less and her reduced drinking helped her stick to her forceful Disputing and rational self-statements.

Reinforcements and penalties to help change dysfunctional feeling and behaving can prove quite efficacious. However, you may use these methods to help you stop excessive drinking, procrastinating, or other irrational activities without fully realizing that your poor cost-benefit *philosophy* has led to those behaviors. Rewards and penalties may help you feel better — for example, to accept yourself conditionally — *because* you stopped your compulsion, so they may well be palliative rather than truly curative.

To genuinely *get* better, *combine* reinforcing and penalties with long-lasting, preventive thinking-feeling-behaving. Remind yourself that the compulsive acting and avoiding are too costly in the long-run. Although reinforcing and penalizing may work as temporary interventions and encourage the long-run benefits of disciplined behaving, they add to short-run costs. Intently *think* about this — and your rational thinking may well enable you to gain and keep higher frustration tolerance (HFT) without the use of penalties and reinforcements.

Using Penalizing Imagery Against Irrational Believing-Emoting-Behaving (IBs)

If penalizing yourself for your dysfunctioning serves you better than rewarding yourself for your good functioning, but you are still reluctant to set actual penalties and go through with them, you can employ *penalizing imagery* instead — as Rian McMullin has suggested. You can discover the Irrational *Beliefs* (IBs) that lead to your emotional malfunctioning and use grim imagery to combat them.

Suppose, for example, you keep irrationally convincing yourself, in order to keep eating delicious meals that are harmful, "I absolutely must not be deprived of my main pleasure — eating gourmet meals! I *can't stand* sticking to ordinary food! It's tasteless and horrible!" Whenever you see that you have these IBs, and that they are practically driving you to eat great-tasting but harmful food, you can quickly penalize yourself with a highly obnoxious image. In this approach, you might see yourself convincing other people that the Holocaust never occurred and that the Jews and Gypsies invented it. Or you could picture yourself having sex with a highly obnoxious individual. Grim images indeed!

If you quickly and invariably counter your Irrational *Beliefs* (IBs) with a thoroughly obnoxious image, this image can serve as a steady penalizer to help you surrender these IBs. This may save you from enacting an actual *penalty* to counter your IBs — or save you from the dysfunctioning to which the IBs are leading. For every time, say, you actually eat a gourmet meal you can promptly nauseate yourself with a penalizing image. Oddly enough, self-nauseating images can sometimes serve as better hindrances to sabotaging thinking, feeling, and acting. Experiment with this kind of imaging.

Utilize reinforcing and penalizing to help yourself avoid phobic and compulsive reacting if you will. But also rip up the nutty philosophizing that leads to your indulging in it. See that you are *able* to change your thinking. Focus on the pleasures of doing so. Realize the freedom you achieve by self-disciplining. See how automatic and easy it ultimately becomes to let go of your irrational fearing and compulsive behaving. Look forward to sensibly restricting yourself today, eliminating endless restriction tomorrow. Make yourself into a *"thinking* long-range pleasure-seeker"— with or without the help of reinforcing and penalizing. Take your actions into your own *reflecting* hands.

Using Relapse Prevention

It's not uncommon for people to give up compulsive dysfunctioning (such as overindulgence in alcohol or overeating), or to surrender silly phobicizing (such as fear of flying in commercial planes or riding in elevators), then fall back to it again in a short time. Why? Because we are biologically prone to create disturbing behaving. You may have habituated yourself to it for several years and therefore miss indulging in it, and, after all, it is still pleasurable and you want to experience it again. You can easily re-hook yourself.

What to do? REBT and cognitive behavior therapy (CBT) have developed a series of techniques to prevent relapse, which are similar to the cognitive, emotive, and behavioral methods you may have used to temporarily overcome your addiction to compulsive or avoidant behaving.

After he gave up six years of using cocaine and then fell back to using it occasionally, but still too often, a year later, Marty used several REBT relapse prevention techniques. First, he looked at the Irrational *Beliefs* that helped drive him back to deciding to snort coke. They were: "It's *too hard* to keep stopping. I *need* the high sexuality I had when under coke! I'm inadequate sexually and less of a man when I stay off the coke!"

Marty strongly disputed these convictions, on tape and in reverse role playing with a friend who enacted them and stubbornly refused to surrender them. Through these therapeutic exercises, Marty finally came up with some powerful Effective New Philosophizing (E) that he put into rational coping self-statements and repeated to himself many times: "It's hard to keep stopping coke, but it's much hard*er* if I don't! Coke is *poison* to me. I *like* my high sexuality when I'm under coke but I don't *need* it. I sometimes am less adequate sexually when I stay off coke but I'm not an *inadequate person.* And I'm a *real man* whether or not I'm less sexy. My manhood doesn't depend *at all* on my sexiness!"

As he acquired these new Effective Philosophizings, Marty identified high risk situations — especially when he was with coke-taking friends — and stayed away from them. He had *realistic expectations* of slipping in these situations, so he monitored how dangerous they were for him. He sometimes used relaxing techniques when he was in danger of slipping, and he used positive imagery — imagining himself refusing coke and feeling okay when he refused.

He discussed with me the long-term effects of readdicting himself, and he also discussed it with some friends who had been but were no longer addicted. He rehearsed in his head what to do when tempted to relapse. He kept checking his *desires* to relapse, but reminded himself that they were not *needs*. He definitely *liked* coke but it did not like him! He made a list of all his "needs" for coke and listed, next to them, his *preferences* for it, which he could handle without giving in to his "needs."

With my help, Marty acquired a vital absorbing interest in helping other addicts not to relapse. He did a great deal of proselytizing to help them get off the coke and prevent relapsing. He joined a Self-Management and Recovery Training (SMART) self-help group and worked with other alcohol and drug-addicting people to show them how not to fall back to their old habits. His long-range goal was to help stop his own and others' addicting, and to marry and raise some sane kids — and he worked steadily at both those goals.

Marty used palliative techniques — like relaxing techniques and social skill-training methods — to help himself feel better and interrupt his coke-taking. But he also changed his *needing* coke into his *desiring* it and being able to be happy (and more effective) without it. So in giving up coke originally, and in dealing with his relapsing, he made a profound philosophic change that helped his *getting better* in both the present and in the future.

Dealing With Addicting and Personality Disorders

Since most of the readers of this book will not addict themselves seriously to alcohol, drugs, gambling, rat-packing, or other compulsive behaviors, and since most of you will not have severe personality disordering that frequently goes with addicting, I will not deal with these kinds of human afflictions in detail. Instead, I refer you to some REBT and CBT-oriented books on the subject, such as my book with Emmet Velten, *When AA Doesn't Work For You: Rational Steps For Quitting Alcohol*, Philip Tate's *Alcohol: How To Give It Up and Be Glad You Did*, and Tom Horvath's *Sex, Drugs, Gambling, and Chocolate*.

If you or your friends or relatives are severely addicting and/or severe personality disordering, let me briefly say some important words about these dysfunctions:

♦ They are likely to include distinct and special biological elements, which strongly predispose people to suffer from them.

♦ They also have definite and powerful environmental factors that encourage them to be addicting.

♦ Important aspects of personality disordering are ubiquitous to human dysfunctioning — easily acquired and difficult to stop.

♦ By the time addicting is discovered and acknowledged, it has usually become habitually ingrained.

♦ For all these reasons, addicting and personality disordering are often most difficult to change — sometimes almost impossible!

♦ They frequently require prolonged individual and group therapy — as well as, perhaps, medical intervention and psychotropic medication.

If you will, learn much more about serious addictions or severe personality disorders. Till then, if you suspect that you are afflicted with them, use many of the feel-better and (especially) get-better methods described in this book. But also seek professional help!

Commitment to Therapy

One aspect of effective therapy and profound self-help is so obvious that it rarely gets mentioned — that is your dedicated commitment to both feeling and getting better.

The importance of clear-cut, and preferably long-range, goals and values is often mentioned. For example, my chapter in Alvin Mahrer's book, *The Goals of Therapy*, shows how REBT particularly stresses goals. It emphasizes *wanting* to change yourself — and strongly *committing yourself* to do so.

Steven Hayes has emphasized the value of commitment in and to therapy since the 1980s and Russell Grieger has emphasized it from an REBT standpoint since the 1970s. If, then, you want to feel better, get better, and stay better you had better commit yourself to these important steps:

♦ Acknowledge your self-disturbing tendencies and don't "happily" gloss over or deny them.

♦ Notice their complex and multiple origins: your biological predispositions to dysfunctioning; outside events that set them off; your uniquely chosen reactions to these people and things; and your habituating and addicting yourself to your defeating reactions.

♦ Admit your difficulty — innate and learned — in seeing and changing your dysfunctioning. Fully face the time, trouble, and effort you will have to take to change, and keep changing, your self-sabotaging.

♦ Firmly decide, determine, and — above all — *act* to achieve the will *power* that REBT advocates for personality modifying.

Is that all there is to your arranging to feel, get, and stay better? Well, maybe not all, but nearly all there is! In the final chapters of this book, I shall further emphasize commitment.

12

Getting Better VI:
Realistic, Logical, and Pragmatic Methods

I t is the thesis of REBT and of this book that certain profound philosophies — or Believing-Emoting-Behavings — can maximally help you to get better and stay better, as well as feel better. These attitudes combine *realistic* and *logical* outlooks. They also include *pragmatic* cost-benefit considerations. Therefore they are most likely to help you feel better, get better, and stay better. If you want to try out these kinds of profound mental health-engendering basic attitudes, here is how they can be applied to the main emotional-behavioral problems you are likely to experience.

Philosophies to Combat Self-Downing

"I may be partly responsible for creating this Adversity and I probably could have done better, but…

"…*realistically*, I am a fallible human who will often make some mistakes and I can now try to correct my lapses."

"…*logically*, I am a person who erred and not a stupid, inadequate person."

"…*pragmatically*, if I think I should be infallible, and if I consider myself worthless for failing in this situation, I will only anxietize and depress myself and become far more likely to fail and be rejected."

Philosophies to Combat Damning of Other People

"You are, as I see it, behaving badly and unfairly, and you could behave better than you do. But in order to prevent myself from raging at you…

"…*realistically*, I can see that you are fallible and therefore likely to act wrongly, and I can see that you cannot *make me* enraging."

"…*logically*, I can show myself that you are not *all* bad and therefore you do not deserve damnation and punishment. I can see that it is highly *preferable* that you act better, but it's illogical for me to conclude that you *absolutely must* do so. I can see that although I'll never *like* your behavior, I'd better not falsely conclude that I *can't stand* it."

"…*pragmatically*, I can figure out that if I believe that you absolutely *must not* do what you do, and if I damn you as a *bad person* for doing it, I shall make myself angry, rip up my own gut, encourage your return raging, and be less likely to help you to change your behavior."

Philosophies to Minimize Low Frustration Tolerating

"This Adversity is decidedly against my interests and I don't want it to exist. But to change it or live better with it…

"…*realistically*, I can see that it's not the end of the world and could be worse. I can do my best to improve it. I can distract myself from focusing on it. I can see that it won't kill me."

"…*logically* I can refuse to jump to the conclusion that it's *totally bad* and *awful*. I can see that I need not let it deprive me of all possible happiness in life."

"…*pragmatically*, I can see that if I define it as devastating, I will have low frustration tolerance, will upset myself unnecessarily, do little or nothing to make the situation better, and most probably make it worse."

To summarize what I have been saying so far: When you emotionally disturb yourself and act in a destructive manner to yourself and/or others, there are many thinking, feeling, and behavioral methods you can use to alleviate your upsetting. As long as you make an effort and really try some of these methods, and preferably a combination of them, you will often feel better — that is, less disturbing, sometimes for a brief and sometimes for a long period of time. So try the methods described in this book and make yourself less upsetting and more capable of living a happy life.

Although self-therapy to enable you to *feel* better may also somehow help you to *get* better, don't count on it. As a human, you often tend to make yourself distinctly more anxietizing, depressing, and raging than necessary. Though you are a born constructivist, and you can figure out many ways to cope with your self-disturbing, you are likely to arrange your life so that self-disturbance has a nasty way of persisting, of only temporarily lessening, and then returning to plague you and your loved ones.

So feeling better is great, but getting better is greater. Not that you will perfectly make it. But you can go a long way toward minimizing your neurotic symptoms and preventing their arising again — that is, to *get* better and *stay* better — if you experiment with a number of the "elegant" techniques that I have described in the previous pages of this book.

Here is a quick review of some of the realistic, logical, and pragmatic philosophies or Believing-Emoting-Behaving that you can use —*forcefully and persistently* — to start you on the road to getting better and staying better emotionally and behaviorally.

Stopping Your Demanding, Musturbating, and Over-generalizing

Strongly suspect whenever you feel and act dysfunctionally that you have conscious or unconscious absolutistic shoulds, oughts, and musts. You are most probably insisting that some of your strong desires and preferences — which are fine and may well add to your life — *absolutely must* be fulfilled.

More specifically, you are probably demanding one or more of these main *musts*: (1) "I *must* perform well at important tasks and projects!" (2) "Other people *must* treat me considerately, fairly, and sometimes lovingly!" (3) "Conditions and Adversities that I dislike *must* not be as bad as they are!"

Any one of these three grandiose demands will create real trouble for you; all three of them will practically devastate you emotionally!

Assume, again, that you most probably have some of these musts and vigorously and persistently dispute them. First, Dispute them realistically, so that you see that however desirable you find that something may be, there is no reason why your desire *has to* be fulfilled. No law of the universe mandates your must.

Second, logically Dispute your demanding, so that you really understand that it never follows that (a) if you don't fulfill it, you are a *worthless person*; (b) if other people don't give you what they "must" they are "no good" and damnable; or (c) the world is a "rotten place" when it does not give you what it supposedly "must."

Third, Dispute your musts pragmatically by showing yourself that they won't work and that as long as you hold them, you will most likely disturb yourself emotionally and behaviorally.

While you are discovering and Disputing your *musts*, consciously realize that inaccurate over-generalizing is easy for you and other humans. Just about all people, including you, are born and raised with a strong tendency to indulge in it, and thereby create considerable self-disturbing.

Monitor your own over-generalizing and nip it in the bud. Clearly see that *failing* never makes you a *failure*. Behaving badly to yourself and/or others doesn't cause you to be a *worthless* individual. Not succeeding several times in a project doesn't mean that it — and you — are hopeless. Being treated unfairly by one or a few people doesn't prove that people and the world are *completely unjust and rotten*. If things are now bad this doesn't mean that they'll *always* be that way and that you can *never* improve them.

When you really upset yourself about anything, closely watch your over-generalizing and see how it creates "horror" and how you can remove this "horror" by going back to logical concluding, instead of illogical "allness" and "neverness." Do your best to think in terms of probabilities, not over-generalized absolutes or certainties. For instance, if you try several times to pass a test and keep failing it, conclude that it is *probable* that you will have a difficult time passing it. But there is no *certainty* that you will *never* pass it and that you *cannot* possibly do better in the future.

Unconditionally Accepting Yourself

It is almost certain that all people are fallible and that, among humans, infallibility and always acting well — not to mention *perfectly* well — do not seem to exist. Therefore, it is quite understandable that you and the people you encounter will frequently act poorly and make a good many mistakes and errors — even when they know the "right" thing to do and make an honest effort to do it.

Among the fallible characteristics we humans share include some we are born with (e.g., various mental and physical handicaps), and some we learn by being raised poorly or exposed to negative influences. So we easily break our own rules and those of the communities in which we reside. Because we are natural constructivists and have some degree of choice or free will, we humans can theoretically choose to act well or badly, and are largely responsible for our behaviors. But biological and social limitations practically insure that most humans will often act erroneously, even when we "know" how to act better.

Moreover, as I have been showing in this book, and as is noted in the previous section on over-generalizing, people who behave "badly" or "wrongly" do not *always* behave that way. Even Hitler was kind to his mother, his dog, and his mistress. So "bad" people are not *all* bad; they also do, with rare exceptions, some good deeds.

At the same time, we can't very well live comfortably in this one life we have unless we evaluate our thoughts, feelings, and behaviors in regard to how well they aid us to survive and be reasonably happy. Therefore, we can legitimately say that some of our *traits* are bad — if we can show that they defeat our important goals and that they sabotage the well-being of others with whom we want to live and work. But we cannot accurately rate our *selves*, our *totality*, our *essences* — for that constitutes an arrant overgeneralization and usually does more harm than good.

For one thing, if you say you *are* bad because of your wrong behavior, then how can a *bad person* like you possibly *change* her or his wrongdoings? And if you say you *are* good because of your good deeds, what incentive do you have to improve those deeds? If you *are* what you *do*, all progress to correct your errors comes to a halt.

Moral: To get along with yourself give yourself unconditional self-acceptance (USA). Don't make your worthiness *as a person* depend on your good performances. Accept yourself as "good" just because you are alive, human, and unique — which you will always be until you die — whether or not you do well and whether or not you are approved by others. By all means *try* to act well and win approval, because you will usually get real advantages by doing so. But don't *demand* that you must succeed in your efforts or else you cannot accept yourself.

As a special REBT variation on unconditional self-accepting (USA), try the experiment of *only* rating your thinking, feeling, and behaving in regard to your chosen goals; but don't rate your *self*, your *being*, or your *essence* at all. You *have* a self — an ongoing process that includes everything you think, feel, and do as long as you live. But you do not *have to* give this self a global rating. Accept it as it is — and then try to change some of its dysfunctioning habits.

"...and Do Unto Others..."

As you work at unconditional self-accepting, you will also tend to achieve unconditional other-accepting (UOA). You will see that other people, too, are incredibly fallible. They often do not realize the harm they do (to you, to others, and to themselves); and when they realize it, they still often do it. Why? Again, because of their human fallibility: their biology, their family and cultural teaching, and their history of reacting foolishly to tense conditions. All humans tend to insist that their desires and preferences *absolutely should, ought*, and *must* be fulfilled — and, sometimes, instantly fulfilled! Just like you, they make innumerable mistakes and errors — and probably always will. Exactly like you, they are hardly superhuman — only human.

Just as you unconditionally accept yourself, then, you had better unconditionally accept all other people. No, not what they *do* — for that is often abominable. No, not what they *say* — for that is often stupid, bigoted, and mistaken. Nor need you accept their feelings — for they may feel joyful while others are suffering. But accept the *fact* that people may behave abominably, say stupid, bigoted, and mistaken things, and have dysfunctional feelings. Don't by any means agree with or endorse many of the things they do, say, or feel. In fact, sometimes oppose them and try to persuade them to behave differently. Try to help them to change, if you dislike their acting, thinking, and feeling.

At the same time, unconditionally accept them, as persons, *with* their disagreeable, unfortunate, and sometimes cruel behaviors. Yes, accept the sinners while deploring and perhaps determinedly fighting against their sins. Why? Well, first, because they are all, like you, fallible humans and if you condemn them for their misdeeds you will encourage condemning yourself for your failings. Who, among us imperfect humans, is to cast the first stone? Unless you really — and I mean really — accept even the people whose behavior you greatly dislike, how will you truly be able to accept yourself with *your* dislikeable activities? Not very easily! Unconditionally accepting others in spite of their unfortunate deeds will give you excellent practice in achieving that truly difficult to achieve attitude — unconditional self-accepting.

Unconditionally accepting others has profound advantages in itself. You have a tendency to disturb yourself with angering, depressing, anxietizing, and self-pitying — all of which often afflict you when you damn others for their "bad" behavior. Thus, if you make them into "horrible people" because of their "abominable" deeds, you often will make yourself rage at them, depress yourself about your conviction that they will always act badly, anxietize when expecting them to act badly, and self-pity about what they may keep doing to you. Your feelings *about* their being prime candidates for hell will do you little good and much potential harm.

If, on the other hand, you fully accept other people with their poor behavior you will have several practical advantages. Without angering yourself at them, you are much more likely to convince them to change their ways. Rather than encouraging them to return your angering with their own, you may help them to be more friendly to you. Accepting them unconditionally may aid them to see that they can unconditionally accept others, too, and be less annoying to these others. Unconditionally accepting others also allows you to forgive and forget — and makes you able to feel love toward others, including some of your close relatives, whom you might otherwise angrily dismiss. Anger begets anger — and surrendering your anger frequently begets love.

Best of all, unconditionally accepting others (as well as yourself) is a main essence of social peace and helps resolve worldwide conflict. People and nations war against each other for many political, economic, religious, and other reasons. But practically all of these reasons include damning other individuals and groups for having different goals and values. Thus, if one country is capitalist and another is socialist and they see each other's systems as "wrong" and "mistaken" but accept the other group *with* its "wrongness," little warring conflict will probably ensue. Perhaps they can both live peacefully with their "wrong" systems.

However, if the capitalist group insists that the socialist group *absolutely must not* be the way it is, and if the socialist group insists on similar demanding, continual bickering and war between the two groups will likely occur. If the citizens of both these warring groups really develop unconditional self-accepting and other-accepting, they will still likely disagree seriously with the ways of the other group — but not tend to make themselves rage at each other and prone to foment conflict and war.

Unconditional self-accepting (USA) gives you the enormous boon of being at peace with yourself — no matter how badly you sometimes behave. But it also tends to encourage you to feel at peace with others — and with the world. Enlightened individualism is a fine thing, and it enables you to be distinctly kind to yourself and not rely too much on help from others. But individualism that is enlightened means that you always acknowledge that you choose to live in a social group and could hardly survive as a hermit. Therefore, you'd better choose to be kind to others, to have real social and community interest, to live happily and help others to live happily — for their sake and for yours.

Especially seeing how conflictual and warring the world is today, with violence and terrorism at frightfully high peaks, and seeing what havoc a few people can wreak with modern technological weapons, the calming of our violent tendencies seems almost imperative for the safe continuation of the human race. Consider that!

Unconditional self-accepting is no panacea. It will not stop all dysfunctional human strife. But the more you achieve it and the less bigoted raging against others you indulge in, the more good you will probably do for all humans — including yourself!

Achieving High Frustration Tolerating (HFT)

As noted throughout this book, people are born and reared awfulizers. They exaggerate minor Adversities and view them as awful. They also take major Adversities and correctly call them very bad, but incorrectly see them as awful, horrible, and terrible. Why incorrectly? Because no matter how bad they are, it is unlikely that they are *totally* bad, as bad as they could possibly be, and absolutely must not exist. Adversities are unfortunate or extremely unfortunate. But when they exist they obviously must exist; and awfulizing about bad conditions not only won't lessen them but will make you feel worse. So first have the courage to try to make things better, then have the serenity to accept what you cannot change about them, and as Reinhold Niebuhr said, have "the wisdom to distinguish one from the other."

High frustration tolerating (HFT) for the hassles, difficulties, restrictions, deprivations, and injustices that you do your best to change, but somehow still fail to improve, is obviously a key to dealing successfully with Adversities. No, you won't turn a sow's ear into a silk purse. But you can *accept* your limitations and stop demanding that you miraculously change them. A sow is a sow; and do you really *need* a silk purse? Beware if your answer to this question is yes!

How do you get HFT? Often with difficulty. But — ironically! — if you *work* at achieving it, and push your ass hard enough in the right direction, you can get a good measure of it. All you have to do is solidly convince yourself — and steadily *keep* convincing yourself, that...

"...I never *need* what I want. I only *prefer* it, albeit sometimes strongly, but even life itself is not a necessity. Only very desirable, especially if I have HFT!"

"...Failing to attain my goals is quite *frustrating and inconvenient.* It is not, except by my foolish definition, a *horror.*"

"...If I miss out on some real satisfactions, I definitely *can stand it* — and find a number of other enjoyments, if I look for them."

"...Doing unpleasant things today (like studying) will often get me future gains (like getting a school degree)."

"...Doing pleasant things today (like smoking) will often bring me future pains (like lung cancer) tomorrow."

"...Finishing distasteful chores (like putting my apartment or office in order) is annoying but not *awful.*"

"...The fact that I abhor doing some required task (such as my taxes) doesn't mean that I *can't* do it."

"...It's often hard to discipline myself (by dieting or exercise) but it's much harder if I don't."

"...I can easily get away with avoiding many social requirements (like getting to work on time). But for how long?"

"...If I think life *always must* be easy, where will that quaint idea get me?"

"...There are no gains without pains." (Benjamin Franklin, *Poor Richard's Almanac,* Vol. 2).

"...My future very rarely plans itself. Time flies."

"...Blame my laziness if I will. But berating myself for my laziness will only convince me that a lazy lout like me *can't* stop being lazy."

"...It's often hard to get up and get going. But it *should be* hard when it is and it's practically never *too hard* unless I *think* that it is."

"...If I force myself to tackle some very unpleasant tasks, I can often get involved in them and actually enjoy what I am doing."

"...I can be reasonably happy with less than what I want when I stop demanding that all my wants be fulfilled."

"...If I deliberately expose myself to uncomfortable things (like making a public speech) I can frequently get over my discomfort, get desensitized to my fear of doing it, and often come to enjoy it."

"...If I keep taking certain risks (like conversing with strangers who may reject me), I may find taking the risks to be interesting, challenging, exciting, and enjoyable."

"...When Adversities inevitably occur and cannot be changed, demanding they must not exist and refusing to accept them will usually make them worse."

Applying a Cost-Benefit Ratio to Pleasures and Misfortunes

Many of the things you enjoy — such as alcohol, delicious foods, and lying in bed after your alarm rings — will sabotage you in the long run. Innumerable pleasures involve painful costs. Why? Because that's the way life frequently is — *both* rewarding and penalizing. With knowledge and experience, you can discover what is good — and bad — for you, a unique individual. Get this knowledge and experience — and use it discriminatingly.

Don't compulsively or perfectionistically weigh the advantages and disadvantages of practically everything you do — for then you are really insisting that you *must* make the "best" moves, and you will always tend to anxietize about making the "wrong" ones. Still, look before you leap and keep these maxims in mind as you decide what to do for increased enjoyment and minimal pain:

- "Practically everything I do has its advantages and disadvantages. There's no free lunch."

- "Perfect choices of what to do and what not to do are utopian. Maybe I will always make them if and when I get to heaven. Not till then!"

- "If I take risks I may lose. If I take no risks I still may get hit by a truck. By refusing to take normal risks I will increase my panicking about taking them and will tend to make my life inert and boring."

- "Nothing ventured nothing gained!"

- "I often will only have the choice of two or more evils. I'd better stop whining and pick what I guess will be the lesser evil."

- "Many pleasures are not worth the trouble it takes to get them. Many are! I'd better discriminate."

- "A stitch in time saves nine."

- "Let me put off till tomorrow what I can do today — and have it uncomfortably hang over my head forever!"

- "I can beat myself mercilessly for procrastinating — and that will help a hopeless incompetent person like me to completely get going!"

- "If I take on impossible tasks and am certain that I can handle anything that can be done, I will accomplish a great deal — badly!"

- "Let me be a control freak — and people will love me for always seeing that they act perfectly well. Until they divorce me."

- "Let me make sure that I always do perfectly well and am on top of things — and die early of high blood pressure and heart problems."

- "For me to have a good social or social-sexual relationship with others entails various costs. I won't sacredize its achievement but figure out whether it's worth it in selected individual cases."

- "I will deliberately choose to reinforce or reward myself after I do some good behavior that I find it difficult to do (for example, let myself listen to music as a reward for socializing when I make myself socially anxious) and/or penalize myself when I make myself anxious to do something (for example, burn a hundred dollar bill each time I avoid socializing). In other words, I will increase the costs of my harmful avoidances."

♦ "Before I depress myself, I can focus on the good as well as the bad possibilities in my life, and how I can enjoy myself despite its Adversities. Yes, I may have real trouble but what are my actual and potential satisfactions?"

♦ "Remember that I often do not have a choice of difficulties that occur in my life and the lives of my loved ones. But I always have a choice of *how I react* to Adversities."

♦ "Having a strong sense of humor can lighten the pain of my displeasures and misfortunes. Even Adversity usually has its funny side."

♦ "There's no law that says I must endlessly put up with obnoxious family members. Blood is often sicker than water. They'll always be my relatives — but I can choose, if I wish, to keep them at a distance."

♦ "If I stop damning the people whose behavior I dislike and accept them with their failings, I can even thoroughly enjoy some of their doings."

♦ "Yes, life has its hassles and pains. But death is boring for a hell of a long time!"

♦ "Whining about difficulties often immensely *increases* their difficulty."

♦ "Focusing on how *awful* and *terrible* it feels to depress myself, and on what a worm I am for depressing myself, will almost certainly augment my misery considerably."

In this chapter, we have explored four approaches for dealing with unhealthy feelings and behaviors:

♦ Inefficient methods that sometimes work.

♦ Distracting methods that may work temporarily and palliatively.

- Realistic methods that offer inelegant or partial solutions.

- Realistic and elegant methods recommended by REBT.

I have shown that the most effective and powerful approach to feeling better, getting better, and staying better is to *avoid* inefficient, palliative, partial methods, and *concentrate instead* on realistic, logical, practical methods advocated and taught by REBT. Simple, short-term solutions may feel good for a while, but it is the elegant long-term approach that will help you *stay* better over the long haul.

In the next chapter we'll look at how you can carry out your resolve to change.

13

Staying Better I: Avoiding Self-Disturbing Beliefs-Emotions-Behaviors

We have been discussing a good many Irrational Believing-Emoting-Behavings (IBs) that contribute significantly to dysfunctional feelings and acting. Your goal, if you want to achieve more of what you want and less of what you dislike, can be to clearly see your *demanding* and then to use several of the thinking, emotive-experiential, and behavioral methods of Rational Emotive Behavior Therapy (REBT) to minimize demanding and replace it with healthy *preferring*.

In this chapter, I will begin to emphasize the importance of *staying* better — making your self-helping changes more-or-less permanent in your life. How can you keep the gains you're making by employing the REBT principles and methods you've learned in this book?

To review and summarize the suggestions for helping yourself I've offered in previous chapters, let me first mention again some of the main Irrational *Beliefs* that you, as well as people all over the world, commonly use to upset themselves — and then to upset themselves about their upsetting. The most basic self-defeating attitude is not only that certain things you dislike (Adversities) are *bad*, but that these Adversities *absolutely should not* exist.

It is rational and self-helping to recognize that a good many things are unfortunate or undesirable. You (and other people) live according to your desires and wishes, and when these are thwarted — by yourself, by others, or by conditions — you can sensibly conclude that that is "bad." It is hardly *good* to want something and not be able to get it, or to dislike something else and have it in your life. As I keep noting throughout this book, your wants and goals are, for the most part, quite healthy, and you would not be happy without them.

As Nico Frijda has shown in a brilliant book, *The Emotions*, your desires and goals are usually life-preserving and life-enhancing. As a member of the human race, you tend to want what keeps you alive and healthy and to dislike what interferes with your living and enjoying. Practically all animals seem to have distinct wishes and preferences, and if they did not have them it is most unlikely that they would survive and have progeny.

"Good" Likes and "Bad" Dislikes

Let's assume, then, that your basic wants and tastes are "good" and that you will tend to live a satisfying life by prioritizing them. Generally speaking, what you like or favor you call "good," and what you dislike or find abhorrent you call "bad." However, self-disturbing does not merely follow from the blocking of your wants and desires, but from dysfunctionally evaluating the undesirable events (Adversities) that happen to you, and consciously or unconsciously insisting that they *must not* exist. Obviously, you — and the human race as a whole — often survive well enough when "bad" things happen — such as when you are hungry or tired. You then are healthily concerned about these Adversities, but not necessarily panicking, despairing, and raging. At the same time, many "good" things happen to you — such as getting a 90 in a course or earning a sizable salary every week — and you still manage to make yourself disturbed about them: depressing yourself, for example, because you didn't get a higher mark or earn a larger salary.

The basis of much of your self-disturbing, therefore, is not the Adversities that happen to you, but your grandiose insistence that these events are *awful, terrible,* and *horrible*; that they *absolutely should not* be as bad as they are; that you *can't stand* or *tolerate* their being that bad; and that you must quickly — immediately! — change and replace them with happenings that you consider good. Almost always, with few exceptions, it is your awfulizing about Adversities, and not their mere occurrence, that upsets you — or, rather, with which you upset yourself.

Does this go for really bad events that may occur in your life — such as violence, rape, incest, war, and terrorism? Probably. You even have a choice how to react to unusually bad events — as shown by the fact that some people actually enjoy or feel only moderately sorry about violence and war. Normally, however, when assailed by unusual Adversities, you automatically view them as, first, *bad* and, second, *very bad*. Being human, you much more often tend to awfulize about conditions you consider very bad than you do about mildly or moderately bad ones.

When something that is quite opposed to your interests occurs and you panic, depress, or rage about it, you not merely assess it as unfortunate and strongly wish that it didn't occur. You also frequently *insist*, in your head and heart, consciously and/or unconsciously, that it absolutely *must not, should not* occur, and that it is *awful* that it does.

Can you indulge in awfulizing about minor, trivial things or small frustrations and slights? Indeed you can, but probably not without viewing them as fairly major. Thus, you can awfulize about missing a shot at tennis, being snubbed by someone you really don't care about, or being rejected for a job you find undesirable. Why do you horribilize about these "slight" frustrations and losses? Because, at the moment they occur, you hardly *view them* as slight. You see the missed tennis shot as "proving" that you are a "very rotten player." You interpret the rejection by someone you don't care about as showing that you are a "loser." You see the refusal of an undesirable job as indicating that you are "hopeless" at job interviewing and will always be rejected if you try for one that you really want.

All of which goes to show, as I keep repeating in this book and as Epictetus said two thousand years ago, *it's not the Adversity that happens that disturbs you but your view of it.* When you disturb yourself, you first view some Adversity as "very bad," even though other people may see it quite differently. Then you insist that because it is *so* bad, that it must not exist — or that because something you want is *so* good that you absolutely must have it. You *assess* an event as quite bad; and then you proclaim, inwardly and/or outwardly, that anything *that* bad absolutely *must not* be.

You are, of course, quite entitled to your assessment — for if you think that missing a shot at tennis is very bad, or even the worst possible thing that could happen to you, you are a free agent who is entitled to that view. If you believe that you *absolutely must* never miss a tennis shot and that it is catastrophic if you do, you are also entitled to that conviction. No one can really deprive you of your *Beliefs*, however irrational or unhealthy they may be.

The problem is that when you believe that your tennis shot is "horrible" and when you believe that it *absolutely must not* be as "horrible" as you find it to be — then, alas, you will dysfunctionally depress yourself about it instead of making yourself healthily and helpfully sorry and disappointed. So go to it, if you will. *Define* various things like bad tennis shots as exceptionally bad; and *demand* that since they are *so* bad they *absolutely must* not occur. Your definitions — for that's what they really are, personal appraisals and definitions — will probably put you into emotional turmoil. Is that what you really want? Is that one of your main goals — to make yourself despairing rather than moderately annoyed? You have a choice of how to feel about your poor tennis shot (or anything else). That's one of the main points of this book.

Disturbing yourself, then, is largely choosing to awfulize and, at the same time, to implicitly command that what you define as "awful" *absolutely must not* occur. When you awfulize about something — particularly something that many people would consider as unfortunate but hardly awful — you tolerate frustration poorly or make yourself experience discomfort. You refuse to tolerate what you don't like. You make a federal case out of deprivation, restriction, and limitation — not getting your own way. No one wants you to *like* these kinds of frustration. But are you really *compelled* to horrify yourself about them and (outwardly and/or inwardly) command that they *must* not exist?

Is your horror likely to do you any good? — likely to remove frustrating situations and get you more of what you want? Not likely! *Disliking* your blocked desires may help you fulfill them. But *awfulizing* and *horrorizing* about them? Hardly!

What's So Awful?

What are some of the main things that you are likely to awfulize and horribilize about and for which you probably demand immediate reduction? Here, so you can easily recognize them, are some of the common forms of awfulizing or refusal to tolerate frustrating conditions and some Irrational *Beliefs* with which you may choose to create your awfulizing:

"What I find frustrating and annoying *absolutely should not, must not* exist!"

"People *shouldn't* act as badly as they definitely do!"

"It's *too much* to bear!"

"I *can't stand* it!"

"These Adversities will *never* stop. It's hopeless!"

"Trouble must cease and not last as long as it does!"

"It's completely bad! There's *nothing* good about it!"

"It's *so* bad that it's actually *more than* bad!"

"Because I can't stand it, I'll fall apart and die of it!"

"I can't be happy *at all* as long as this Adversity lasts!"

"I'm overwhelmed with it! I can't cope with it at all!"

"The whole world is evil because it frustrates me!"

"I must avoid this misfortune *at all costs*!"

"It's so bad that I can't help feeling very depressed about this loss!"

"I can't do anything to cope with this 'horror!' And I *must* fix it!"

"Because I *can't stand* frustrating conditions, I *absolutely must* change them!"

"I absolutely *must* find something to distract myself from this *awful* happening."

"It's so bad that I can't face it and I must deny that it exists!"

"It's *so* bad that I must keep complaining about it instead of trying to improve it!"

"It's *so* bad that I must endlessly express my disturbed feelings about it!"

"It's *so* bad that I must make it disappear!"

Practically all these forms of terribilizing and awfulizing about situations that you don't like make you *less* able to change what you can change about them. Horribilizing, in fact, not only makes you intolerant of frustration — it also increases your frustrations — makes unfortunate events seem *more* unpleasant than they are. Even when you acknowledge that you are foolishly demanding that misfortunes *must not* be as bad as they are, you still may continue your demands — and may thereby make Adversities worse!

Self-Disturbing Philosophizing

Many of your disturbing feelings may include self-downing philosophies, such as the following ones:

"I can't deal well with these bad events. Therefore, not only are they *awful*, but my inability to deal with them makes me *a worthless person!*"

"Bad conditions overwhelm and disrupt me and thereby *make me* no good!"

"I *should have* been able to prevent these bad events from happening, and since I was not able to prevent them, I am an *inadequate individual!*"

"I should be able to stop these bad events, now that they have occurred. Since I am not able to stop them, I am an *incompetent person!*"

"Because I *should* be able to cope with these bad events, I *shouldn't be* disturbing myself about them!"

"I should only, at most, be slightly upset about these misfortunes and *should not be* as upsettable as I am!"

"Since not all people are as disturbed as I am about these bad events, I am a weakling for making myself so disturbed about them!"

"These events are bad because I am a bad person and because bad things always happen to a bad person like me! If I were really a good person these bad things wouldn't occur!"

"Because I am worthless, I deserve to suffer, as I am suffering from these misfortunes."

"God or Fate has it in for me, and that is why these bad things are occurring and making me suffer."

"Because I am unable to cope with and handle these Adversities, God or Fate must help me cope with them, and it is *awful* if they do not rescue me!"

When you have self-downing Irrational *Beliefs* such as those just listed, you not only awfulize about Adversities but additionally awfulize about your part in contributing to them and/or not being able to deal with them. You then make yourself doubly and triply self-disturbing!

Don't You Believe It!

When Adversities occur in your life, you also may have Irrational *Beliefs* that lead you to blame other people and be angry at them. Anger is about people (rather than about things and events). When you anger or enrage yourself, you demand that other people must give you what you want and never seriously deprive you. Else, of course, it is *awful*; and else they do not merely *act* badly but they also *are* vile people. You can poorly tolerate happenings in your life that you consider "bad" and you can also enrage yourself at people who, presumably, *absolutely must not* frustrate you and who *absolutely must* help you when you are deprived.

Here are some typical *Beliefs* that you may self-defeatingly create when you denigrate other people for the unfortunate conditions they may inflict on you and thereby make yourself angry at them:

"It's other people's fault that these bad events are happening to me and they should be severely damned and punished for doing so!"

"Other people should stop these awful things that are happening to me, and since they are not doing so they are rotten people!"

"I need help from other people to make things better and they are not helping me as much as they *should* and are therefore bad people!"

"God is bringing about the misfortunes I encounter and is not helping me enough with them. Therefore He is evil!"

Are You Bringing It on Yourself?

In three (or more) important ways, then, you may disturb yourself with your *absolutistic demands* that:

- Adversities *must* not happen to you,

- you *should* be able to prevent them and cope with them, and

- other people *have to* help you stop them or help you handle them.

You may have three major contributions to your self-disturbing that lead you to awfulizing about Adversities, to self-downing, to other-damning. These are your three absolutistic, dogmatic musts. Then, when you use these grandiose demands to help create anxietizing, depressing, and raging, you probably insist that you *absolutely must not* bring about your self-disturbing — so you disturb yourself about that. A pretty picture! — but one, fortunately, that *you have the ability to revise and reconstruct.*

Now I am not contending that *all* your possible disturbing is sparked by your grandiose shoulds, oughts, and musts. Some of it may be aroused by different kinds of neurophysiological or biochemical imbalances — for example, hormonal problems, neurotransmitter deficiencies, nervous system anomalies, food allergies, hypoglycemia, and other physiological problems. So if you have any of these neurophysiologically caused difficulties, you may not be creating your disturbing Consequences with your Believing-Emoting-Behaving. Even then, however, once you become upset for physical reasons, you can easily demand, "I *must not* be dysfunctioning!"

Or you may live in extenuating and oppressive social circumstances — extreme poverty, racism, homophobia, bigotry, political or religious extremism. Although others have found rational ways of dealing with such conditions (see, for example, Viktor Frankl's classic, *Man's Search for Meaning,* about survival in Hitler's death camps), some degree of disturbance is certainly expected and rational in these cases.

You can bring on a secondary disturbing even when your primary problem does not result from your own absolutistic demanding. You're still better off to give up *insisting* that you not react by creating problems. In short, *refuse to upset yourself about your upsetting.*

Assuming that you are using absolute musts, shoulds, and oughts to contribute to your emotional and behavioral malfunctioning, let me summarize, in the next two chapters, some of the main attitudes you can acquire that will help you, first, inelegantly and second, elegantly make yourself get and stay better.

14

Staying Better II:
Avoiding Inelegant Methods of Change

s Nicco Frijda has noted in *The Emotions*, humans ingeniously figure out, by ourselves and with the assistance of therapists and other helpers, many ways to change our dysfunctional emotions.

We have definite feelings *about* our feelings: we like some of our feelings and try to enhance them and we dislike others and try to reduce or eliminate them. Thus, we like feelings that go with loving and of being loved, and we try to increase or preserve them; and we dislike feelings of severe anxietizing and depressing and we try to decrease those.

Because this is a self-help book, it deals with negative feelings and how to minimize them. Not all negative feelings, to be sure, for REBT is one of the few therapies that clearly holds that some negative feelings — sorrow, regret, disappointment, frustration — are usually healthy and self-helping. These healthy negative emotions prepare you to deal constructively with negative events — especially failure, rejection, and discomfort — to remedy them and not unduly upset yourself about them. But REBT shows you how to cope with your unhealthy emotions — especially panicking, depressing, and raging.

To sum up what I have been explaining in this book, I shall briefly review four different ways you can use to deal with your unwanted and unhealthy negative feelings and behaviors:

* Methods that are unrealistic and relatively inefficient but that sometimes work.

* Methods that are forms of distracting and that tend to work temporarily and palliatively.

* Methods that consist of realistic attitudes, but that give you inelegant or partial solutions to disruptive emotions.

* Methods that are realistic and elegant, and that REBT usually recommends as better solutions to self-defeating emoting and behaving.

Unrealistic and Relatively Ineffective Methods of Dealing With Unhealthy Feeling and Behaving

If you strongly believe in one or more supernatural philosophies, they may have a placebo effect and may help you reduce your anxietizing or depressing — *because* you believe in them and not because they have any real power. Thus, you may believe that God or fate is personally interested in you and will come to your aid. Or that some special talisman, charm, incantation, or guru will specially be on your side. Or that some other kind of magical ritual or formula will drive away your disturbing feelings.

You can also believe that however troublesome your problems are in this life, you can count on an afterlife in which they will be resolved. Or you can have other super-optimistic, faith-unfounded-on-fact philosophies that may help you.

None of these kinds of *Beliefs* is realistic — in the context of the physical world — and all of them mostly consist of faith in supernatural forces, which you can hold but never empirically substantiate or falsify. Nonetheless, you can choose to uphold these convictions and they may, as long as you devoutly affirm them, relieve your disturbed feelings. They are not based in fact, however, and you will tend to hold them tenuously. You might well be better off with some of the more solid and realistic attitudes that are described in this and the next chapter.

Distracting Methods That Tend to Temporarily and Palliatively Interrupt Your Unhealthy Feelings and Behaviors

As I have noted previously in this book, you can use a number of cognitive, emotive, and behavioral methods of interrupting and distracting you from your unhealthy negative thinking, feeling, and acting. These include meditating, relaxing procedures, breathing exercises, Yoga, busyness, sports, exercising, and other techniques of mental and physical focusing. Some of these distracting techniques, such as transcendental meditation and Yoga, have a philosophic aspect that may — or may not — encourage you to make a profound philosophizing change such as the kind REBT favors. Most of them, however, use the principle that if you concentrate heavily on one thing, you have trouble focusing, at the same time, on other (e.g., negative) things, such as your anxietizing and depressing thoughts. This is a realistic notion — since that's the way the human mind usually works: one main concentration at a time.

The trouble with distracting techniques for reducing your disturbances is that they tend to work temporarily and palliatively. While they may remove or diminish your self-disturbing ideas — such as, "I must always perform outstandingly or else I am worthless!" — they do not provide instead self-helping, Rational *Beliefs* — such as "It's good to perform outstandingly well *but* I am a worthy individual even when I perform badly." What is more, certain kinds of distracting activities — such as engaging in sports — may even tend to reinforce the dysfunctional conviction that your worth as a human depends on your excellent performances.

Distracting methods, then, are practical and realistic — but largely enable you to feel better and not get better. They are usually not profound or elegant paths to mental health. Nevertheless, they often work beautifully — in the short run.

Realistic But Philosophically Inelegant and Limited Methods of Dealing With Your Unhealthy Negative Feelings and Behaviors

When you disturb yourself, you often have unrealistic Believing-Emoting-Behavings, such as, "Failing an important test will mean I'll always fail, and I'm worthless if I fail!" and "If I risk going in an elevator and it stops between floors, I couldn't stand the anxiety. Therefore, I must never take 'terrible' risks like going in elevators!"

You can effectively challenge these dysfunctional convictions with realistic Disputing, and sometimes you can quickly change them. You can question them and see that failing an important test hardly means that you will always fail and that going in an elevator that stops between floors does not mean that you could not stand the anxiety and would be trapped forever with it.

Your realistic or empirical Disputing of the horror of failing an important test or being trapped in an elevator doesn't, however, entirely solve or prevent your *terribilizing*. For you could prove that failing an important test doesn't mean that you'll fail *every* test — but you can still be dysfunctionally convinced that you are worthless if you fail *any* important test. Even if you see that you will probably, if you keep trying, pass most tests, you can still devoutly believe that failing *any* test makes you worthless. If you do, you may make yourself so anxious about test-taking that you *make yourself* fail practically *all* tests!

Again, you may realistically prove to yourself that the probability of your being trapped *forever* in an elevator and dying of anxiety is very low. You easily may be able to see that this idea is quite ridiculous and that might well help you with your elevator phobicizing. But you may still hold a strong Irrational Belief that being trapped in an elevator — even once for only a matter of several minutes — is "terrible," and you would still have your phobia.

Empirical or realistic Disputing of some of your dysfunctional convictions is fine, and is often used in REBT; but it is sometimes not enough. It is better if supplemented by logical, pragmatic, and other forms of Disputing. Thus, logical Disputing takes your Irrational *Beliefs* to some of the worst possible extremes, and comes to the self-helping conclusion that no matter how often you fail at important tasks or get rejected by significant others you are still logically a *person who* failed and never illogically a Failure with a capital F or a *bad person*. It doesn't follow that because failing is against your interests, you are an *inadequate person* for failing.

Logical Disputing also shows you that if and when people treat you extremely unfairly and thereby really harm you, it is illogical to jump to the conclusion that they *absolutely should have behaved better* and that they are *rotten people* if they didn't. It shows you that they are, at the worst, *people who* acted badly and are not totally worthless humans. Logical Disputing also shows you that however unfortunate Adversities are — and they really may be *very* bad — you cannot sensibly conclude that they *absolutely must not exist* and that it is *totally bad*, or *awful* that they do.

Realistically, then, many Adversities can occur — but it is unrealistic to assume that they will always occur, that they will be exceptionally bad, that they will last forever, and that they will have no saving graces. So if you take a thoroughly realistic or empirical attitude, you will ward off much anxietizing, depressing, and raging.

By all means, be as realistic as you can be about possible and actual Adversities and your ability to cope with them. At the same time — and perhaps more importantly — also be logical about Adversities. Assume that if, by some unusual chance, some of the worst things you can imagine do occur, you can most probably accept them, handle them, and not be utterly devastated *because* they happen. No matter how bad they may be, you can logically (and empirically) figure out some ways to cope with them and still find happiness in life.

The logical philosophy that you use to cope with actual and possible Adversities can also be used to take a practical and pragmatic outlook toward upsetting yourself *about* such Adversities. For you can always ask yourself the empirical question, "What will probably happen if I take an unrealistic and illogical view of Adversities and seriously upset myself about them?" Your answer to this question, if you honestly ask it, will usually be: "Such a view will help me to panic, depress, rage, and self-pity, and will encourage self-defeating avoiding and/or compulsions. Then I will tend to make my life more difficult than the Adversities I deplore already make it."

If you forcefully and persistently employ a combination of realistic, logical, and pragmatic Disputing of your core Irrational Believing-Emoting-Behavings, and if you do this Disputing together with some of the emotive-evocative and behavioral methods described in this book, you will have a good chance to make yourself feel better — and *get* better — by becoming less disturbable.

In spite of the limitations of using only realistic Disputes to counteract your Irrational Beliefs, these realistic emphases can be helpful in getting yourself to *feel* better when faced with Adversities. There are several main realistic philosophies you can use to cope with Adversities and that will help you feel healthily sorry, disappointed, and frustrated, but not seriously self-disturbing when they occur. They will help you temporarily and sometimes may lead to a profound getting better. Thus, you can tell yourself:

"This Adversity that is happening is bad…

…*but* it is not as bad as it could be and might be a lot worse than it is." Example: "It is bad that the storm is bringing 12 inches of snow! But it could produce twice as much!"

…*but* it also has some advantages." Example: "My job is pretty rotten but it pays well and I am learning a lot by it."

…*but* I can use various relaxing techniques so it won't bother me so much." Examples: Meditating, Yoga, Jacobson's progressive relaxation technique.

…*but* I can use various kinds of physical and bodily distractions, so it won't bother me so severely." Examples: Exercise, sports, massage, sex.

…*but* I can keep myself very busy to distract myself from it." Examples: Work, studying, playing bridge.

…*but* I can devote myself to a vital absorbing interest or cause that will distract me from it for much of the time."

Examples: Raising a family, building a business, devotion to a political, social, or religious cause.

...*but* I can probably get help from working with others to make it better or cope with it." Example: get tutoring to improve my grades.

...*but* I can learn some skills that will possibly make it better." Example: "I can practice tennis so that I rarely lose."

...*but* I can work hard and possibly make it better." Example: "I can work hard to improve my job evaluations."

...*but* as I grow older and get more experience, I will probably be able to cope with it better. Example: "Getting used to a difficult job and improving my ability to cope with it."

In the following chapter, we'll take a look at ways you can put into practice your plans for change.

15

Staying Better III: Implementing Your Resolve to Change What You Can Change

L et us assume that you have read this book so far and that you largely — not necessarily wholly — agree with it. You would like to feel better when you anxietize, depress, and enrage yourself; and you also take my main message seriously — you want to get better, to stay better, and to stubbornly refuse to seriously upset yourself even when unusual Adversities occur. So you resolve to work at — to not only insightfully *see* but also to effectively *practice* — the self-help techniques of REBT. Fine! But now what? How can you persistently implement REBT's behaviorally-oriented Insight No. 3: There is no way but work and practice — yes, w-o-r-k and p-r-a-c-t-i-c-e — to change what you can change about your irrational thinking, your disturbing feeling, and your destructive behaving?

Okay — how?

The answer is: *Not easily!* It is often relatively easy for you to *see* that you largely upset yourself, to *learn* REBT and discover *how* you do this, and to *know* that if you think and act differently you will most probably change. But insight and knowledge is still not action, just a prelude to action. To change, you still have to PYA — push your ass. Yes, act!

How? How do you *act* differently, even when you "know" what to do and how to do it? Hmm!

No one can give you a precise answer to this question. Theoretically, you can give yourself reinforcements or rewards *after* you act on helping yourself or give yourself stiff penalties *after* you refuse to act. Thus, you could allow yourself to eat only *after* you stopped procrastinating on your taxes and burn a ten-dollar bill for every minute that you actually procrastinate. Either or both of these reinforcements or penalties may work. The problem, however, is: how will you make yourself actually *use* these planned reinforcements and penalties? If you won't act without them, what will lead you to actually enforce your plan to use them? What?

So you still have a problem of choosing, determining, and planning to act to change yourself — *and* of actually doing this planned action. The first part — the contemplating and the choosing — *gets you ready* for acting; but it doesn't exactly *make* you act. What, then, does?

That's a hard question to answer. You may see the answer by clearly calculating the cost-benefit ratio between acting and not acting. But even then, you may not act upon what you see.

Suppose, for example, your doctor tells you to stop eating fatty foods — or else you may well have a heart attack. So, not wanting to have a heart attack, you *see* she is right, you *choose* to cut down on fats, you *determine* to follow your choice, and you *plan* a low-fat diet. Good. We may say that if you see the "disbenefits" of a high-fat diet *clearly enough*, you choose to adopt a low-fat one *strongly* enough, you determine to follow it *powerfully enough*, and you plan to stick to it *well enough*, you will probably then change your eating habits. But you *still* may not act!

Why? Because you're human, and you tend to *strongly* choose, determine, and plan to follow the course of inaction (or the wrong action). Thus, you *forcefully* decide, despite planning to diet, that you *need* those good-tasting fatty foods, that you *can't* live happily without them, that you can *get away with* ignoring your doctor. Your *choice* and *determination* to diet is overruled by your *stronger* choice and determination to eat fatty foods. You contradictorily *choose* to act by dieting but you *more powerfully* choose to act by eating more fat than you "see" is good for you.

How common! You "see" a certain action, such as eating too much fat, as "bad" and you *choose* not to do it. But you *more strongly* "see" the actual taste of the fatty foods as "good" or as a "need," and, darn it, you actually do what you told yourself you wouldn't do. Or we can say that you "see" fatty foods as bad for your health but you more strongly "see" them as good for your taste — and you foolishly *refuse* to push them away.

What, again, to do in such a dilemma? While no one absolutely knows, the best answer I can think of is simple but difficult: determined action. *Strongly, forcefully, and powerfully* take responsibility for your own life, convince yourself to act, act, act in your major long-term interest, no matter how unpleasant some of your action may be. And with equal strength, force, and power, decide to accept the fact that *you'd better refrain from acting against your important goals and values.*

Well, that seems pretty obvious. Millions of people have followed this rule and have voluntarily — without therapy or support groups — quit smoking, overeating, gambling, and other harmful addictions. Millions more have by themselves — without any support to speak of — forced themselves to exercise, diet, write term papers, get to work on time, rise before dawn to begin their chores, and do many other things which they find unpleasant but which they benefit from doing. So changing your acting or stopping procrastinating, though hard, is something you can definitely do.

As I noted in chapter 12, the key is not will but will *power*; and will power invariably seems to include *acting*. No pain, no gain; no action, no will *power*. But acting to do "good" things that you don't like to do and to stop doing "bad" things that you distinctly enjoy involves thinking — and often *heavy* thinking. To *choose* to act is relatively easy; to *determine and resolve* to act is harder. Both are choices, decisions, and desires. But the second process — strongly determining and resolving to act — will get you much further toward pushing yourself and acting than will *lightly* choosing to do so.

Here, therefore, are several attitudes and philosophies that, if you *strongly* hold them, will probably help you choose to change, to determine to change, and to resolve to change some of your self-defeating thinking, feeling, and behaving. Yes, if you hold them *strongly*:

- "Talk, including self-talking, is cheap. Only talk backed by *acting* will get me better and keep me better."

- "To change my ways I often have to make myself *un*comfortable before I start to feel comfortable and enjoying. Too bad, but I'd better court some *dis*comfort."

- "I am habituated to thinking, feeling, and behaving dysfunctionally. I can only break these habits by forcefully breaking them a hundred times. And, if necessary, more than a hundred!"

- "The longer I've indulged in my self-defeating behavior, the longer I'd better work to disrupt it. Persistently!"

- "It's easy to stop overeating. I've done it a thousand times!"

- "It's hard to stop smoking and stay stopped, but it's easy to die of lung cancer."

- "After I die of lung cancer I won't have any trouble stopping smoking."

- "Drinking alcohol will rid me of my social anxietizing — until I sober up again."

- "If I put off today what I can do tomorrow, I'll have an incredibly crummy tomorrow."

- "Avoiding acts I am afraid to fail at will temporarily lessen my performance anxiety— and permanently augment it."

- "The more I think I am worthless for failing, the less I will try to succeed."

* "God helps those who help themselves."

* "My fairy godmother is having too hard a time with her own life to devote much time and energy to mine."

* "If I want to find peace and joy in heaven, I'd better work my butt off to get there."

* "If I demand that I be perfect, I'll create perfect nonsense and act perfectly foolishly."

* "A balanced life avoids extreme goals."

* "If I need support and approval from others to get myself going, I will keep setting up roadblocks in my way."

* "*Desiring* to achieve and to relate will push me forward. *Needing* to succeed and relate will halt me in my tracks, make me panic, and help push me backward."

* "Frustration can motivate me greatly — if I stop whining about it."

* "*Desiring* is the mother of invention; *necessitizing* is the mother of anxietizing and anguishing."

* "If I don't push my tush no one else really will. Will they?"

* "Procrastination and frustration reinforce each other. In the long run, the former increases and prolongs the latter."

* "Self-actualization means hard work."

* "Scientists, artists, performers, and entrepreneurs get somewhere in life by sitting on their asses — once in a billion times."

* "It's easy to hate people when they make mistakes. I win many friends this way."

* "I can quickly and easily upset myself about Adversities in my life. What a difficult — and great — challenge it is not to do so!"

- "Yes, working to better my life is often annoying and frustrating. But what about the pains of letting my life slide?"

- "If I can do onerous tasks for rewards or reinforcements, that at least proves one thing — that I *can* do them."

- "If I forcefully tell myself I absolutely can't do something doable, I'll most probably get a self-fulfilling prophecy."

16

Final Wisdom on Feeling Better, Getting Better, and Staying Better

As I have been showing throughout this book, when you behave disturbedly, you can choose many ways to feel and to get better. Review them. Try them. See how they work in your unique case. *What works best for you may be radically different than what works for other people.* Nothing is effective marvelously and all the time for every one of the billions of people on earth — or, probably, for those who will inhabit it later. No, no cure-alls or panaceas.

So? So try several — perhaps many — of the thinking, feeling, and behavioral methods of Rational Emotive Behavior Therapy, and of other systems of therapy as well. As I noted before, experiment! See if the methods you choose do work for you. See if they keep working. Do personal research on them. Be your own scientist. Test your results. Keep checking!

Is that all? Yes. But while you are testing out your best personal ways of feeling better and getting better and staying better, here are a few hypotheses which I would advise you to investigate. They are prejudices of mine that I have derived from almost 60 years of doing psychotherapy and counseling with over 15,000 people. Some I only saw for a single brief demonstration, others I saw for several to several hundred therapy sessions. Most of them were American citizens but hundreds were born and reared in countries around the world — almost any country you can name. Their diagnoses? Almost every one imaginable. So they were — and still are — a motley crew!

From this large sample of troubled people, as well as from supervising the therapy of hundreds of clients of other practitioners, attending many talks and workshops, and reading thousands of articles and hundreds of books on human personality and its problems, I have naturally made numerous inferences and deductions — many of which I have stated in the previous chapters of this book. Now let me summarize some my major ideas — hypotheses, not proven facts — for you to consider and think about in treating your own difficulties. I believe, on the basis of my long experiences in the field of psychotherapy, that they can be very helpful. See if you find them so.

To Choose or Not to Choose

I have stressed before in this book that no humans have complete "free will" or unhampered choice in what we think, feel, and do because we all have some important biological limitations and social-environmental restrictions. None of us, as far as we know, is totally free, unhampered, and unlimited. We all have natural — human — limitations; if any of us are godlike and supernatural they have not exactly shown that characteristic yet.

Okay. So you, I, and other people are limited in our freedom and our choices. But not completely! We do have some "free" choice. Other animals, especially mammals and vertebrates, seem to have some, too. They can *choose* to eat or not eat, fight or not fight, flee or not flee from danger. But we humans have much more choice, partly because of our larger cerebral cortex, our superior ability to invent and use language, and our unusual (probably unique) aptitude for thinking about our thinking, and at times even thinking about thinking about our thinking. These propensities do not completely free us — but give us more choice — sometimes much more — than the other animals. We can be unusually constructivist.

Making Conscious Choices

Let's assume that you and I have considerable choice — selective determining — in what we think, feel, and do. Not total, not complete choice. But some.

If so, and we want to *choose* to be less disturbing, less disturbable, and often happier, we had better do many kinds of thinking-feeling-behaving — as I have shown in this book. Moreover, much of our healthy, self-helping efforts had better be conscious rather than unconscious, mindful rather than mindless, deliberate rather than automatic. For we often get by in life — survive and stay reasonably happy — with considerable unconscious, mindless automatic thinking. In fact, very often! So we'd better not strive to be *completely* conscious and deliberately choosing — no, not all the time. Preconscious thought — sensing danger when we do not see it very consciously — is often quite useful. The same is true of much unconscious thinking — such as occurs in dreams, hypnosis, forgetfulness, and other intellectual processes which happen without our full awareness.

Good. But what I seem to have mainly learned in my many years of studying psychology and doing therapy is that *conscious* choice or discrimination isn't sacred and isn't a cure-all for all emotional ills. It can, however, greatly help you to feel better, get better, and stay better — to rarely fall back into serious self-disturbing. *Conscious* choice, deliberation, and discrimination? Yes.

I am going to show you exactly what I mean by conscious choice. I am going to hypothesize that if you make yourself deliberately, intentionally, and willfully *aware* that you have certain self-helping (healthy) and self-defeating (unhealthy) choices about how you think, feel, and act; and if you then consciously *choose* to have "good" rather than "bad" Believing-Emoting-Behavings, you will considerably improve your chances of feeling better and — especially! — getting better.

Choosing Individual vs. Social Values

First, however, let me deal with the ticklish question of your picking fundamental goals, purposes, and values. Practically all of us — including, probably you — pick the general goals of choosing to stay alive, and trying to be reasonably happy and free from pain when you are by yourself or with other people, including those few people with whom you are intimate, such as your family members, mates or lovers, and close friends. You also, in general, probably try to be reasonably happy and productive educationally, vocationally, and recreationally.

Well and good. But you are a *unique* individual, with your specific biology, with your family and cultural upbringing, and with your special history of habituating yourself to a certain definite set of desires and distastes. So how can I or anyone else properly advise you to keep your present goals and purposes — or to set new ones? We can't. You basically have to *choose your own* future aims — and that is not as easy as it might first appear. Let me show you why.

You can choose to stop following an old set of purposes or follow a new set. Sometimes startlingly. Thus, antisocial people sometimes makes themselves into social benefactors, and frantic competitors may turn to procrastinating and ass-sitting. You, too, can work at changing — if you determine to do so. The problem is this: If you want to change your habitual ways, what direction shall you take?

Sometimes changing is fairly obvious. You distinctly desire people's approval — but you often anger yourself and act punishingly to them. Well, that won't work! Or you want to be a diligent entrepreneur or writer but you crave frequent relaxing with marijuana. No go! Something has to give if you steadily indulge in one of these desires and still insist on getting the opposing one fulfilled.

If you have conflicting goals, such as just described, and they block your own enjoying, you can choose between them or compromise. But you still have to choose! Moreover, your choices will be somewhat unique to you; and you will have a hard time, often, in figuring out, first, what seems to be the best choice to take and, second, to act on the one you choose. With the best conscious intentions, you may pick one road, but actually take another.

Aren't there, however, some socially approved goals that almost everyone would tend to agree would be best for your community and therefore best for you? Yes, there are — but not everyone will agree with them and those that the majority might endorse might have real disadvantages — for both you and your community.

Consider social action for community causes, or being kind and beneficial to selected others. Nice. Yes, by most people's standards. But if you focused too much on community causes, you might not be able to concentrate enough on using your unusual talent for composing music or inventing a better mousetrap — and your community might suffer a real loss. And you yourself might lose out on achieving maximum creativity and joy in the one brief life you'll ever have. So devoting yourself to community work or to being kind and loving to a few intimates may have its distinct drawbacks.

Or suppose you follow the REBT recommendations for your own mental health by giving up your hatred and damning of other people. Sounds great doesn't it? But then you might give up your hatred of some tyrant — such as Hitler or Stalin — stop working on your plans to block him or her, and thereby fail to benefit humanity. You might also stop being a revolutionist against a fascist or Nazi state, and help to perpetuate the evils of that state. That can be your choice, of course; but would it be entirely a "good" one?

Again, take humanitarian goals and purposes. Let us say you fight against tyranny, war, the bombing of civilians, terrorism, rape, clitoridectomy, discrimination against women, and other things that most enlightened people consider unmitigated evils. You are surely entitled to do so, can get real pleasure from pursuing your goal, and may help some people considerably by actively espousing these causes. But not everyone will cheer you on. Some conservatives and reactionaries — who in a democracy are entitled to their views — will damn you, and perhaps try to severely punish you, for what you call your humanitarian goals.

How can you be certain that your critics are wrong and that they are less humanitarian than you?

Individualistic or "selfish" goals and purposes also have their disadvantageous side. You may be too much out for yourself — narcissistic and antisocial, for instance. You may miss out on the joys of helping and caring for others. You may be hung up on short-range pleasuring and ignore longer-range enjoying. You may indulge in smoking or excessive drinking and may harm others and your social community. Well??

How about choosing the goal of making yourself flexible, scientific, and unmusturbating. Usually, as I have shown in this book, if you choose this kind of thinking and doing, you will not contradict yourself and will acknowledge social reality. You will thereby arrange less inner turmoil, less outer conflict, and more enjoying.

But not always! Some people enjoy being rigid and inflexible — they minimize their anxietizing that way. Some people avoid scientific, realistic thinking — and happily concentrate, instead, on romanticizing, fictionalizing, and fantasizing. Obsessive scientism may itself be rigid and restricting. Be careful!

Some people also benefit — at least temporarily — from musturbating. They absolutistically insist, "I *must* achieve greatly!" — and their dogmatic insistence motivates them to achieve. Or they command, "I *must* get married!" or "I *have to* have children!" and they determinedly push themselves to have a successful marriage and to rear loving children. So even risky musturbating sometimes works.

So does supernaturalizing. You may devoutly believe that supernatural forces, your fairy godmother, or even the Devil, solidly favor you and will help you conquer Adversity or succeed at some goal you pursue. No such supernatural force may exist — but your profound *Belief* that it does may encourage you and help you. Don't count on it — but your dogmatic faith may work.

Balancing Act

What about having the goal of balancing your desires, avoiding extremes, and trying for the mean between the extremes? What about avoiding black-and-white thinking and seeing both sides of important questions?

Thus, you can work for social causes and devote yourself to helping others — and also concentrate on your own individual interests and enjoyments. You can unconditionally accept other people, avoid hatred and fighting — and still determinedly discourage and try to stop others from committing what you consider wrong or evil acts. You can be flexible and scientific and also cultivate romanticizing in literature, art, music, or your imagination. You can musturbate to some extent about achieving your fondest goals, but not insist that Adversities must not exist when they do exist and not rate your self as a person, your being, as "bad" or "inadequate" when you are not doing as well as you supposedly *must* do.

Yes, you can choose to be moderating and balancing, considering the means between the extremes — why not try that path? It has many advantages and REBT often recommends it. But not sacredly or dogmatically. Maybe it works pretty well much of the time for most people. But for you in particular? Maybe!

Perhaps you really like and get a lot out of taking things to extremes. You'd rather be black or white — not gray. You can't be very high and excited, which you greatly enjoy, without risking and even experiencing some lows. You find middle-grounding relatively dull. You are just that kind of a person — and eager to stay that way. Perhaps you even prefer a short life and a merry one. If you really do, why not try it and see? Many other people will think you are crazy. But are you?

Choosing Health Over Disturbance

Where do we go from here? Are there no absolute, invariable rules for you to best follow in seeking to be less self-disturbing, minimally disturbable, and maximally happy? Most likely not. What can you do then? You can try several procedures that will help you choose.

♦ Ask yourself what you think — yes, guess — you will choose for your major goals and purposes. Ask about others' aims and purposes and consider them for yourself.

♦ Think about the possible advantages and disadvantages, benefits and disbenefits, of your choices. For yourself. For others you love. For your community. For the world at large. Do a cost-benefit analysis for each goal you consider seeking.

♦ When you are about to pick a goal do some research on what others have found by following it. Ask others. Perhaps go to the library or to some Internet sites.

♦ Tentatively try for the goal you choose. Try it in your imagination and try it in practice. Experiment. Give yourself a chance. Don't drop it too easily. Don't needlessly hang on to it because you picked it. More trials, more experimenting.

♦ Check your results. Check the good results and the bad results you get. Check, if you can, your short-term results and your long-term results. Keep checking.

♦ Commit yourself to one or more goals that you think are important for you, that seem feasible, and that will probably work out. Be optimistic — and realistic!

♦ If one or more of your purposes doesn't work out or prove satisfying, don't beat yourself for picking it. A bad *choice*, perhaps — but not a bad *you*. Besides, you usefully *learned* that it was not for you; and may have learned several valuable things about what you tried, and about *you*, and about *other people*.

♦ Keep choosing goals, purposes, ideals, interests, and involvements and trying them out. You have little to lose by trying — and a major part of your life to possibly lose by *not* trying. Choose!

Helping Yourself Feel, Get, and Stay Better

Now let us return to the main theme of this book. You presumably have had some emotional-behavioral problems, and you wish to improve them. Moreover, you are deciding to feel better, *and* get better, *and* stay better. That is, to reduce your cognitive, emotional, and behavioral upsetting, to keep it removed, to use the best methods you have learned if perchance the upsetting returns again. You've chosen to refuse to upset yourself again even if major Adversities occur in your life and interfere with your aims and interests. What can you possibly do now to aid your goal of achieving minimal self-disturbing and maximum undisturbability?

You're a unique individual with somewhat unique purposes and interferences, so no general plan I could offer may work for you. But there are several common thinking processes or ways to discriminate that have worked well with people somewhat like you and that may work for you as well. Here are some of them with which you can experiment. Try them!

Choose to discriminate between your feeling healthy negative emotions, such as feelings of concern, disappointment, sorrow, regret, frustration, and annoyance, when you are faced with actual or potential Adversities; or to experience unhealthy negative feelings, such as severe anxiety, depression, rage, and self-pity. You can't very well eliminate all unhealthy negative feelings, but you can work at reducing many of them.

Choose also to discriminate between your healthy interest in and some degree of devotion to people and things, such as your enjoyment of social relations, love, sex, work, and recreations; and see if you are unhealthily obsessively-compulsively addicted to one or more of your interests and you therefore self-defeatingly spend too much time and energy pursuing it to the detriment of important other aspects of your life.

Choose to discriminate between your desiring and preferring, on one hand, and your dire needing and demanding, on the other hand. Whatever you desire or want, with few exceptions, is natural to you and legitimate and whatever you dislike and don't want is also legitimate. You are you and are entitled to weak and strong tastes and distastes. But your absolutely needing what you strongly want is likely to get you into trouble — because other people and world conditions often do not favor your desires and sometimes clearly block them. Your demanding fulfillment that may not come will likely lead you to anxietize, anger, and depress yourself. These are not exactly healthy negative feelings!

Choose to discriminate between self-interest — primarily looking out for your own interests — and social interest — importantly caring for the interests of other people. They need not seriously conflict with each other, since you can have much of both; and choosing to extremely favor one against the other may get you in difficulties. Being only self-interested may alienate others, lead to unethical and immoral behavior, make you miss out on the joys of loving and caring for others, and may possibly sabotage and help destroy your social group — which would do you yourself little good. On the other hand, being only concerned with loving and caring for others and hardly favoring your own interests might well get you little of what you really want, encourage others to take advantage of you, and lead you to neglect your own safety and survival. Consider! — and perhaps pick some middle ground between these two extremes. Or choose *both* self-interest *and* social interest, not either/or.

Discriminate between short-range and long-range hedonism. There is nothing wrong in seeking for pleasure and happiness, both long-range and short-range. But some immediate satisfactions — such as smoking, overeating, heavy drinking, and over-spending — easily lead to lung disease, poverty, other handicaps, and severe trouble. At the same time, focusing mainly on disciplining yourself at the expense of immediate pleasures may lead to compulsive saving that will only do your heirs much good and compulsive dieting that will make your meals unenjoyable. Again, if you can find a mean between these two extremes and that would be best for your happiness, do some research and find it!

Discriminate — though this is often difficult! — between your beliefs and your dogmas. As a human, you may well be inclined to strongly believe in many purposes and goals and invent "facts" that support them. Be skeptical and suspicious of your devout Belicving-Emoting-Behavings. From time to time rethink them and the "facts" behind them. Look at alternative or even opposite convictions. Get more "facts." Reconsider! Remain flexible!

Even the "best" rules that you choose for yourself and others may have some unusual exceptions. Don't follow — or ask others to follow — them absolutely and invariably. They may be fine in general — but not in some specific instances. Consider some possible exceptions.

Science and reason are good and useful. But so are art and emotion. Reason often implements desire and emotion; and feelings can also implement reasoning. Both/and rather than either/or!

All things can change — including your goals, values, and purposes. See whether you *now* find them useful and practical as you *once* did. They need not be written in stone! Strive to fulfill them today — but not necessarily tomorrow.

Experiment and experiment. Try several paths before you settle for one. Change may not be easy — but it usually possible. What works best for you and for other people? Explore!

Selected References

The following references include the works of some of the main authors mentioned in this book, but by no means all of them — since a good many of them, such as Fritz Perls, are famous in their own right and including them would make the list too long. An additional number of items on Rational Emotive Behavior Therapy (REBT) and Cognitive Behavior Therapy (CBT) have been included because they may be useful for self-help purposes. Many of the items in the references may be obtained from the Albert Ellis Institute, 45 East 65th Street, New York, NY 10021-6593. The Institute's free catalogue, that includes materials it distributes, may be ordered on weekdays by phone (212-535-0822), by fax (212-249-3582), or e-mail (orders@rebt.org). The Institute will continue to make available these and other materials, and it will offer talks, workshops, and training sessions, as well as other presentations in the area of human growth and healthy living and will list these in its free regular catalogue.

Adler, A. (1964) *Social Interest: A Challenge to Mankind.* New York: Capricorn.

Alberti, R., & Emmons, M. (1970/2001). *Your Perfect Right.* 8th ed., Atascadero, CA: Impact Publishers, Inc.

Bandura, A. (1997). *Self-Efficacy: The Exercise of Control.* New York: Freeman.

Bargh, J. A, Chartrend, T. L. (1999). The unbearable automaticity of being. *American Psychologist*, 54, 462-479.

Beck, A. T. (1976). *Cognitive Therapy and the Emotional Disorders*. New York: International Universities Press.

Beck, A. T. (1988). *Love is Not Enough*. New York: Harper & Row.

Beck, J. S. (1995). *Cognitive Therapy: Basics and Beyond*. New York: Guilford.

Bernard, M. E. (1993). *Staying Rational In An Irrational World*. New York: Kensington Publishers.

Bernard, M. E. & Wolfe, J. L. (Eds. 2000). *The RET Resource Book for Practitioners*. New York: Albert Ellis Institute.

Broder, M. S. (1990). *The Art of Living*. New York: Avon.

Burns, D. D. (1980). *Feeling Good: The New Mood Therapy*. New York: Morrow.

Burns, D. D. (1993). *Ten Days to Self-Esteem*. New York: Morrow.

Chess, S. (1997). The temperament program. In J. K. Zeig (Ed.), *The Evolution of Psychotherapy: The Third Conference*. New York: Brunner/Mazel.

Consumer Reports editors (1995). Mental health: Does therapy help? *Consumers Reports*, 60, 734-737.

Csikszentmihaly, M. (1997). *Finding Flow: The Psychology of Engagement with Every Day Life*. New York: Basic Books.

Dryden, W. (1999). *How to Accept Yourself*. London: Sheldon Press.

Dryden, W. (2000). *Rational Emotive Behavior Therapy: A Training Manual*. New York: Springer.

Dryden, W., & Gordon, J. (1991). *Think Your Way to Happiness*. London: Sheldon Press.

Ellis, A. (1957/1975). *How to Live With a Neurotic: At Home and At Work*. New York: Crown. Rev. Hollywood, CA: Wilshire Books.

Ellis, A. (1958). Rational psychotherapy. *Journal of General Psychology*, 59, 35-49.

Ellis, A. (1960). *The Art and Science of Love*. New York: Lyle Stuart & Bantam.

Ellis, A. (1962). *Reason and Emotion in Psychotherapy*. Secaucus, NJ: Citadel.

Ellis, A. (1972). Helping people get better rather than merely feel better. *Rational Living*, 7 (2), 2-9.

Ellis, A. (1972/1991). *Psychotherapy and the Value of a Human Being*. New York: Albert Ellis Institute.

Ellis, A. (Speaker). (1973). *How to Stubbornly Refuse to Be Ashamed of Anything*. Cassette recording. New York: Albert Ellis Institute.

Ellis, A. (1976). *Sex and the Liberated Man*. Secaucus, NJ: Lyle Stuart.

Ellis, A. (Speaker). (1977). *A Garland of Rational Humorous Songs*. (Cassette recording and songbook). New York: Albert Ellis Institute.

Ellis, A. (1979). *The Intelligent Woman's Guide to Dating and Mating*. Secaucus, NJ: Lyle Stuart. Orig. ed., 1963.

Ellis, A. (1988). *How to Stubbornly Refuse to Make Yourself Miserable About Anything — Yes, Anything!* New York: Kensington Publishers.

Ellis, A. (1994). *Reason and Emotion in Psychotherapy*. Revised and updated. New York: Kensington Publishers.

Ellis, A. (1999). *How to Make Yourself Happy and Remarkably Less Disturbable*. Atascadero, CA: Impact Publishers, Inc.

Ellis, A. (1999). *Rational Emotive Behavior Therapy Diminishes Much of the Human Ego*. New York: Albert Ellis Institute.

Ellis, A. (2000). *How to Control Your Anxiety Before It Controls You*. New York: Citadel Press.

Ellis, A., & Abrams, M. (1994). *How to Cope With a Fatal Disease*. New York: Barricade Books.

Ellis, A., Abrams, M., & Dengelegi, L. (1992). *The Art and Science of Rational Eating*. New York: Barricade Books.

Ellis, A., & Becker, I. (1982). *A Guide to Personal Happiness*. North Hollywood, CA: Melvin Powers/Wilshire Books.

Ellis, A., & Blau. S. (1998). (Eds). *The Albert Ellis Reader*. New York: Kensington Publishers.

Ellis, A. & Crawford, T. (2000). *Making Intimate Connections*. Atascadero, CA: Impact Publishers, Inc.

Ellis, A. & Dryden, W. (1997). *The Practice of Rational Emotive Behavior Therapy.* New York: Springer.

Ellis, A., Gordon, V., Neeman, M., & Palmer, S. (1998). *Stress Counseling.* New York: Springer.

Ellis, A., & Harper, R. A. (1961). *A Guide to Successful Marriage.* North Hollywood, CA: Wilshire Books.

Ellis, A., & Harper, R. A. (1997). *A Guide to Rational Living.* Rev. ed. North Hollywood, CA: Melvin Powers/Wilshire Books.

Ellis, A., & Knaus, W. (1977). *Overcoming Procrastination.* New York: New American Library.

Ellis, A., & Lange, A. (1994). *How to Keep People From Pushing Your Buttons.* New York: Kensington Publishers.

Ellis, A., & MacLaren, C. (1998). *Rational Emotive Behavior Therapy: A Therapist's Guide.* Atascadero, CA: Impact Publishers, Inc.

Ellis, A., & Tafrate, C. (1997). *How to Control Your Anger Before It Controls You.* New York: Kensington Publishers.

Ellis, A., & Velten, E. (1992). *When AA Doesn't Work For You: Rational Steps For Quitting Alcohol.* New York: Barricade Books.

Ellis, A., & Velten, E. (1998). *Optimal Aging: How to Get Over Growing Older.* Chicago: Open Court.

Ellis, A., Wolfe, J. L., & Moseley, S. (1966). *How to Raise An Emotionally Healthy, Happy Child.* North Hollywood, CA: Wilshire Books.

Esterling, B., Libate, L., Murray, E. & Pennebaker, J. W. (1999). Empirical foundations for writing in prevention and psychotherapy: Mental and physical health outcomes. *Clinical Psychology Review,* 19, 79-96.

FitzMaurice, K. E. (1997). *Attitude is All You Need.* Omaha, NE: Palm Tree Publishers.

Frank, J. D. & Frank, J. B. (1991). *Persuasion and Healing.* 3rd ed. Baltimore, MD. Johns Hopkins Univ. Press.

Frankl, V. (1959). *Man's Search for Meaning.* New York: Pocket Books.

Fried, R. (1999). *Breathe Well, Be Well.* New York: Wiley.

Glasser, W. (1998). *Choice Theory.* New York: Harper Collins.

Glasser, W. (2000). *Reality Therapy in Action.* New York: Harper Collins.

Goleman, D. (1995). *Emotional Intelligence.* New York: Bantam.

Gollwitzer, P. M. (1999). Implementation intentions: Strong effects of simple plans. *American Psychologist, 56,* 493-503.

Hauck, P.A. (1973). *Overcoming Depression.* Philadelphia: Westminster.

Hauck, P.A. (1974). *Overcoming Frustration and Anger.* Philadelphia: Westminster.

Hauck, P.A. (1975). *Overcoming Worry and Fear.* Philadelphia: Westminster

Hauck, P.A. (1991). *Overcoming the Rating Game: Beyond Self-love — Beyond Self-esteem.* Louisville, KY: Westminster/John Knox.

Horvath, A. T. (1998). *Sex, Drugs, Gambling and Chocolate.* Atascadero, CA: Impact Publishers, Inc.

Jacobson, E. (1938). *You Must Relax.* New York: McGraw-Hill.

Kirsch, I. (1999). *How Expectations Shape Experience.* Washington, D.C.: American Psychological Association.

Korzybski, A. (1933/1990). *Science and Sanity.* Concord, CA: International Society of General Semantics.

Lazarus, A. A. (1989). *The Practice of Multimodal Therapy.* Baltimore, MD: Johns Hopkins.

Lazarus, A. A., Lazarus, C. N. (1997). *The 60-Second Shrink.* Atascadero, CA: Impact Publishers, Inc.

Lazarus, A. A., Lazarus, C., Fay, A. (1993). *Don't Believe It For a Minute: Forty Toxic Ideas That Are Driving You Crazy.* Atascadero, CA: Impact Publishers, Inc.

Lazarus, A. A., (2001). *Marital Myths Revisited.* Atascadero, CA: Impact Publishers, Inc.

Lazarus, R. S. (1999). *Stress and Emotion: A New Synthesis.* New York: Springer.

Mahoney, M. J. (1991). *Human Change Processes.* New York: Basic Books.

Maultsby, M. C., Jr. (1971). Rational emotive imagery. *Rational Living,* 6 (1), 24-27.

Maultsby, M. C., Jr. (1986). *Coping Better…Anytime, Anywhere.* New York: Prentice Hall.

McMullin, R. E. (2000). *The New Handbook of Cognitive Therapy.* New York: Norton.

Meichenbaum, D. (1977). *Cognitive-Behavior Modification.* New York: Plenum.

Miller, T. (1986). *The Unfair Advantage.* Manlius, NY: Horsesense, Inc.

Mills, D. (1993). *Overcoming Self-Esteem.* New York: Albert Ellis Institute.

Nielsen, S. L., Johnson, W. R., & Ellis, A. (2001). *Counseling and Psychotherapy with Religious Persons: A Rational Emotive Behavioral Approach.* Mahwah, NJ: Erlbaum.

Perls, F. (1969). *Gestalt Therapy Verbatim.* New York: Delta.

Peters, D. L. (1998). Going rapport and a common base of understanding. In H. G. Rosenthal. (Ed.) *Favorite Counseling and Therapy Techniques.* Philadelphia, PA: Accelerated Development.

Palmer, S., & Dryden, W. (1996). *Stress Management and Counseling.* London and New York: Cassell.

Rogers, C. R. (1961). *On Becoming a Person.* Boston: Houghton-Mifflin.

Russell, B. (1950). *The Conquest of Happiness.* New York: New American Library.

Seligman, M. E. P. (1991). *Learned Optimism.* New York: Knopf.

Simon, J. L. (1993). *Good Mood.* La Salle, IL: Open Court.

Skinner, B. F. (1971). *Beyond Freedom and Dignity.* New York: Knopf.

Tate, P. (1997). *Alcohol: How to Give It Up and Be Glad You Did!* 2nd ed. Tucson, AZ: See Sharp Press.

Tillich, P. (1953). *The Courage to Be.* Cambridge, MA: Harvard University Press.

Vernon, A. (1989). *Thinking, Feeling, Behaving: An Emotional Education Curriculum for Children.* Champaign, IL: Research Press.

Vernon, A. (1999). *The Passport Program.* Champaign, IL: Research Press.

Walen, S., DiGiuseppe, R., & Dryden, W. (1992). *A Practitioner's Guide to Rational-Emotive Therapy*. New York: Oxford University Press.

Wolfe, J. L. (1992). *What to Do When He Has a Headache*. New York: Hyperion.

Woolfolk, R. L. (1988). *The Cure of Souls: Science, Values, and Psychotherapy*. San Francisco: Jossey-Bass.

Young, H. S. (1974). *A Rational Counseling Primer*. New York: Albert Ellis Institute.

Zettle, R. D. (1994). Discussion of Dougher: On the use of acceptable language. In S. C. Hayes, N. S. Jacobson, V. M. Fonnette, & M. J. Dougher. (Eds.), *Acceptance and Change: Content and Context in Psychotherapy*. Reno. NV: Context Press.

Index

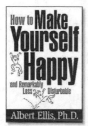
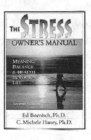
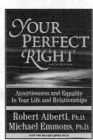
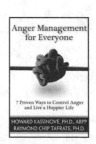

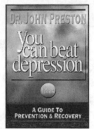